Word, Sound, Image

EXPLORATIONS IN ANTHROPOLOGY
A University College London Series

Series Editors: Barbara Bender, John Gledhill and Bruce Kapferer

Joan Bestard-Camps, *What's in a Relative? Household and Family in Formentera*

Henk Driessen, *On the Spanish-Moroccan Frontier: A Study in Ritual, Power and Ethnicity*

Alfred Gell, *The Anthropology of Time: Cultural Construction of Temporal Maps and Images*

Tim Ingold, David Riches and James Woodburn (eds), *Hunters and Gatherers*
  Volume 1. *History, Evolution and Social Change*
  Volume 2. *Property, Power and Ideology*

Bruce Kapferer, *A Celebration of Demons* (2nd edn.)

Guy Lanoue, *Brothers: The Politics of Violence among the Sekani of Northern British Columbia*

Jadran Mimica, *Intimations of Infinity: The Mythopoeia of the Iqwaye Counting System and Number*

Barry Morris, *Domesticating Resistance: The Dhan-Gadi Aborigines and the Australian State*

Thomas C. Paterson, *The Inca Empire: The Formation and Disintegration of a Pre-Capitalist State*

Max and Eleanor Rimoldi, *Hahalis and the Labour of Love: A Social Movement on Buka Island*

Pnina Werbner, *The Migration Process: Capital, Gifts and Offerings among Pakistanis in Britain*

Joel S. Kahn, *Constituting the Minangkabau: Peasants, Culture, and Modernity in Colonial Indonesia*

Gisli Pálsson, *Beyond Boundaries: Understanding, Translation and Anthropological Discourse*

Stephen Nugent, *Amazonian Caboclo Society*

Barbara Bender, *Landscape: Politics and Perspectives*

Christopher Tilley (ed.), *Interpretative Archaeology*

Ernest S. Burch, Jr. and Linda J. Ellanna, *Key Issues in Hunter-Gatherer Research*

Daniel Miller, *Modernity – An Ethnographic Approach: Dualism and Mass Consumption in Trinidad*

Robert Pool, *Dialogue and the Interpretation of Illness: Conversations in a Cameroon Village*

Cécile Barraud, Daniel de Coppet, André Iteanu and Raymond Jamous (Eds), *Of Relations and the Dead: Four Societies Viewed from the Angle of their Exchanges*

Christopher Tilley, *A Phenomenology of Landscape: Places, Paths and Monuments*

Victoria Goddard, Josep Llobera and Cris Shore (Eds), *The Anthropology of Europe: Identity and Boundaries in Conflict*

Pat Caplan, *Understanding Disputes: The Politics of Argument*

Daniel de Coppet and André Iteanu (Ed.), *Society and Cosmos: Their Interrelations or Their Coalescence in Melanesia*

Alisdair Rogers and Steven Vertovec (Eds), *The Urban Context: Ethnicity, Social Networks and Situational Analysis*

Word, Sound, Image

The Life of the Tamil Text

Saskia Kersenboom

BERG PUBLISHERS
Oxford • Washington, D.C.

First published in 1995 by
Berg Publishers Limited
Editorial offices:
150 Cowley Road, Oxford, OX4 1JJ, UK
13950 Park Center Road, Herndon, VA 22071, USA

© Saskia Kersenboom

All rights reserved.
No part of this publication may be reproduced in any form
or by any means without the written permission of
Berg Publishers Limited.

Library of Congress Cataloging-in-Publication Data

A catalogue record for this book is available from the Library of
Congress.

British Library Cataloguing in Publication Data

A catalogue record for this book is available from the British
Library.

Cover Photograph: © Marco Borggreve, Stadhouderslaan 27,
Utrecht.

ISBN 0 85496 424 X (Cloth)
      1 85973 008 6 (Paper)

Printed in the United Kingdom by WBC Bookbinders, Bridgend,
Mid Glamorgan.

In memory of

Shri Kandappa Ganesan
(1924–1987)
genius of time

Contents

Acknowledgements	ix
Note on Transcription and Transliteration	xii
List of Abbreviations	xiii
Preface	xv
1 Introduction	1
Part I: Habitus	25
2 Text	27
3 World	41
4 Performer	82
Part II: Praxis	117
5 Speech Artefact	119
6 Form	143
7 Content	159
Part III: Representation	169
8 Orientation	171
9 Reproduction	178
10 Objectification	196
11 Translation	211
Conclusion	226
Select Bibliography	241
Glossary	246
Index	254

Acknowledgements

The debt incurred while developing this theme and the subsequent publication is enormous. It covers years of trust, friendship and teaching, hospitality and care that I received from my teachers in India and abroad. In seniority, Shri T. Sankaran, Smt. P. Ranganayaki, the late Dr V. Raghavan, the late Shri V. S. Tyagaraja Mudaliar and his wife, the late Shri K. Ganesan, Pulavar R. Kannan, the late Shri M. Nageswara Rao, Shri B. Krishnamoorthy, Smt. R. Ramani, Smt. Nandini Ramani and Smt. Vinita Venkataraman have all allowed me to be part of their artistic heritage and traditional erudition and thereby shaped my perception to a great extent for almost twenty years. The wealth of these thrust me into an intellectual challenge to my own academic milieu. This challenge raged to the full at the then still-existent Indological Department at Utrecht University (Prof. Dr K. V. Zvelebil, Dr Sanjukta Gupta and Dr Emmie te Nijenhuis) and at the Anthropological Sociological Centre at the University of Amsterdam (Prof. Dr J. Fabian), where I found several bold and bright students who never failed to prod further and further into my intellectual struggles to make both worlds meet. My classes with them, as well as their own attempts to apply these ideas in their fieldwork, proved to be invaluable touchstones for the vitality of my ideas. Therefore I remember all of them with gratitude. The toughest challenge, surely, was the ten months at the Netherlands Institute for Advanced Study in the Humanities and Social Sciences (NIAS, Wassenaar, Holland). During the academic year of 1991/2 I was generously offered the opportunity to form a theme group that was to study the phenomenon of Orality as a systematic strategy of communication. At a later stage this theme group was extended to Orality versus Literacy, and, indeed, the *versus* proved to be a paradigmatic controversy of the first order. It was the inspiring fire and commitment of Prof. Dr Bruce Kapferer and Prof. Dr

René Devisch that kept my spirits up. The relentless insistence of Bruce Kapferer on the conceptualisation and propositional communication that enable a true exchange of ideas instead of a cascade of erudite data are ever fresh in my mind. I thank him for never slackening his demands and forcing my thinking to move beyond. I thank NIAS for this opportunity to 'think one's maximum for the sake of intellectual survival'.

The road that finally led me to the Compact Disc-interactive has been a long, winding and hazardous one. The number of 'short sketches of the project', 'the size of about one A-4', has escaped the grasp of my memory. A seemingly unending series of keen, interested faces has encouraged me from 1988 onwards to pursue my vision. An almost equally large number lost their enthusiasm when the project revealed its financial consequences. At this point I would like to thank those who have helped me to concretise my conviction that CD-i is ideally suited to represent cultural expertise: the Centre for Knowledge Technology (University of Utrecht), Mr Jaap ten Hoope (Digital Equipment, then Philips), Drs J. Nolthuis (Educa Video, Utrecht), Mr B. R. O. Naeyaert (Philips Media), Mr Rene F. J. van den Bichelaer (CODIM), Mr Wim van der Linden (then CODIM), Drs Johan Vos (Transferpunt, University of Amsterdam), who tamed all the adverse forces in the turmoil of business negotiations, and, especially, Gert-Jan van Ratingen, software engineer, and Ger de Vries, graphic designer, at CODIM, without whose talents and perseverance this CD-i Bhairavi Varnam would not have materialised. In the end, it is they who did the real job.

I would like to express my deeply felt gratitude to the committee of recommendation that assembled to save the project from financial catastrophe: Drs K. J. Gevers, President of the University of Amsterdam, Prof. Dr D. J. van de Kaa, Director of NIAS and His Excellency the Ambassador of India to the Netherlands, Shri I. P. Khosla, gave their invaluable support to the realisation of the CD-i. Also, I would like to thank Prof. Dr Ing R. Scha (University of Amsterdam, Alfa-Informatics) and Prof. Dr J. Renkema (Catholic University Brabant, Discourse Studies) for their encouragement and support. This joint publication of the monograph *Word, Sound, Image: The Life of the Tamil Text* and the *CD-i Bhairavi Varnam* would not have been possible without the financial support of the International Institute for Asian Studies (IIAS), the Netherlands Organisation for Scientific Research (NWO), Philips Media and Rabo Merchant Bank N.V. The underlying research was sponsored by generous fellowships of the Royal Academy of Arts and Sciences and of the Netherlands Institute for Advanced Study in the Humanities and Social Sciences, by stipends from the Netherlands Organisation for Scientific Research (NWO) and by tenure at the University of Amsterdam.

Throughout the entire process my husband, Alfred J. van Duren MBA, has encouraged me as well as criticised my work with sobering common sense and sharp insight. His support has preserved my stamina and endurance of it all. Moreover, he is the reassuring embodiment of the world outside one's study, a world full of life, vitality, beauty and love.

Note on Transcription and Transliteration

The transcription used for Tamil technical terms and names of texts, music and dance compositions, is based on a strict transliteration according to the system adopted by the *Tamil Lexicon* (Madras University, 1982). The transcription of Sanskrit terms follows the *Sanskrit–English Dictionary* of Sir M. Monier-Williams (Oxford University Press, 1970). In the case of personal names we have adhered to the transcription preferred by the person in question. If a firsthand record of such choice was not available, we have preferred to transcribe names as literally as possible, either from Tamil or from Sanskrit. Loanwords from Sanskrit in Tamil or mixed terms have been rendered as employed in their specific contexts. Place names follow mostly the commonly used anglicised version. For the sake of readability Sanskrit, Telugu and Tamil diacritics have not been used in the main text; these details can be found in full in the glossary.

List of Abbreviations

AI	–	Artificial Intelligence
CD	–	Compact Disc
CD-i	–	Compact Disc Interactive
CD-ROM	–	Compact Disc Read Only Memory
DED	–	Dravidian Etymological Dictionary
Ka.	–	Kannada
NS	–	*Natyasastra*
Skt.	–	Sanskrit
Ta.	–	Tamil
Te.	–	Telugu
TP	–	*Tolkappiyam*

Preface

Enta prayogam? 'What's the use?' – a wary question often heard while trying to get one's data 'straight'. Literally, *enta prayogam* means 'Which application?';[1] and, indeed, how do we apply the knowledge that was gathered at such high costs? What do our painstaking efforts amount to? To the scholar his or her[2] publication may be a result to be proud of: it constitutes the proof of understanding the subject-matter of one's research. But to the Tamil expert and informant scholarly interest, research and its products are by no means a hard proof of insight. *Prayogam*, or application, brings out the notion of a pragmatic nature of understanding.

Originally, *enta prayogam* hit me as a question that I tried to answer in scholarly terms. Such answers never satisfied their audience. Thus, the question transformed itself into a demand for scholarship to satisfy. As a student of Indology I witnessed the grandeur of Philology and Literary Sciences in the examples set by Jan Gonda and Kamil Zvelebil. Classes in Sanskrit and Tamil with them were full of erudition, vision and inspiration that instilled awe and excitement over the new horizons they were able to open up before our eyes. However, Philology-at-large seemed to create a puzzling sense of *vacuum*. When confronted for the first time, in 1975, with the lush South Indian reality, it dawned upon me that my uneasiness 'back home' might have something to do with our type of scholarship. In the same year I began my apprenticeship in South Indian traditional dance, called Bharata Natyam, with Smt. Nandini Ramani, student of the legendary Smt. T. Balasarasvati. At Utrecht University, the training in dance and the study of Indian languages seemed to many to be miles apart and incompatible. Now, almost twenty years later, the continuous training in South Indian traditional dance and music has proved to be crucial fieldwork in Tamil literature.

The Tamils speak a language that belongs to the Dravidian family. It can claim a 'classical status' on account of its early, indigenous grammars and its textual continuity over two thousand years. As early as the sixth century AD the Tamils defined their language as being threefold: *Muttamil* (literally 'three Tamil'), comprising word, music and mimetic dance. The natural consequences of this definition imply that the Tamil language assumes its full scope only in expressions cast in three medial *forms* and in the dimension of *time*. Tamil texts share these features. Their multimedial character, the fourth dimension of time, and their 'doubly interactive setting' between sender and receiver form the core of the problems that Western scholarship encounters when trying to describe, analyse, interpret and represent Tamil literature.

Until today, the concept of *Muttamil* has not been pursued logically, nor has Tamil literature been allowed a conclusive, rigorous, genre-based classification. This failure cannot be attributed to any individual scholar, but rather to methods of research. Generally, textual data are recorded and analysed in line with their final mode of representation, that is, publication. The format of a book did not only colour the perception of textual data, it provided as well the guiding principles of description, analysis and interpretation. If data were understood to form a book, then surely 'meaning' should be elicited by reading. The twin 'reading-and-writing' that constitutes a vital paradigm in the Humanities does not form a natural pair in Tamil scholarship. Here, writing does not necessarily give rise to reading; it rather serves as a memory aid to a performance of the text. The full representation of a text is therefore not found in a document but in an event. As a result meaning is produced in an entirely different manner. One might say that the Western proof of solid textual scholarship is voiced by the academic 'must' *publish or perish*, whereas the traditional Tamil expert adheres to the ultramodern saying, popular at the MIT, *demo or die*, i.e. demonstrate or die![3]

In 1987 I received a fellowship from the Royal Netherlands Academy of Arts and Sciences to investigate the concept *Muttamil* and its implications for the Tamil language and its literature. From the start I decided to accept the self-definition of Tamil as being literally threefold. This meant to pursue its practical consequences and to become a student in Tamil prosody and in instrumental music. Early Tamil grammarians regarded the large lute as vocal cords made visible, and refer to it in matters of phonology.[4] The *vina* is considered its direct descendant. Side by side I continued my training in dance and in vocal music. Here, as elsewhere, people kept asking me *enta prayogam* 'Which application?' The only convincing argument for studying *Muttamil* was actual demonstration. My 'official debut' in dance took place in March 1989 in Shri Krishnaganasabha (Madras). Quite often *pulavar* R. Kannan prompted me to substantiate my point of studying Tamil prosody by reciting medieval Tamil poetry and grammars on the art of prosody. The same demand was felt by my music teachers Shri B. Krishnamoorthy (vocal), Smt. R. Ramani, Smt. Vinita Venkataraman and the late Shri M. Nageswara Rao (*vina*); I am sure they will not approve until they hear and see me performing before a Madras audience as well. Such is the pressure of application as proof of analytic capacity, synthetic grasp, comprehension, understanding and 'feel' of style and nuance in interpretation that the search for an apt representation of knowledge other than performance became increasingly difficult.

My first confrontation with computerised multimedia, in 1988, proved to be an eye-opener that took me in the direction of the very recent invention of CD-i: the Compact Disc-interactive.[5] After the success of CD-audio, CD-ROM (Read Only Memory) digitalised the printed word. Now, Compact Disc-interactive has succeeded in combining the earlier Video Disc and Compact Disc functions into one disc comprising word, sound and moving image. Multimedia have reached a point where they can truly be called 'secondary orality'. Predictions made some thirty years ago by Marshall McLuhan and others have come true.[6] The object of research, being 'primary orality', poses new demands for a new type of scholarship. Philological precision falls short when studying the phenomenon of real-time communication by which an oral tradition is shared and transmitted. Linguistic Anthropology afforded me new, broader and more generous parameters to analyse and comprehend such phenomena.

With the advent of CD-i anthropological and linguistic fieldwork are offered a chance to represent their data, which depend on word, sound and image as their existential condition, as well as their analyses, in one comprehensive exteriorised form. CD-i picks up the above challenge where Video alone has to let go. Although film, video and audio recordings serve an excellent purpose on the descriptive level, they do not offer any possibility of interacting with the program and asking questions of an analytical, compositional or semantic nature. An attempt to interfere with a video or audio recording results in a stop, a still, a slowing down or a close-up, but not in an answer nor in a 'research trajectory' behind the still. CD-i can do all that film, video and CD-audio achieved separately, plus providing the traditional facilities offered by the book: we may enter the domain of transcriptions, translations, prose, graphs, drawings, commentaries – in short, the entire apparatus inherited from the technology and culture of writing. CD-i invites scholarship to add to the huge heritage of the book, the treasure house of three-dimensional form that belongs to the sphere of Fine Arts, as well as the mysteries of time as they are known to the Performing Arts. Thus it poses a challenge to the Humanities as a demand for a truly interdisciplinary study. CD-I as a knowledge representation synthesises scientific analyses that gradually fragmented into lives of their own. These various lives are moulded now, once again, into one organic whole.

Word, Sound, Image: The Life of the Tamil Text is a book and is not a book. *As a book* it takes up one Tamil text as an example of Tamil literature. The 'oral genius' of the Tamil textual tradition is brought out by the fact that the three lines that form the manuscript of this text may take thirty or more minutes to perform. Philology and Hermeneutics are at a loss here, and are forced to enter into a new dialogue. This monograph is the playground for that dialogue. The INTRODUCTION juxtaposes the two traditions of *erudition* by reassessing the concept of 'text'. Part I, HABITUS, highlights the text as *textus*, that is, as a weave interweaving with the world. Part II, PRAXIS, examines the text as a *speech artefact*, as a product of artisanal skills, chiselled into a dynamic, meaningful form. Finally, Part III, REPRESENTATION, questions the nature of data *storage* as well as of the *representation* of knowledge. Embodiment, transmission and performance are contrasted with abstraction, custody and lasting objectification.

As a vehicle this publication holds an 'incremental future': its dust-jacket contains a CD-i demonstration disc. The 'demo' offers five minutes out of the total half hour it takes to perform the full Tamil text discussed in the monograph. It aims to be a mini-size demonstration of what a new textual scholarship might look like when facilitated by CD-i. At the descriptive level we find the integral recording of a sentence of Tamil words, sounds and images. Questions at the descriptive level are answered by transcription of the three separate layers of the sound, the word and the image, as well as by the translation of the latter two. At the analytical level the user may choose to enter the worlds behind the event: on the one hand the world of FORM, and on the other, the world of CONTENT. Questions concerning the first open up the formative grammars of Tamil prosody, music and dance, whereas questions about the second move through semantic networks that connect the five minutes of the Tamil text with the conventions of the Tamil universe. At the interpretative level, the 'speech artefact' emerges as a concrete moment in the continuous, ever-active movement between forming and meaning.

The question 'Which application?' is being challenged by the present attempt. Apart from the live training and performance that make up the age-old method of storing, maintaining and analysing oral tradition, this experiment instantiates a new way of studying texts, on the one hand, by committing philology to the praxis of 'participant participation' as a praxis of anthropology; and, on the other hand, by representing these texts together with the analyses of their praxes and cultural world through a medium that is as flexible and true to the real-life event as possible. To conceptualise 'culture' as a 'performing art' demands an application that differs from writing taken alone. This experiment proposes such an application by combining graphic and multimedial publication. Thus one part of the question *enta prayogam*, namely 'Which application?', has been answered; the other part, 'What is the use?', is to be answered by the interactive reader.

Notes to the Preface

1. The Tamil term *pirayo kam* (Skt. *prayoga*) is of crucial importance in the present intellectual pursuit; it questions the methodological grounds and aims of academic research. In a broader context it may mean: 'discharge – as of weapons', 'use, application to a purpose, use of means', 'practice of magic', 'medicine', 'authority, quotation', 'example,

illustration'. Its derivation *prayojana* (Ta. *pirayocanam*) indicates the result of such practice: 'usefulness', 'profit, advantage', 'result of actions', 'reward'.
2. For reasons of stylistic economy and ease the general use of the masculine third person singular should be understood as indicating both male and female gender.
3. See Brand, S., *The Media Lab, Inventing the Future at M.I.T.*, p. 4. 'Students and professors at the Media Laboratory write papers and books and publish them but the byword in this grove of academia is not "Publish or Perish". In Lab parlance it's "Demo or Die" – make the case for your idea with an unfaked performance of it working at least once, or let somebody else at the equipment. "We write about what we do", comments Director Negroponte, "but we don't write unless we have done it."'
4. *Tolkappiyam*, Chapter *Eluttu atikaram*, Stanza 33: aḷapiṟan-tuyirttalum oṟṟicai nīṭalum/ uḷaveṉa moḻipa icaiyoṭu civaṇiya/ narampiṉ maṟaiya eṉmaṉār pulavar// 'the experts say that it belongs to the secret knowledge of the string that joins with sound, to resonate the latent realities of both breathing passed into measurement and the lengthening of realised sound'.
5. Harvard University, Special Program in the study of Oral Tradition and Literature, then organised by Prof. Dr Albert Lord and Prof. Dr Gregory Nagy.
6. See the chapters 'The Making of Typographic Man' and 'The Galaxy Reconfigured' in Marshal McLuhan's *The Gutenberg Galaxy*; also the chapter 'Print, Space and Closure' on 'secondary orality' in W. J. Ong's *Orality and Literacy, The Technologizing of the Word*, pp. 117–38.

Chapter 1

Introduction

Wos lejgner a blinder lebt, alz mer set er.

– Yiddish proverb

'The longer a blind man lives, the more he sees!' A paradox for an answer. Throughout his entire work George Steiner poses the question about the merit of literary studies. In his essay *To Civilize our Gentlemen* (Steiner 1969, 77–91), he sets out to identify such presumed merit in terms of 'the source and essence of a truly humanizing culture',[1] only to conclude the very opposite:

> It is at least conceivable that the focusing of consciousness on a written text which is the substance of our training and pursuit diminishes the sharpness and readiness of moral response ... The capacity for imaginative reflex or moral risk in any human being is not limitless: on the contrary, it can be rapidly absorbed by fictions, thus the cry in the poem may come to sound louder, more urgent, more real than the cry in the street outside (Steiner 1969, 83–4).

The urgency in Steiner's quest resembles the Tamil insistence on *enta prayogam?* 'What's the use?', or, 'Which application?' He seriously doubts the moral idealism that inspired and validated the Humanities in the eighteenth and nineteenth centuries. The concatenation of wars, cruelties and human violence makes it painfully clear that the old premises and optimism do not work in our times. Reading 'great literature' bears no moral fruit. Perhaps because 'literature takes a great deal of living with and living by' (Steiner 1969, 77). But how do we perform such 'living with and living by'? As a profession, a career,[2] or as an identification and embodiment?

From the angle of a professional occupation with the text, we may observe that the existential condition of scholarship is the text – reading the text, writing the text.[3] Such life is determined by a 'permanent game of references referring mutually to each other' (Bourdieu 1990, 103). The scholar weaves from himself a web of intertextuality, suspended between the works of others. It constitutes the 'symbolic capital' of the intellectual, standing out on its own without any root in the experiential world. The currency of this symbolic capital is coined in terms of erudition and academic power.[4]

This self-enclosure of the textual life and of the text as a sign of knowledge and as a password to power is telling in the light of Foucault's interpretation of the sign, that is, the sign as word and its relation to the world.[5] In his terms, the 'ancient sign' is merged with the world. To utter the word is to enter the thing. Activated by the mysterious powers of language, the word opens up the very experiential reality it refers to. In contrast, the 'classical sign' splits into two: a natural sign that is given by natural phenomena, and a conventional sign that is discerned and attributed by mankind. The latter sign craves representation in order to communicate and survive. Language, once more, becomes representation: at this point, however, no longer as speech, but as script. The classical sign emerges as a crystal-clear, visible description of the conventions of the world. It takes the shape of a treatise, a 'grammar' that is systematically codified and that aims to be conclusive. The treatise is solidly concrete and paper-bound, so that form and content may last for mankind to hold, see and read and to educate society.

Bourdieu (1990, 70) remarks that the ambition to codify and represent in a systematic manner should be accompanied by a theory of the effect of codification. This warning is to be taken seriously: as the classical sign bifurcated into two signs, pursuing two different directions, it entered into two fundamentally different lives. The natural sign continued to live and breathe with the world: water remained water, fire continued to be fire as it continued to be hot. But the other, new sign turned away from the world – just a quarter: the treatise describes the conventions of the world and allows the reader to study the text and to compare it with the sunlit world. Such contemplation and comparison no longer draw their vital energy from roots cast into the natural, wet and smelly soil, but from their suspension in an abstracted realm. Professionally speaking, the expert of the world no longer takes the world for reference, but concentrates, instead, on his own textual orbit.

Introduction

The third sign spins off from the conventional sign. The ambition of the classical sign, to offer a treatise that should be conclusive, proved to be insatiable. Any conventional sign produced by one generation provides ground for interpretation to the next. Thus, the genesis of one text from the other turns into an endless chain of rebirths that crave a life of their own, cast into individual textual representation. The fragmentation of the ancient sign, at this point, reached a hectic pace. The old situation of speech, of word as utterance, was marked by a unity of sender, receiver, time and place. The text as sign suspends these four coordinates in no man's land: writer and reader have turned half a circle away from the world. With their backs to the circumstance of seasons, of dawn and dusk, untouched by the five senses, they live a professional life of their own, individually, in a world fashioned by man-made conditions and imperatives. Here indeed the blind man does not need eyes to see: the inner sweep of his imagination suffices: in fact, it is richer, louder, more urgent and more real than the world outside.

With the 'classical' and the 'modern' sign Bourdieu's warning assumes its full implication. The force of textual entropy of scholarship makes not only Steiner gasp for breath. The ardent plea of Said in his *Orientalism*[6] demonstrates what havoc such a literary attitude has brought about in the study, description, analysis and interpretation of non-Western literatures and cultures. Said argues that, to some, the Orient was a career caught up in a network of political power; to others, poets and moral idealists, the Orient was an intoxicating vision, a *fata morgana* that could never disappoint nor be dismantled, as they never attempted to get physically close.[7]

After some five centuries of Western Tamil scholarship a reassessment of very basic notions of Tamil texts and their production and reception is inevitable, if only for pragmatic reasons, such as an adequate description of their form, let alone as an adequate representation of the communicative power of their content. By reopening the questions of the *status, nature, reality, representation and raison d'être* of the Tamil text, we part company with traditional Western Philology and Hermeneutics. By processing a sample of Tamil textual activity on a Compact Disc-interactive, we explore new ways of representing texts, away, again, from the modes of representation that were almost synonymous with the methodologies mentioned above. As a 'new sign' deeply rooted in real-life praxis, it hopes to complete the circle that was started five centuries ago. Thus back again, facing the world, this 'new sign' may do more justice to a literature that insisted for two thousand years on maintaining a fully-fledged relationship with the sensuous, experiential world.

Texts

The confrontation of Western scholarship and indigenous Tamil learning resulted in an impressive output of grammars, dictionaries, lexicons, editions of Tamil texts, translations and interpretations over a period of almost five centuries. But these were rarely transferred into a dialogue.[8] All activities were marked by an explicit agenda on both sides: ranging from religious fervour, missionary zeal, scientific positivism and administrative ambition to the demarcation of group and national identity. These motivations derived their vitality from other sources than Tamil textual creativity 'on its own terms'. Their relevance was clear from the start and in some cases continues to be so. What remains today, when missionary and administrative aims have ceased, and the belief in the positivist ideals of literary science has abated? Mere description, translation, a historical cabinet or museum? Perhaps, Tamil verbal art – again? As a novice student of Bharata Natyam I made the eager mistake of enquiring from the great dancer Smt. T. Balasarasvati what she thought of the 'future' of Bharata Natyam. The answer was stunningly different from what I could imagine: 'Tcha, what is there? Dance has always been, so it will continue. If you are a dancer, you dance.' This shattered my confident enthusiasm for interpretation and explanation on a 'meta' level. In analogy, Tamil literature has been there, notably, for twenty centuries. Like the dancer who dances, a vital literature will be, if only because of its acute immediacy.

Examples of such tenacity are found in lyrical poems that go back to the earliest strata of Tamil literature. Two thousand years ago courtesans performed *varnams* for the Tamil king; in the twentieth century performing artists still do so. It is in the synchronic immediacy of experiencing the performance that all validations merge and blur. No philological, historical, religious,

Introduction

moral, hermeneutic, psychological, functional, structuralist, semiotic, receptionist, sociological or (neo)-Marxist analysis and interpretation can represent what that textual event is. If all interpretation boils down to reductionism that falls short of the event, then why try? Or should we search for the crucial difference elsewhere, in another methodology and another mode of representing the Tamil text? The gap between nineteenth-century and earlier orientalist Philology or Hermeneutics and the indigenous Tamil expert must have been unbridgeable. We realise this, in retrospect, when we take a critical look at their respective agendas, expressed in and on their own terms. First, the agenda of the Humanities, because they pleaded so explicitly and eloquently for their own cause. Ricoeur summarises Philology and Hermeneutics as follows:

> ... hermeneutics comprises something specific; it seeks to reproduce an interconnection, a structured totality by drawing support from a category of signs which have been fixed by writing, or by any other process of inscription equivalent to writing. So it is no longer possible to grasp the mental life of others in its immediate expressions; rather it is necessary to reproduce it, by interpreting objectified signs. This *Nachbilden* (reproducing) requires distinct rules since the expressions are embedded in objects of a particular nature.... it is philology – the explanation of texts – which provides the scientific stage of understanding.
>
> For both thinkers [i.e. Schleiermacher and Dilthey: SK], the essential role of hermeneutics consists therein: 'to establish theoretically against the constant intrusion of romantic whim and sceptical subjectivism ..., the universal validity of interpretation upon which all certainty in history rests.[9]

In moments of actual encounter with alien textual activity, this agenda proved to be a hidden one: phenomena were not studied in order to detect their individual coherence and autonomy, but rather for the sake of something hidden, behind them: a *universal-validity-of-interpretation-upon-which-all-certainty-in-history-rests*. This cascade of concepts was bewilderingly strange to Tamil experts. The secular character of historical and philological analysis, as much as the romantic spirituality of Hermeneutics, was unknown and unloved in Tamil company. Both, however, developed powerful material tools, such as grammars, dictionaries, text-editions, libraries and museums, that were to be admired; mental tools, such as the concepts: interconnection, comparison, structured totality, fixation, *Nachbildung*, *Auslegung* and *Interpretation*, produced constructs that had no physical shape or presence, but were nevertheless there, influencing the quality of life. Orientalism developed a life of its own, reigning supreme in the West and as an obnoxious reminder of difference in the East. The agenda of Tamil experts was a straightforward one: their language, and *eo ipso* their literature, were of divine origin, of divine substance and directed at a divine aim. The gift of 'threefold Tamil' is a gift from God. Even today students of Tamil learn by heart a prayer to the elephant-headed god Shri Vinayaka, Lord of Obstacles:

> pālum teḷiteṉum pākum paruppum ivai
> nālum kalantuṉakku nāṉ taruvēṉ kōlañcey
> tūṅka karimukattut tūmaṇiyē
> nīyeṉakku caṅkattamiḻ mūṉrum tā

> Milk, clear honey, coarse sugar and porridge – these all four in a mixture
> I give to you, O pure Ruby, whose elephant head is striking because of its swaying decorated trunk;
> you, in return, must give to me the Academic Tamil that is threefold.

This stanza is ascribed to the poetess Auvaiyar (twelfth century AD), and is taught as reminder of the divine origin of the Tamil language. Only through mediation of the gods can Tamil be absorbed by human beings. The knowledge of Tamil, the words, the sound and its enactment instantiate the divine: Appar, a poet-saint of the late sixth century AD, describes the god Shiva as muttamiḻum nāṉmaṟaiyum āṉāṉ (*Tevaram* 6.23.9.1.), 'the One who has become *Muttamil* and the four *Vedas*'. In other words, God incarnates into the threefold Tamil. The very utterance of Tamil is vibrant with divine presence and power. The threefold nature of Tamil is believed to generate such conditions of divine presence.

Not all Tamil is capable of doing so. The ordinary, everyday Tamil, spoken at home and in the market-place, does not have these powers. It is called *kotum tamil*, 'bent, uneven, crooked Tamil'. In order to acquire a divine quality it has to be chiselled, as the goldsmith melts and forms his precious metal. It was in the so-called *cankams*, Academies or gatherings of experts, that the standards for 'good artisanship' were set and tested. As a result 'qualified Tamil' was also *cankattamil*, implying a triple expertise: *iyal* (natural word), *icai* (musical rendering) and *natakam* or *kuttu* (mimetic rendering). The last two modes of expression, especially, safeguard the divine powers of the language. In order to hear and see, one must be there as a witness; and, in the case of a god, one's incarnation must be committed to an experiential, sensorily accessible presence.

This promise of interconnecting the momentary physical with the metaphysical eternal is held by the threefold Tamil. Its formula of natural word, musical rendering and mimetic rendering is chiselled according to the standards of the experts in the community, as *cem tamil* or *centamil*, 'auspicious Tamil'. *Centamil* always stood in contrast to *kotuntamil*, not as 'literary' to 'spoken' Tamil, as we are told by early and contemporary Western grammarians,[10] but as 'holy, auspicious' Tamil to 'ordinary, rough' Tamil. It is therefore not surprising that the traditional aim of Tamil texts was not reading but 'presencing', that is, making the text present.

In this vein, the philosopher-saint Tirumular (late sixth century) says in stanza 15 of *Tirumantiram*

> ennainan rāka iraivan pataittānān
> tannainan rākat tamil ceyyu mārē
>
> The Lord has made me well /
> in order that (I) make Him well in Tamil //

This stanza is uttered in the context of describing himself as 'one who has been ruminating rare food, i.e. the knowledge of *Muttamil* that forms the essence (literally 'that-ness') of the Eternal in the form of the god Shiva'. Taking the divine as its origin, substance and aim, Tamil textual activity followed an agenda that was totally incompatible with Western literary sciences. As a result the two traditions mainly followed their own tenets, sometimes because of lack of understanding but more often because they found it hard to take each other seriously. Interesting 'cross-breeds' have seen the tropical light, such as Father Beschi's *Paramartta kuruvin katai*, 'the story of Guru Paramartta', composed in Tamil poetic conventions and dealing with Christian themes. Or the many *Histories of Tamil Literature* that added to the prestige of Tamil, but not much to History in Western terms. In short, the confrontation between Western Linguistics and Literary Sciences on the one hand, and Tamil and its textual achievements on the other did not evoke any factual recognition. The secular, Western object called 'text' that functioned as a building-block in an epistemological or moral–spiritual edifice, and the Tamil divine presence of the word had close to nothing in common.

Data

Which data formed the basis of these respective agendas? First, the agenda of 'establishing theoretically the universal-validity-of-interpretation-upon-which-all-certainty-in-history-rests'. Here, however, agreement on the methods appropriate to the construction of scientific theories is by no means unanimous. In his *Thematic Origins of Scientific Thought* (1988) Gerald Holton offers a scheme that reflects both general and popular understanding. It moves in five steps:

1 Tentatively, propose as a *hypothesis* a provisional statement obtained by induction from experience and previously established knowledge of the field.
2 Refine and structure the hypothesis (...) by making a mathematical or physical *analogon*.
3 Draw *logical conclusions* or *predictions* from the structured hypothesis which gave promise of experimental check.
4 *Check* the predicted consequences (deduced from the analogon) against experience, by free observation or experimental arrangement.
5 If the deduced consequences are found to *correspond* to the 'observed facts' within expected limits (and not only these consequences, but all different ones that can be drawn) then a warrant is available for the decision that 'the result is postulated as universally valid'. Thus, the hypothesis, or initial statement, is found to be scientifically 'established'.[11]

When we apply this theory to the agenda of Philology and Hermeneutics, the first confrontation is constituted by the contact with a field of life in its 'immediate expressions'. The signs that emerge from that field have to be made into an object for reflection, as stated earlier, through a process of inscribing these signs on lasting materials such as paper. Step two is refining and structuring the hypothesis by making a mathematical or physical *analogon*. How do the Humanities go about this task? Ricoeur informed us that the *Nachbilden* (reproduction) required distinct rules. And, indeed, Philology claims to be the scientific basis for the representation of the text, that is, for the construction of the *analogon*. All further testing depends on the *analogon's* precision and adequacy. In a scientific agenda, the *analogon* demands a central and critical concern. Therefore Holton continues:

> ... if we try to understand the actions and decisions of an actual contributor to science, the categories and steps listed above are deficient because they leave out an essential point: to a smaller or larger degree, the process of building up an actual scientific theory requires explicit or implicit decisions, such as the adoption of certain hypotheses and criteria of preselection that are not at all scientifically "valid" in the sense previously given and usually accepted. One result of this recognition will be that the dichotomy between scientific and humanistic scholarship, which is undoubted and real at many levels, becomes far less impressive if one looks carefully at the construction of scientific theories. This will become evident first at the place where explicit and implicit decisions are most telling – namely, in the formation, testing, and acceptance or rejection of the hypotheses.[12]

If the formalisation and objectification of life into signs inscribed in writing constitutes the hypothesis of the Humanities in the confrontation with the field in its immediate, live expressions, and if, further, this structured text can be considered the *analogon*, then our scrutiny of the *analogon* has to address the writing of the text first. *What* is the 'text', *where* does it come from? Via a short cut, Ricoeur takes us through the vast territory of the theory of interpretation by linking it with the theory of language. The premiss of this theory is a fundamental distinction between system and discourse. He analyses discourse as a field composed of an internal dialectic between 'event' and 'meaning'. The Hermeneut distinguishes between two dimensions of meaning: the subjective aspect of what the speaker means and the objective meaning of what the sentence means. This objective meaning can be understood as an 'ideal sense' and as a 'real reference'. Only at the level of the sentence is language held to refer to something that is related to the extralinguistic world. The hermeneutic method now proceeds to elicit the objective meaning of the sentence through the 'semantics of discourse', to which we will return later. At this point we will restrict ourselves to mentioning its result: an emergent meaning. This emergence is accompanied by a transformation of the referential dimension and by a power to redescribe reality.[13] The nature of this transformation . . . is clarified by the concept of the text. The moment of the emerging transformation of the referential dimension and the power of redescription is crucial: it has to be caught and saved from the ephemeral nature of discourse-as-speech-event. It has to be objectified through inscription: thus the text comes into being. Its realisation in writing involves a series of characteristics that effectively distance the text from the conditions of spoken discourse. At this point the *analogon* is being constructed. Its method of construction is called *distanciation* or 'distancing', and involves four movements:[14]

1 surpassing the event of saying by the meaning of what is being said. It is this meaning which is inscribed in writing;
2 separation in the relation between the inscribed expression and the original speaker: 'what the text signifies no longer coincides with what the author meant. . .';
3 a similar separation between the inscribed expression and the original audience: the text 'decontextualises' itself from its social and historical conditions; and
4 the emancipation of the text from the limits of ostensive reference: whereas the reference of spoken discourse is ultimately determined by the shared reality of the speech situation, in the case of writing this shared reality no longer exists.

Thus the text emerges from the linguistic field.

The equivalent of the mathematical or physical *analogon* emerges as discourse in the objective meaning of the sentence in its ideal sense inscribed as text. Steps three and four in Holton's agenda dictate 'logical conclusions or predictions from the

Introduction

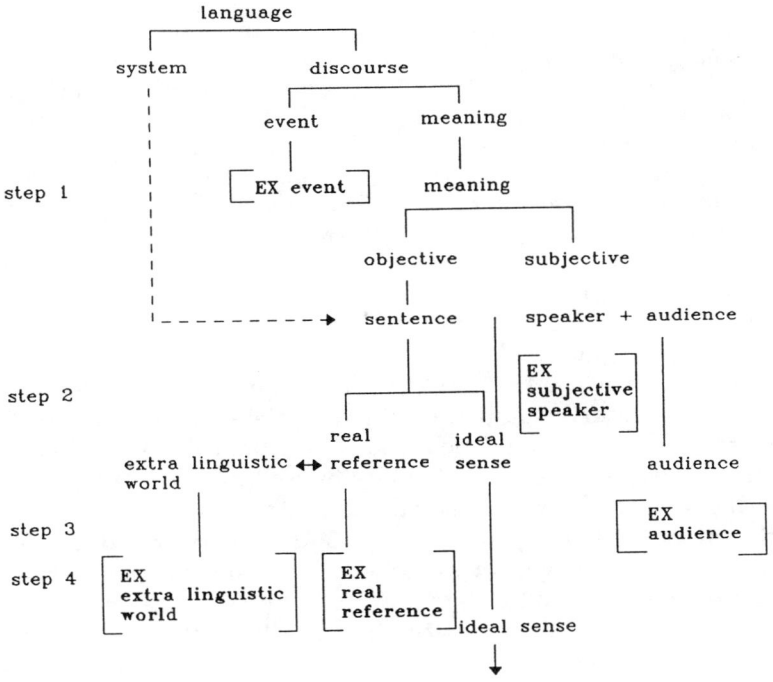

Figure 1 – the emergence of the text from the linguistic field

constructed hypothesis which have promise of experimental check', and the actual checking of the 'predicted consequences (deduced from the *analogon*) against experience, by free observation or experimental arrangement'. It is precisely at these 'scientific' steps that the nature of the Hermeneutic *paradigm* is revealed: *reading as the recovery of meaning* forms not only the drawing of logical conclusions or predictions but also their experimental check against experience, as well as the free observation or experimental arrangement! The explanation of texts and their interpretation erect a so-called Hermeneutical arc, encompassing an understanding that blossoms into appropriation:

> ... the process of interpretation culminates in an act of *appropriation* which forms the concluding counterpart of *distanciation*. To appro-

priate means "to make one's own" what was initially "alien", so that interpretation binds together, equalises, renders contemporary and similar. The act of appropriation does not seek to rejoin the original intentions of the author, but rather to expand the conscious horizons of the reader by actualising the meaning of the text. This theory of interpretation demands not only the initial suspension of the referential relation but also the initial relinquishment of subjectivity – this is a precondition for the ultimate expansion of consciousness under the objective guidance of the text.[15]

It seems hard to plead for 'free observation' and 'experimental check' under these circumstances. How on earth can we expect an 'objective guidance' of a text that has been constructed by the reading research community outside its dimensions in space and of time, without an audience, without a referential relation to the extra-textual, extralinguistic world, and, ultimately, even without a subject who consciously involves himself in the text? Such an *analogon* certainly will not stand the test of Holton's step five: 'If the deduced consequences are found to correspond to the "observed facts" within expected limits (and not only these consequences but all different ones that can be drawn) then a warrant is available for the decision that "the result is postulated as universally valid".' It seems that the implicit and explicit decisions that went into the Hermeneutic scientific theory, its *analogon* and paradigm were conditioned more by the wish to control the relationship of researcher and object of research than by scientific openness and equilibrium. Bourdieu holds that such a relationship is often an unconscious one, and that the discourses on the object of investigation are in fact often mere projections of the objective relation from subject to object.[16] This argument rings true when it comes to literatures other than Western ones. The elicitation of universal-validities-upon-which-all-certainty-in-history-rests from Tamil literature must be scrupulously held with open-minded scepticism. To Holton, universal validity remains fragile: 'The scientist does not take a dogmatic view of his assumption, he does not herald it abroad, but keeps the question open and submits his opinion to the dedication of nature itself, prepared to accept this decision without reserve.'[17]

Similarly Western scholarship is ready for a renewed confrontation with nature itself, that is, with the living textual tradition of the Tamils. After having invented and worked out sharp analytical tools such as grammars, dictionaries, lexicons and precise descriptions of the verbal substrate of Tamil texts, the time seems ripe for Hermeneutics to head for a confrontation with the live event that includes sound and image. Only then will step five of Holton's scheme be taken.

What does the Tamil linguistic field look like? In terms of Ricoeur's mapping, five characteristics immediately stand out: first, as a language Tamil claims to be threefold: word, sound and mimetic image. In consequence we are confronted with the second feature: the system of language is threefold as well. The Tamil term employed to indicate the systematicity of language is *ilakkanam*, 'marker'; and indeed, we find markers, or 'grammars' in our terms, of the verbal, musical and dramatic arts that constitute Tamil. Third, discourse is termed 'the marked' (*ilakkiyam*). Discourse is a marked event, marked by the markers of word, sound and visual image. This might be compared to Ricoeur's 'life in its immediate expressions' and thus create an expectation of eliciting from the flow of discourse systematicity on the one hand, and 'meaning' on the other. Tamil theory on discourse thwarts that hope, causing a critical rift between Tamil and Western literary concepts. In the relationship between system and discourse, the Tamils hold that discourse always comes first, it precedes system.[18] The initial confrontation is with *ilakkiyam*, the 'marked'; *ilakkanam*, the 'marker', inheres in it, and can be evaluated only in its live context. Not only is discourse considered to be the vehicle of system; the latter cannot even survive without it. In other words, couching it in terms of theory and praxis: praxis is always the condition for theory, and without it there is no locus for theory to exist! Discourse as praxis is a marked event, composed of a confluence of words, images and sounds. It is hard to abstract this flow into an 'objectified sign' that represents meaning. The entire relationship and balancing of constituent parts that are at play in Tamil literature frustrate Ricoeur's agenda.

And if we take this agenda as characteristic of Western literary studies, then they frustrate Orientalism as well. This becomes painfully clear when we examine the data that formed the basis for Western Oriental scholarship. The edition and translation of Tamil texts was based on access to Tamil manuscripts. This policy is well within European traditions; but, as can be understood by contemplating the whole field of Tamil textual creativity, it does not hold for Tamil literature. The culture of maintaining and studying manuscripts, in a way that we are familiar with from medieval monasteries, cannot be assumed automatically to be followed everywhere. One glance at a palmleaf manuscript may suffice to bring out its fragility and vulnerability to the ravages of a tropical climate and voracious ants. Moreover, the way of recording the Tamil text, without capital letters, makes the 'reading and studying' of manuscripts highly improbable. Tamil manuscripts, simply called 'leaf', *olai*, were used as memory aids mostly by those who already knew the text anyhow but who would use the leaves for reference or as an object of worship in their houses or in a shrine. *Olai* are not literature.[19] Yet it was exactly these leaves that formed the basis of Western text editions and translations. The equivalent of 'literature' is the phenomenon *ilakkiyam*. When referring to Tamil literature Western scholars referred to Tamil palmleaves, while the Tamils themselves conceive of their literature as *ilakkiyam*; in other words, as Tamil discourse marked by the markers of word, sound and image. The functional slot of the 'objectified sign' cannot be formed by the Tamil object of inscription but has to be the event itself. The multimedial interactive, dynamic and especially synthetic nature of such a communicative event made it difficult for the Western scholar to continue with the subsequent steps of his original agenda. Instead of a full stop, the manuscript provided a plausible way out.

The fifth feature of the linguistic field that startles the Western scholar is the Tamil concept of 'meaning'. The idea of eliciting an 'objective meaning' of the sentence in its 'ideal sense' seems truly 'meaningless' in the Tamil context. Their term that is used in this functional slot is *porul*, literally indicating 'thing', 'matter', 'object of reference'. Here Tamil reveals its character of 'ancient sign' in terms of Foucault: the relationship between words and things is certainly not an arbitrary one. On the contrary, the word and its referential basis in the world are tied together, breathing in unison. To activate the word is to activate the thing. Therefore, step four of *distanciation*, namely, severing the ties of the sentence with its referential, real-life meaning, and thus with the extralinguistic world, seems as unimaginable as it is unattractive.[20]

The Tamil text lives in symbiosis with the world; its testing ground is not its objectification as inscription, but its being performed in communication. Instead of lifting the word out of human interaction, Tamil literature depends on exposure to an interactive audience for its validation. Truth in terms of the universal-validity-upon-which-all-certainty-in-history-rests, takes a definite shape in Tamil terms: *mey* is used for translating the concept 'truth', but means literally 'body'. In fact, it is an inevitable 'quality of being', not an abstract entity on its own. Truth must be experiential in order to be true; thus it can be experienced only by the body. Such a state of experiencing is called *meyppatu* 'affecting the body' or *cuvai* 'tasting', as if tasting the 'taste of being'. Such tasting is the highest aim of Tamil discourse.

Two metaphors are used to suggest this experience. On the one hand, the idea of cooking is worked out in great detail. In this context we encounter the logic of a recipe (here, a compositional formula), ingredients and cooking instructions (here, the 'markers') and finally the characteristic dish (here, the 'marked') that is offered for tasting. The recipient should be a knowledgeable expert who is capable of tasting and appreciating the tasteful work of art. Such an audience is also called 'tasters' (Skt. *rasika*).

The other metaphor is taken from the art of painting. The literary composition that forms the central object of our discussion is termed *varnam*, literally meaning 'colour'. We will see how the *varnam* is created gradually in the activity of painting. The painting is conceived of not as a static end-product, but as an ongoing creation displaying the live canvas of the world. In the metaphor of painting by means of word, sound and image the character of Tamil literature as an 'ancient sign' that maintains its umbilical relation to the world is worked out best.

Both metaphors are sensuous, performative metaphors, rooted in a sharing of time and place. They follow a logic that guides us through Ricoeur's map of the linguistic field exactly along those routes that were closed off by him. Instead of erasing that quality of coordination by the parameters of time and place that marks the event of discourse, the event is considered a *conditio sine qua non*. Instead of eliciting systems out of discourse, systems are located exclusively in discourse. Instead of the text's usurping the role of the speaker, the speaker turns out to be the embodiment of the text. Instead of removing audience and historical context, the speech event interlaces with the moment, actively influencing it. Instead of abstracting truth it inscribes 'truth' in the world, in the sensory receptivity of actor and audience, invigorating the world by becoming its living sign. Thus, the text becomes the world in the course of performance, testing its own creation for effectivity in the world.

In other words, when we compare the data that underlie the two types of text, the two agendas of empirical testing, the two methods of doing so and their actual results, we are confronted with irreconcilable differences. While the nature of the Western text is static, an object of analytical abstraction, and takes the form of a document, the Tamil text is organic in nature, a process of synthetic absorption, living a reality of performance. The application of both differs as well: while the document adds to a database that eventually will produce the ultimate interpretation as truth, the performance offers a becoming, an embodiment of life, here and now. These extremes are substantiated in their material representations.

Knowledge Representation

> It is not worthwhile remembering
> that past
> which cannot become a present
> — Kierkegaard

> If there is a substitute for love,
> it is memory.
> To memorize then, is to restore intimacy.
> — Brodsky

The question that underlies and connects these two quotations is the question of the representation of knowledge. The form that is considered to be adequate and efficient tells us something about the 'temperament' of the knowledge it conveys. Such temperaments are revealed by the type of life that these forms of representation live; they bespeak implicitly their *epistemes* and ends. The two representations that we have been confronted with, namely, the document and the bodily event, are extreme polarities in a spectrum that shows one common denominator: the Sign as 'database'. This modern metaphor comes in handy while examining where and how we store our knowledge of ourselves and of the world. We will return to the question of knowledge and data as other than 'information' at several occasions in this work. Here, it suffices to examine that spectrum of databases that have been employed in the Humanities.

'It is not worthwhile remembering that past which cannot become a present' critically questions the actual merit of treatises, interpretations upon interpretations, proliferating in a seemingly endless spiral out of the humanly graspable orbit. It requires Humanistic idealism to believe in the Utopia of the 'ultimate community' that will appropriate the 'ultimate interpretation'.[21] The Philological and Hermeneutic texts spiral upwards along with this hope. The need to transcend the present as well as the past is a vital tenet in that creed: the more transcendent the knowledge, the more persistent and lasting it will prove to be. The book serves merely as a concrete, objective, non-interfering, stable base for that knowledge to remain intact and survive. The method for endowing the prose of the text with that transcendent quality is outlined by Ricoeur: it is termed 'the semantics of discourse'. It is believed to shed light 'on the primitive processes of creativity and interpretation in ordinary language'. 'The basic condition of creativity is the intrinsic polysemy of words, that is, the feature by which words in natural languages have more than one meaning.' Polysemy can be grasped only by a semantics of the sentence. Exposing the sentence to various contexts results in a vast array of meanings. The task of the Hermeneut is now to 'filter out' the surplus meaning, so that a univocal discourse can be produced from polysemic words. 'To grasp this filtering effect is to exercise interpretation in its most primordial sense.' How should we imagine the actual practice of this filtering? Ricoeur proposes a 'violation of the linguistic code' that creates a tension between two terms within the framework of the sentence:

> The metaphorical statement then appears as a reduction of this tension by means of a creative semantic pertinence within the sentence as a whole. Hence Ricoeur suggests that 'metaphor is a semantic innovation that belongs at once to the predicative order (pertinence) and the lexical order (paradigmatic deviation)'. The emergent meaning can be grasped only through a constructive

interpretation which makes sense of the sentence as a whole, building upon and extending the polysemy of metaphorical terms. The emergence of sense is accompanied by a transformation of the referential dimension, endowing the metaphor with its power to redescribe reality. The nature of this transformation which affects not only metaphor but literary works in general, is clarified by the concept of the text.[22]

This method of sifting the polysemy of words, making them clash with each other within a sentence until a univocal meaning emerges, is the way in which the 'objective meaning' of the sentence is elicited. The ultimate result, i.e. the ideal sense of the objective meaning of the sentence, is laid out in the 'text'. In his essay 'The Model of the Text' he outlines this progression from discourse event to the text in terms of *meaningful action considered as text*. Such text is not just a 'database', it forms the locus and opportunity for 'work'. The act of reading a text is an interpretative endeavour, an involvement that, according to Ricoeur, can be compared to the interpretation of a 'musical score'. However, at this point the shape of the knowledge representation and its related labour are revealing the nature of its content. We may observe the reader entering and leaving the pages of the book. As a result he neither speaks nor interacts with nor affects his surroundings in any way. The musician who picks up his musical score may glance through it; but soon he will seat himself behind the piano and start working on interpreting the text of the music. Any musician will be heard, vocally or instrumentally. He will affect his surroundings even while practising, and will look forward to sounding out his interpretation to an audience. Only then his music lives, carried by sound, reaching an audience. To postpone playing until one has found the 'ultimate interpretation' makes no sense – because there is no such interpretation. 'Music is like nature, it always moves and changes.'[23]

Thus the comparison between a written text and a written score and the activity of interpretation that follows is asymmetrical. While the text is the impetus and destination of the art of interpretation, the musical score is the impetus to a movement outwards into the world. Firstly, in the form of sensory expression (sound), next as sensory sharing (playing out) and finally as interpreting in performance (concert). The

Introduction

asymmetry is not only caused by the movement of the interpretative action, but also by the expertise it takes to perform such action. Reading a text is a minor skill that accompanies us almost throughout our lives; the inner sweep of imagination is easily triggered off and conducted almost spontaneously. To read a musical score is not an automatic skill, nor is the playing of a musical instrument or the use of the voice. Skill, training, talent and practice are the natural ground from which meaning may emerge. Apart from these personal qualifications of the interpreter of the score, a sympathetic audience is a must. No musician survives a concert in which the audience is unacquainted with the traditional aesthetics of his music, let alone taste. An amount of concentrated attention and shared presence are equal preconditions for the eloquence of his interpretation. In this way the music score is 'read' in interpretation. This type of reading is a remembering that constitutes a new, shared present. It is its capacity to renew itself in an actual, experiential present that makes this past worth remembering. Such shared re-enacted memory carries an aura of intimacy. This is a highly subjective emotion closely related to love. 'If there is a substitute for love, it is memory. To memorise, then, is to restore intimacy' holds true not only for Brodsky but also for the performance of a music score as well as for the ever-repeated performance of Tamil texts. In his collection of essays *Less than One* (1986) Brodsky describes and evokes Nadezhda Mandelstam, widow of the great Russian poet.

> By memorizing his poems, reciting them incessantly they gradually became her identity: repeating day and night the words of her dead husband was undoubtedly connected not only with comprehending them more and more but also with resurrecting his very voice, the intonations peculiar to him, with a however fleeting sensation of his presence. . . . once set in motion, this mechanism of memorisation won't come to a halt (Brodsky 1986, 150).

Similarly, the Indian notions of *smara* (Sanskrit) and *marapu* (Tamil) combine love, memory, tradition and worship. They refer to reverential acts of ritual attendance, but also to the passionate longing of love. *Smara* is one of the names for the god of desire, *Kama*. This Cupid is known too as *Pancabana*, 'the one with five arrows'. These five arrows take as their target the five senses. As love invades the entire sensory reality of the victim, the god of love appears to be bodiless (*Ananga* 'the one without limbs'). He seems to attack and enter from everywhere, as if the entire experiential world, nature, man and beast, are bespeaking infatuation and love. As Brodsky observes: 'Of course she loved him, but love is the most élitist of passions. It acquires its stereoscopic substance and perspective only in the context of culture, for it takes up more space in the mind than it does in the bed.' If we were to attempt to speak of Tamil textual creativity in terms of *epistemes*, then it would certainly not be a universal-validity-of-interpretation-upon-which-all-certainty-in-history-rests, nor would it operate on the basis of reading-as-the-recovery-of-meaning. It would rather figure as loving-memory-that-keeps-the-Tamil-tradition-alive. The meaning of the tradition is its quality of presence.

This meaning is brought about, too, by means of metaphor; but not by metaphor in the sense given by Ricoeur. The Tamil use of metaphor is closer to the medieval Western use than to the modern concept. In traditional Western rhetoric, metaphor is regarded as a type of trope. A trope substitutes a figurative function for a 'literal' function on the grounds of an apparent resemblance. There are no tensions between the two terms; on the contrary, a deepening of the meaning of a word by means of 'embellishment' 'mellows' its character. Trope in terms of the Gospels meant a 'sensuous rendering of the word'. Liturgical drama developed from this very process.[24] The earliest medieval Gospel trope *Quem queritis?* 'Whom do you seek?' is part of the Liturgy of the Resurrection of Christ. It was widespread by the tenth century in Northern Europe, England, the North of France, the Rhineland and most of Frankish territory. Over six hundred versions of the Easter dialogue survive, with and without music, spanning six centuries and the whole of Europe. The Biblical words *Quem queritis?* are amplified, as a trope, into an entire dramatic dialogue of the three Marys who visit the tomb and the angels of the tomb. At a deeper level this is the dialogue between the worshippers of Christ and the dwellers in heaven.[25] This contrast between the two uses of metaphor even within our own Western tradition reveals the bias that is hidden in modern Western scholarship. Of these two uses, one is a polysemy of words, violating linguistic codes and thus giving birth to an emergent 'objective', 'ideal sense' meaning, all located in the mind of the reading individual. The other is a sensuous, infatuated presencing that deepens the relationship between the words, speakers, audience, community and cosmology. It is certainly no wonder that the medieval use of metaphor ceased by the sixteenth century. It is at this *nexus* that Foucault observes the *prose of the world* transforming into the *prose of the text*.[26] In terms of knowledge representation this means that the textual life transforms from the living, sensuous, colourful pageant, that is, the word in its all encompassing presence, into the mentalistic iconoclasm of meaning. In short, from a vibrant artefact into an authorised mentifact.

Coda

In the previous pages we took up the challenge of facing the question *enta prayogam* 'What's the use?', firstly, by examining the aim of literary studies expressed by late Western scholarship. The 'text' was understood to be a Sign of knowledge maintaining a particular relation to the world. We observed the Western sign turning away gradually from the experiential world. In consequence the validation of its presumed moral, humanising status proved to be feeble. The Tamil sign remains firmly rooted in the world and cosmos, convinced of its divine status and metaphysical powers. In order to understand these vast differences we contrasted their respective agendas. Testing the idealist and positivist aims of eighteenth- and nineteenth-century Philology and Hermeneutics against a truly positivist agenda of Physics, the Western construct, named 'text', proved to fall short; its data, empirical ground and empirical testing could not meet the necessary scientific standards, thereby losing the 'universally valid' fruit of its endeavours. The Tamil agenda proved to be pragmatist, turning data into its very existential mode, and testing its 'hypotheses' right in the empirical field by becoming its interactive sign. This empirical check of textual products was conducted in the human, 'doubly interactive' setting of performer and audience, revealing its communicative efficacy.[27]

Agenda, data, empirical experiment and testing procedures brought out the contrasting characteristics of these two textual 'Signs': the late Western sign is static in nature, manifesting its reality as a document; the Tamil sign is organic, manifesting itself as an event. The status of the first is secular, although highly idealist; that of the second cosmological. The two agendas resulted in different forms that represent culturally cherished knowledge. Such representations reveal *episteme* and *telos*: thus, the book holds and safeguards the essence of meaning for future generations, while the performance brings alive past, present and future in a shared commemoration of presence.

The next step in challenging the demand 'What's the use?' will be the attempt to unfold the Tamil tradition of textual expertise. One applied example, namely a *varnaprabandha* set in *raga bhairavi* and *tala rupakam*, will take us through Parts I, II and III, that is, through Habitus, Praxis, and Representation.

The third step consists of the author's plea for relevance. This plea is expressed in the Conclusion, and is substantiated by the CD-i demonstration disc.

Notes

1. See 'To Civilize our Gentlemen' in George Steiner's *Language and Silence*, in which he quotes Henry Sidgwick.
2. 'The Orient is a Career' figures as a motto in *Orientalism, Western Concepts of the Orient* by E. Said.
3. See *Writing Culture, the Poetics and Politics of Ethnography*, ed. J. Clifford and G. Marcus, University of California Press, 1986.
4. This argument is worked out in several contexts by Bourdieu; his *Homo Academicus* takes this theme as its central concern.
5. See Foucault, *Les mots et les choses*.
6. Said, *Orientalism*, Chapters II and III: II-'Silvestre de Sacy and Ernest Renan: Rational Anthropology and Philological Laboratory'; III-'Oriental Residence and Scholarship: The Requirements of Lexicography and Imagination'.
7. The examples set by Max Müller, Goethe and Schlegel were still followed by Jan Gonda and his students who could become Professors of Sanskrit without taking an active interest in fieldwork until the reorganisation of Academic priorities in the 1980s disturbed the philological equilibrium.
8. Kamil Zvelebil traces Tamil literary historiography back to the sixteenth century; see *Companion Studies to the History of Tamil Literature*, pp. 1–11.

9. See 'The task of hermeneutics' in Ricoeur's *Hermeneutics and the human sciences, Essays on language, action and interpretation*, p. 51.
10. Zvelebil voices the common notion that Tamil can be divided into 'literary' Tamil and 'spoken' Tamil when he translates *valakku* with 'spoken, colloquial (style)' and *ceyyul* as 'poetic literary (style)'. Earlier European grammarians have often translated *kotuntamil* and *centamil* as 'low' and 'high' Tamil; cf. Zvelebil 1974, pp. 132–3, nn. 4 and 2, and the grammars of Father Beschi and Julien Vinson.
11. This scheme is taken from Gerald Holton, *Thematic Origins of Scientific Thought, Kepler to Einstein*, pp. 31–2.
12. Holton, *ibid.*, pp. 32–3.
13. Ricoeur, *Hermeneutics and the human sciences, Essays on language, action and interpretation*, p. 12 and 'Metaphor and the Central Problem of Hermeneutics', pp. 165–82.
14. Ricoeur, *ibid.*, p. 13 as well as 'The Hermeneutical Function of Distanciation' (pp. 131–45), 'What is a Text ? Explanation and Understanding' (pp. 145–65) and 'The Model of the Text: Meaningful Action Considered as Text' (pp. 198–203).
15. Ricoeur, *ibid.*, pp. 18–19 and 'Appropriation' (pp. 182–97).
16. Cf. Bourdieu, P., *In Other Words, Essays Towards a Reflexive Sociology*, p. 94.
17. Holton, G., *Thematic Origins of Scientific Thought, Kepler to Einstein*, p. 32.
18. Zvelebil 1992, pp. 129 ff.
19. Ricoeur, *Hermeneutics and the human sciences, Essays on language, action and interpretation*, p. 184, speaks of 'ideality', as 'the meaning of a proposition is neither a physical nor mental reality'.
20. Cf. Ricoeur, *ibid.*, p. 164, 'Within this chain of interpretants, the first interpretants serve as tradition for the final interpretants which are the interpretation in the true sense of the term (...) The idea of interpretation is not, for all that, eliminated; it is simply postponed until the termination of the process.'
21. Cf. Ricoeur, *ibid.*, p. 11, and 'Creativity in Language', trans. David Pellauer in *The Philosophy of Paul Ricoeur*, ed. Charles E. Reagan and David Stewart (Boston: Beacon Press, 1978), p. 25.
22. Cf. Ricoeur, *Hermeneutics and the human sciences, Essays on*

language, action and interpretation, p. 11 and pp. 156–7 in *The Rule of Metaphor: Multi-Disciplinary Studies of the Creation of Meaning in Language*, trans. Robert Czerny (London: Routledge and Kegan Paul, 1978).
23. Personal communication from Naum Grubert, Russian concert pianist and at present professor at the Royal Conservatory and the van Sweelinck Conservatory, both in Holland.
24. Cf. the very thorough study by John Stevens, *Words and Music in the Middle Ages, Song, Narrative, Dance and Drama 1050–1350*, p. 330.
25. Cf. Stevens, *ibid.*, pp. 330–6.
26. Cf. 'The Prose of the World' in Foucault's *The Order of Things*, pp. 17–46.
27. The terms 'double interact' and 'double interactivity' are taken from Karl E. Weick. In his *The Social Psychology of Organizing*, p. 89, he defines 'double interact' as follows: 'Processes contain individual behaviours that are interlocked among two or more people. The behaviours of one person are contingent on the behaviours of another person(s), and these contingencies are called *interacts*. The unit of analysis in organizing is contingent response patterns in which an action by actor A evokes a specific response in actor B (so far this is an interact), which is then responded to by actor A (this complete sequence is a *double interact*)'. Communication is characterised by strategic organisation of maximal double interactivity. In Indian terminology, this 'resultant' double interact can be understood as *rasa* 'tasting' or *meyppatu* 'affect of the body' which permeates the entire process and all its participants. In contrast to live communication, reading is a 'single' interact and can never move beyond that position, owing to the lack of that shared proximity that is a *conditio sine qua non* for the emergence of double interaction, and because of the static nature of the message, which cannot reciprocate the live address by the reader. What remains is the processual nature of the activity of reading; but this process is directed one-sidedly by the reader alone.

Part I
Habitus

Chapter 2

Text

> mōkamāṉa eṉmītil nī inta vēḷaiyil; mōṭiceyyalāmō eṉ cāmi metta//
> nākarīkamāṉa tirunakaril vācarē; pōkatyākēcā aṉupōkam ceyya vā kiṭṭa//
> māraṉ kaṇaikaḷ tūvurāṉ caramā riyāy//

> At this moment your presence fills me with the intoxication of love; ignoring me could that be, my Lord? it is hard to bear//
> The elegant holy town is your residence; Bhogatyagesha to delight me too, you must come to my side //
> Lethal arrows of love descend like pouring rain //

This text forms the central object of our discussion. It appears in an edition of manuscripts ascribed to the so-called *Tanjore Brothers* (early nineteenth century). Its three lines form a *varnam* (literally 'colour') and are set in the tonal scale *bhairavi* and the rhythm cycle *rupakam*. *Varnam* is classified as a type of *prabandham*, a large and important genre of Tamil literature. This particular *varnam* survives in many oral versions followed by various schools and in one printed version; its original author is said to be Ponniah (1887–1945).[1]

An introduction like this immediately reveals the difficulties that are peculiar to oral verbal art. 'Text', 'classification', 'genre' – all terms sound familiar and adequate. However, when applied to *bhairavi varnam*, they hold on paper but not in praxis. Earlier we discussed the discrepancy between the types of data that served as a basis for literary analysis and criticism. Whereas it is a quite self-evident move to the Western scholar to accept the manuscript as a point of departure, this attitude lands us in deep trouble when followed in a Tamil context. The Tamil palmleaf manuscript, the *olai*, does not correspond to the product that the

Tamils themselves regard as literature. How does this product, termed *ilakkiyam* (lit. 'the marked'), relate to the manuscript? In short, as three lines to thirty minutes: the *olai* manuscript serves as a *residuum* of the performance *bhairavi varnam*. Thus the application of the manuscript may take half an hour or more.[2] During this process the palmleaves are converted into a marked sign. According to Western criteria, it is hard to consider a *varnam* 'literature'; after all, it turns out to be dance, music and mime. It seems to be an either/or situation: either a text is literature, i.e. written and received as such; or, a text is Art and expressed in performance. However, a third possibility is available: *varnam* as literature is literature as applied science. The logic of application allows a *varnam* to reach its full expression in the course of performance. The difficulties in analysing the *varnam* reflect the difficulties literary criticism has encountered in trying to analyse the 'genre' *prabandham*. Kamil Zvelebil (1992) assesses the 'state of the art' as follows

> It is my conviction, though, that the very 'basics' mentioned above – the 'particles' making up the complex dynamic structure of Tamil verbal art – have still not been dealt with adequately, even in approximation. We may have very deep-going, detailed and supremely intelligent studies of individual works (. . .), but entire epochs (e.g. sixteenth, seventeenth, eighteenth centuries), not to speak of hundreds of individual authors and works, and of the oral dimension of verbal art, have been left virtually untouched by serious scholarship.[3]

The hypergenre of *prabandha* (Skt.), *prabandham* (Tamilised Sanskrit), or *pirapantam* (Ta.) in fact falls into every one of the lacunae mentioned above: *prabandham* flourished and expanded into a megagenre precisely during this period; crucial questions regarding the form, nature and generic logic of *prabandham* remained unanswered in Western criticism because of the oral character of this type of texts. Even the question of 'genre' has been problem-ridden: how should we account for a genre that is first mentioned in a normative treatise of the tenth century as comprising 36 subgenres,[4] that expands in the course of six centuries into 96 subgenres, and eventually attains the stupendous total of 248 subgenres by the nineteenth century. The examination of this particular *varnaprabandham* gives a surprising turn to the immobility of the scientific discussion on the genre at large. Literary scholarship got stuck in the seemingly insurmountable problems of inorganic growth, lack of inner coherence and megalithic status. The normative work (*pattiyal*) by Cuvaminatam (eighteenth/nineteenth century) and the *Pirapantatipikai* by Muttuvenkata Cuppaiya Navalar (nineteenth century) mention *varnam* as a composition that belongs to the genre *prabandham*.⁵ The *varnaprabandham*, and especially the *padavarnaprabandham* that we deal with here, depicts one of the many love situations that make up lyrical poetry. Our *varnam*, too, speaks of the intense longing for the beloved and moves from hope to despair and back within the range of melancholy. The Tamil experts' analysis of the form of *varnam* shows the following progression:

1 Invocation of the gods
2 Praise of the hero
3 The town and the country of the hero
4 and 5 The hero meets a woman in his garden and enjoys himself with her.
6, 7 and 8 (and more: SK) Further erotic descriptions.

In the last parts, there may be a description of a 'Gandharva marriage' (i.e. a marriage without ceremonies and without the permission of relatives).⁶ At first sight it seems hard to accommodate our three-line manuscript into the eight-part scheme given above. However, when we follow the logic of application and, in consequence, we observe the performance of these three lines, then a new text appears. The term *ilakkiyam* begins to make sense as a 'marked event' the moment the *olai* manuscript unfolds in practice into the following 'libretto':

1 At this moment your presence fills me with the intoxication of love;
2 ignoring me, could that be, my Lord? It is hard to bear//
3 The elegant holy town of *Arur* is your residence;
4 Bhogatyagesha, in order to delight me too, you must come to my side//

Now, a line appears in the application which is not to be found in the manuscript text. It functions as a transition to the second part of the *varnam*.⁷

5 Contamuṭaṉ eṉai kūṭiṉa vintaiyai niṉaintē tiṉam vāṭi
maṉam nāṭi umai tēṭi uravāṭa mikavum eṉatutalatu
patarutē iṉi arai nimisamum
yukamākutu atarasāramatu tara itē camayam caraca
catkuṉaṉē//

5 (Translation:) As your very own you embraced me; that splendour I remember every day; my heart quivers searching for you, just as if you were intimately related to me; inside, I am all trembling, half a minute turns into an aeon; your sweet lips, please do grant me these; this is the right moment, O You whose nature is the Experiential (Skt. *sa-rasa*), the Embodiment of Being (Skt. *sat-guṇa*).

The third line of the manuscript māraṉ kaṉaikaḷ tūvuṟāṉ caramāriyāy unfolds into four further performance sentences:

6 Lethal arrows of love descend like pouring rain (free translation) unfolds into 7, 8, 9 and 10, thus

7 māvēril kuyilkaḷ kūvutē iṉi eṉ ceykuvēṉ // (māraṉ . . .)
In the garden love-birds are cooing; now what am I to do?

8 mārutam orupuram vīcutu iravinil tamasam eṉai aṉaivāy iṉi vacamalla// (māraṉ . . .)
The (cool) breeze is blowing on one side; without delay you might embrace me during the night, now my strength ebbs away.

9 Cōmantaṉal mika cōriyayil rāmā iṉi cakiyēṉaṭa kāmaṉ kalavikku cintaiyai nāṉ cāmi maṉatu vimmutaṭā// (māraṉ . . .)
The rays of the moon pour down like fiery cinders; alas, I can't bear any more, my Lord, my heart overflows with the thought of a love tryst.

10 Curēcaṉ aṉutiṉamum pukaḻ varēca muṉivar paṉiyum jakatīcaṉ akaṇṭa pūraṇa vilācaṉ aṭiyavarkkaruḷ puriyum īcaṉ akila puvaṉamatil vācaṉ ari aiyaṉ ariyāta īcaṉ varaṅkaḷ tarum tiru tyākēcaṉ kaiyilai puvaṉamatil vācaṉ eṉtaṉai aṉaiya ippō// (māraṉ . . .)
Sureshan, Lord of Lords daily praised, Lord of boons, worshipped by sages, Lord of the universe, encompassing the

entire expanse, showering grace on his devotees, Isha!, unfathomable to Hari and Ayan, Tyagesha!, bestowing all wishes, living in the realm of Kailasa, embrace verily me, *now*!

The branching out of three written lines into a performance of ten lines poses an enigma to Western textual scholarship. All parameters of criticism seem to be uprooted. Which is the text: the manuscript, the libretto, or each interpretation it receives in performance? Where is the text located: in the palmleaves, in the memory of the performers, or in the performance itself ? Once more, such questions may be tackled best when posed in the context of indigenous categories and terminology. The manuscript of the *varnaprabandham* employs three terms for the three lines that reveal the nature of the text. These are: *pallavi*, *anupallavi*, *caranam*, and can be understood as 'branch', 'twig' and 'tail of a peacock'.[8] This terminology indicates the dynamic nature of the text: the three lines noted down in the manuscript serve as seeds for the organic growth of the stem, branches and foliage of a tree. The text develops branches, sub-branches and rich foliage that fans out like a peacock's tail, displaying the splendour of its imagery. This process explains the amplification of three lines into thirty minutes of performance. How this process is achieved is described in Part II of this work.

What matters in this context is the remarkable discrepancy that occurs between the foci of attention and criticism: whereas the Indian expert has analysed the *application* of the three lines in the course of their being performed, the Western scholar has tried to analyse the *document*, taking the manuscript for the text. The difference between the application and the document is the difference between coordinated activity and its formula. The manuscript yields the formula *pallavi*, *anupallavi*, and *caranam*, while its application in performance yields coordinated, meaningful action as its product. In short, text considered as meaningful action is the Tamil model of a text, and thus an exact opposite of Ricoeur's model of the text that was discussed earlier.[9]

The object of exegesis on this model transforms itself; we pass from exegesis of a document to exegesis of a colourful event. The text dwells in its colouring activity. This activity is *varnana* 'colouring'; *varnam* as 'literature' does not equate with its formula, but with the event of concerted action. The colouring of the event contains words, sounds and images. All three have their 'formulaic still' that demands to be committed to interactive communication.

Just as the word stratum has an *olai*, the dimension 'sound' is registered in the form of graphemes. These are the initial letters of the name of the note; thus, they do not differ from the graphemes of the alphabet. Tonal scales therefore read like the written word, which does not do much justice to their tonal quality. In addition the total gamut of the codified tonal scales, that is seventy-two scales, is represented in a huge circular chart called the *melakkartta*. This complex chart shows the scales in their relative relation to each other.[10] The very complexity of this scheme would surely discourage any non-performer from reading it. The mimetic rendering of the word-text has its 'stills', too. On the walls of South Indian shrines one may find huge columns of sculptures termed *karana*, depicting 'dance poses'.[11] None of these three 'objectified signs' can be considered a text or the notation of a text. They are formulae, codes and codifications that go into the colouring of the *varnam*.

The etymology of the term 'text' turns out to be very felicitous in the light of the activity of *varnana*, the 'colouring' that shapes *varnam* into *ilakkiyam*. The original meaning of *textus* as 'weave' enables us to apprehend the Tamil notion of textual creativity as 'colouring' or as 'weaving a colourful weave' of expressive meaning. Moreover, this etymology not only turns out to be an example of happy coincidence, but seems to share the very concept of textual culture. The 'colourful weave' resounds as an echo in the latin *textus* and in its Tamil counterpart; there, a folk etymology glosses 'verse' and 'weave' in *pa*. The logic of weaving permeates the logic of textual creativity. Another example of this shared imagery shines through in the term *nul*. *Nul* is usually translated as 'book'. Literally, though, it means 'thread', and indicates a theoretical treatise that may be employed in the process of the 'weaving of the text'. The learned tradition distinguishes between primary, secondary and supportive treatises.[12] According to tradition a Tamil *nul* is produced in the way illustrated in Fig.2.[13]

The number of theoretical treatises that may go into the weaving of Tamil texts is impressive. The Tamils analysed the coherence and interdependence of several communicative systems that we would gloss as *langage*. And, indeed, their

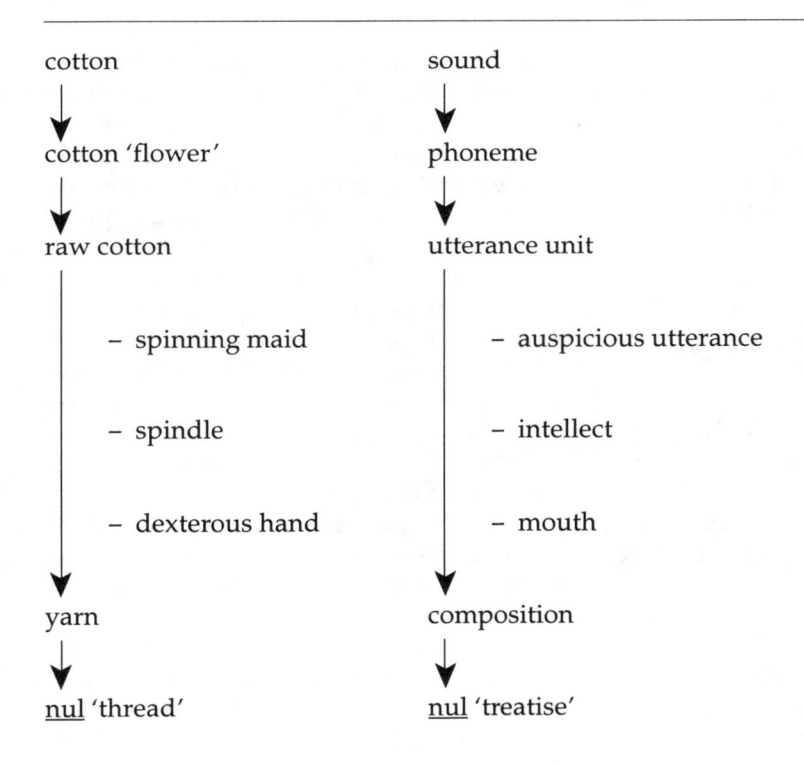

```
cotton                          sound
  ↓                               ↓
cotton 'flower'                 phoneme
  ↓                               ↓
raw cotton                      utterance unit
  │                               │
  │    – spinning maid            │    – auspicious utterance
  │                               │
  │    – spindle                  │    – intellect
  │                               │
  │    – dexterous hand           │    – mouth
  ↓                               ↓
yarn                            composition
  ↓                               ↓
nul 'thread'                    nul 'treatise'
```

Figure 2 – spinning the Tamil book

meticulous systematicity would make them feel at home in structuralism and semiotics. The greatest and most striking difference seems to be in the attribution of a 'first' in the dialectic tension between discourse and system, or, in other words, between process and structure. In modern terms, the Tamil experts feel that structure inheres in process; it has process as its existential base and is rendered meaningless without it. In a similar vein application outweighs system: speech comes first, grammar dwells in it. Tamil experts hold *ilakkanattukku mun ilakkiyam*: before the markers – the marked.[14] In a free translation this means: language-as-speech precedes language-as-grammatical system.

Earlier we encountered the term *ilakkiyam* for 'literature'. The example of *varnaprabandham*, its formula, technical terminology, and its application *'bhairavi varnana'*, revealed the dynamic nature of the term *ilakkiyam*. This, coupled with the theoretical discussion on the relationship between *ilakkanam* and *ilakkiyam* may throw new light on the problems around the 'genre' *prabandham*. Firstly, literary criticism has treated samples that are listed, traditionally, as *prabandham* as if they were a type of *literary text*. To them the 'marked product' (*ilakkiyam*) was a product marked by the grammatical markers of the language system. The French nuance between *langue* (language system/ grammar), *parôle* (speech, i.e. applied grammar) and *langage* (i.e. the expressive scope of 'communication', including, for instance, music, gesture and facial expressions) comes in handy here. The *prabandham* text, in these terms, is *parôle*. Secondly, it is an example of speech that is marked by the markers of *langage*, not exclusively of *langue*. To accept the systematicity of *langage* as grammar means to commit *parôle* to the dynamic conditions of sound and image. The text that seemed to be a document turns out to be a cue for action. In short, *prabandham*, too, is not a document but an event.

The character of these compositions as 'action poems' comes out beautifully in the woodblock prints that illustrate the edition of the *Tiruvacakam* (lit. 'Holy Utterance') by Manikkavacakar (ninth century AD). His work contains several compositions that date back to the earliest stratum of Tamil textual culture and appear from the twelfth century onwards under the title *prabandham*. The quality that they share throughout almost twenty centuries is the quality of action, whether in the form of royal, sacral or folk custom. Four examples of such 'action texts' are depicted here: *Tiruvempavai* – 'waking up' the beloved king or god from his sleep by verses sung in the early morning;[15] *Tirukkottumpi* – 'sending a bee as love messenger';[16] *Tiruppuvalli* – 'string of holy flowers', each flower evoking the recitation of the grandeur of the hero;[17] and *Tiruponnucal* – 'holy golden swing', songs sung while swinging the god and goddess, the hero and the heroine, or a bridal couple.[18]

These themes are as ancient as the old, bardic literature that we will discuss later on.[19] In the work of the poet-saint-singer Manikkavacakar they appear as devotional poems; as such they are a kind of *proto-prabandhams*. The poet himself is depicted, too, as part of the scene: the singing and dancing is conducted by his beating of the rhythmic structure of the texts. In the woodblock illustrations we encounter again and again the little male figure, clapping or beating his cymbals in accompaniment to the performance.[20] From this angle *prabandhams* make sense, not as a written testimony, but as the activity of *prabandhana*, i.e. of 'composing, connecting, tying'. *Prabandhana*, too, is an event not a document. The joy, the beauty and thus the meaning of the *prabandhana*, or *varnana*, of connecting and colouring, is in its creative, doubly interactive, doing. 'Appropriation' in this context means a merging of worlds: those of composer,

Plate 1 *Tiruvempavai* – 'Holy waking up'

performer, and audience; a merger of the past, present and eternity; of the worlds of gods, demons, man, beast and nature, into the world they 'live with and live by'.[21]

Now, what is it that *bhairavi varnam* weaves, that it paints in its 'colouring'? What are the strands, and what are the motifs of the weave? The strands, basically, are provided by the threefold Tamil: *iyal* 'word', *icai* 'sound' and *natakam* 'mimesis', or, 'image'. The motifs woven in the weaving evoke Time, Space and Creation, as we will see further on. Composer, performer and

Plate 2 *Tirukkottumpi* – 'Holy bee'

audience weave, connect and colour their world in interactive creation and reception. The activity of *prabandhana* is indeed a 'tying', a 'connecting' of various, even infinite layers of meaning. The process of expressive orchestration renders the *varnaprabandham* into a powerful sign, affecting world, audience and performer. Such 'emergent meaning' has indeed the power to redescribe reality, not in the form of a manuscript, of a formula, of a text giving the gist of the action, nor as a grammar yielding all the technicalities of the event. This power does not

Plate 3 *Tiruppūvalli* – 'Holy string of flowers'

Plate 4 *Tirupponnucal* – 'Holy golden swing'

result from a violent clash of words in the sentence; it emerges from the physical foregrounding of the text. Such a metaphor searches and investigates the possible meanings of the text as they live in the world, in the hearts and in the memory of the community. In this confrontation of text, performance and world, with all that lives in it, a 'double-interact' builds up sending a 'magic touch' through the entire experiential realm. The text has become meaningful action.

Notes

1. *Bhairavi varnam 'mohamana'* is known in many versions. This particular one was handed down to me by my teacher Smt. Nandini Ramani. It was 'set' by Kandappa Pillai, the father of Shri K. Ganesan. Among the various renderings that survive in oral form, one version has been edited by K. P. Kittappa and K. P. Sivanandam, two other descendants of the Tanjore Quartet.
2. Cf. W. J. Ong in *Orality and Literacy*, p. 10: '... the relentless dominance of textuality in the scholarly mind is shown by the fact that to this day no concepts have yet been formed effectively, let alone gracefully, conceiving of oral art as such without reference, conscious or unconscious, to writing.'
3. K. V. Zvelebil, 1992, pp. xx–xxi.
4. K. V. Zvelebil, 1974, pp. 193 ff.
5. M. Muilwijk, 1992, Ph.D. dissertation, University of Utrecht, *The Divine Kuṟa Tribe, Kuṟavañci and other Prabandhams*, pp. 175–7.
6. M. Muilwijk, 1992, pp. 179–80. See also K. V. Zvelebil, 1974, p. 217, listing the *varnaprabandham* as no. 85 in the total of 96 'subgenres'.
7. This section is termed *muktayisvarasahitya* 'ending-notes-words'. It divides the first and the second half of the *varnam* by means of a rhythmical transition: from the steady, slow first tempo of the *pallavi* and *anupallavi* lines to the second tempo and complex rhythmical organisation of the *caranams*.
8. Ta. *pallavi, pallavam* 'sprout, shoot, extremity of a bough', 'chorus of a song'; Ta. *anupallavi, pallavi* plus the prefix *anu* 'after, together with'; Ta. *caranam* 'foot, reverence', 'peacock, peacock's tail', 'line sung between choruses'.
9. See Introduction, p. 1.
10. See CD-i Content-Sound-Time-Text.
11. See CD-i Content-Image-Time-Text.
12. K. V. Zvelebil, 1992, p. 229.
13. Cf. K. V. Zvelebil, 1992, p. 228 for the inspiration of the present generic chart.
14. See K. V. Zvelebil, 1973, p. 139, fn. 1, and 1974, p. 4, quoting Smt. Kokilam Subbiah as well as the ancient grammar *Akattiyam*: ilakkiyattiṉ ṟetuppaṭumilakkaṇam 'from the marked is taken the marker', and *Nannul* st. 140: ilakkiyaṅ

kaṇṭatak ṛilakkaṇam *iyampal* 'the ancients say: to those who observe the marked the marker [becomes clear]'.

15. The ceremony of waking up a 'cult-hero' goes back to the bardic period where *Cankam* poetry depicts the *aubade* for the king. Such songs are composed even nowadays in the ritual context of waking up a god or goddess by wishing him or her a 'bright day' (Skt. *suprabhatam*).
16. The theme of sending a *postillon d'amour* is ubiquitous in both Tamil and Sanskrit literatures. The messengers Skt. *duta* or *duti* and Ta. *tutu* can be almost anyone and anything: gods, men, women, bees, birds and even clouds.
17. Even today litanies are accompanied by decorating the god or goddess. Shri Tyagarajasvami receives such an offering called *Mucukunda sahasra nama*, that is enumerating 1008 names of the god while placing a flower or its petals at the recitation of each name. This ritual takes a little more than two hours.
18. The custom of swinging the auspicious pair is honoured every day in temples where the god and goddess are 'swung to sleep', and, during the elaborate wedding ceremonies that include the swinging of the bridal pair accompanied by so-called 'swing songs' sung by 'auspicious women' (Skt. *sumangalis*), and formerly by *devadasis*, 'courtesans'.
19. The *Tiruvacakam*, 'Holy utterance', contains the following 'proto-*prabandhams*': *tiru ammanai* – 'holy ball-game', *tiru untiyar* – 'holy kite', *tiru empavai* – 'holy morning', *tiru kotumpi* – 'holy bee', *tiru catakam* – 'holy 100', *tiru calal* – 'holy clapping of hands', *tiru tacankam* – 'holy ten limbs', *tiru tellenam* – 'holy sifting of sand to rhythmical beats', *tiru tonokkam* – 'holy hitting the shoulder', *tiru puvalli* 'holy string of flowers', *tiru porcunnam* – 'holy gold dust', *tiru ponnucal* – 'holy golden swing'. Most of these are performed in the context of daily and festival worship in temples.
20. Cf. *Tiruvacakam* by Manikkavacakar, edited by B. Irattina Nayakar and sons, no date, Madras.
21. Cf. Introduction, p. 1.

Chapter 3

World

'Reality is Fantasy that works' is the trump-card of Frank Smith in trying to break away from the model that perceives language as synonymous with communication, communication with the transmission of information and the brain as the repository of that information.[1] This paradigm of cognitive psychology regards thought as 'information-processing', and learning as the mechanism by which new information is acquired. His critique proposes that (a) very little of what the brain contains can be appropriately thought of as information; (b) very little of the brain's commerce with the world (including other people) can be appropriately regarded as the exchange of information; (c) learning is rarely a matter of acquiring information; (d) the brain is not very good at acquiring information – it is not the most 'natural' thing for the brain to do; and (e) language is not a particularly efficient means of transmitting information; again, it is not the most 'natural' thing for language to do. What is the alternative metaphor that corresponds more closely to the natural functioning of the brain? Smith holds that the brain contains nothing less than 'a theory of the world'. The world in all its dynamic complexity never ceases to impress our senses with a vast array of signals. All these signals would constitute information according to the information theory mentioned above. This is not so: only those signals that can be interpreted can yield certainty; the rest is considered 'noise'. In such a sense, information can only exist in the world, not in the brain. What the brain must contain is the understanding that can interpret signals, that can transform noise into certainty – thus, a theory of the world.[2]

How does the brain learn to form such theory? As an alternative to the data-storage, information model, Smith sees the brain as an 'artist': the brain learns the way an artist learns, not by accumulating facts, but by exploring possibilities, by testing its own creations. In fact, the brain learns best when it is most creative. This creativeness brings out the brain's talent to create experiences for itself and for others. These experiences are experiences of worlds that the brain creates on the basis of its own theory of the world. The data for its creative theory are all past experiences interpreted in a sense that makes sense, and that forms the basis not only of our present understanding of the world but, more importantly, for a prediction of the future. It contains all our knowledge, beliefs, and expectations about the objective world in which we find ourselves. As the world around us, life as such, is dynamic, and seemingly ever changing, therefore the theory in the head must be dynamic, too. The perceived world is a vast and dynamic colourful canvas that the brain receives, explores and changes according to its own criteria of logic, intention and aesthetic preference, with a minimum necessary regard for the demands of 'reality'. It does so by creating new experiences that elaborate and modify the theory in the head.

How is the theory in the head expressed, shared and mediated? Basically, by language, not by language-as-writing but by language-as-speech. The strength of the latter is the close interaction of sender and receiver, which guarantees the sensory participation in the creative event, and ensures exchange within a shared 'grounding'.[3] Thus language that is spoken has more resources than language that is written. A written text serves primarily as a vehicle by which the perceiver's own constructions of the world are promoted. According to Smith, writing is not good for communicating information; it is only good for codifying it.[4] In this way, 'knowledge' is easily quantified. If the value of a model is determined by the rigour with which it can be evaluated, then the metaphor of the brain as an artist will undoubtedly receive less credit in circles of scientific 'objectivity', as creativeness is not easily quantified. Moreover the contents of the human mind and activity of the brain are so vast that sheer description is out of the question, nor can the relative value of metaphors be assessed 'objectively'. There is no statistical test that will decide which is 'correct'. The question is which metaphor is the most productive one, and the answer will depend on what one's intention is in the first place: to measure and control the world and human behaviour or to understand it.[5]

This plea for an alternative model of cognition and fruition of knowledge by Frank Smith fits our plea for modes of understanding that evoke the Tamil modes as well as our analysis of the role that our *varnaprabandham* plays in it. A number of aspects of Smith's proposal correspond to the Tamil postulates that we discussed earlier. They concern the relationship between Sign and World, the epistemological work that the artist puts forward and the terms in which knowledge is received.

First, the relationship between the text as Sign and the world at large. The discussion concerning a 'first' in the dialectic between marker and marked, or structure and process, yielded a 'first' for *ilakkiyam*, the marked process. This point of view reveals the philosophical tenet that the world – as a dynamic canvas – comes first; the markers, the *ilakkanam*, inhere in that natural first and are bound to change with it. The concept of an 'ongoing process' resembles the nature of 'Reality' better than its abstracted structures. These, literally, have no basis for existing, and thus, no argument to convince.

Second, in terms of Smith, the Tamil brain is certainly an artist at work, not aiming at measuring and controlling the world but at understanding it. This understanding is not couched in mental concepts alone: it rather aims at a sense of belonging, a 'feel' of the world and being at 'home' there. Thus the brain travels through the vast marked sign of the perceived world, experimenting and testing its experiences. The Indian term for this activity is *manodharma*, freely translated as 'realm of the mind'; it is used mostly in Western translation as improvisation in music and mime, but in fact constitutes the artistic research of the brain, making sense of the world. The activity of this artistic research is by nature a dynamic process that enters into the sign and discovers ever deepening layers of the 'that-ness' of a situation, the feelings involved in it and its meaning to the affected experiencer.

Third, knowledge, understanding and meaning are terms that are all couched in categories of experience, 'feel' and ultimately 'taste': tasting the quality of existence. We will return to this remarkable position later in Part II.[6] At this point, it suffices to draw the curtain on 'meaning' as contextual information, and to give the stage to 'meaning' as artistic research penetrating ever deeper into the canvas of the perceptual world, turning it into a place of intimacy, belonging, splendour and rapturous beauty. Without this mental relocation it is hard to understand the weaving capacity of the *varnam*, how it connects world, composer, audience and artist in the course of its performance.

In terms of cognitive psychology, the playground of the brain is in fact the world in the head. This is, so to say, the workshop where the brain forms its theory of the world; here it spots its opportunities for experiencing this theory in interaction with the live canvas outside and with everything that operates in it. The medium that inhabits both is language: language as the idiom of the interior discourse coining a theory of the world, language as medium of expression for such theories, and language as the doubly interactive medium for negotiating, testing and experiencing the world in the head in relation to the world as such. Thus the practice of the brain as artist is basically the practice of language.

Once more we invoke the perceptive French distinction between *langue* 'language as grammatical verbal system', *parôle* 'language as speech', or applied language; and *langage* 'that composite field of human expression that enables communication'.[7]

On the one hand, there is Smith's argument that language is not a particularly efficient means of communicating information. Against language speaks its own ambiguity, and the fact that the surface structures of language construct a kind of syntactic and semantic interface between the datum and its receiver or reader. But, on the other hand, language-as-speech is excellently suited for communication. The close interaction between sender and receiver, the multisensory impact of the speech-event, guarantee the live workshop for the brain to test and experience its own creation in communication with the world and the other. Ambiguity, and the contextual situatedness of speech make this praxis of language the treasury from which the world emerges as a meaningful creation making its theory felt. In short, the praxis is the world itself, the theory of the world and the creation and communication of that world. Such speech is not only applied verbal grammar, it is applied *langage*. We identified the *varnam* as such an example of applied *langage*. The performance of the *varnaprabandham* provides the artist an opportunity to practise this praxis. While the codifications in terms of grammar and syntax that go into its making do not reflect the natural function of the brain, the practice of the praxis of *langage* does so. In the course of performance the brain searches and experiments, winding its way into the world. It is in this practice that the world is constituted as perceived, interpreted and lived.

The concept *habitus*, reintroduced by Pierre Bourdieu, offers us a dynamic field that encompasses a world that is inhabited, perceived, conceived and lived by. Such a world finds its expression in *langage*. The practice of such *langage* can therefore be considered the practice of the *habitus*, or, more succinctly: *langage* is praxis is habitus in practice. We have arrived at the root of the question *enta prayogam?* 'What application?' In asking for an application, implying that application is the vehicle of 'use' or 'sense', the Tamil expert inquires after a practice that is permeated by a praxis and, in consequence, by a world. Such a dynamic field allows improvisation and creativity within a consensus that is felt as natural. Its guiding principles are rules that dwell in a 'feel' for the field but that are not prescriptive

> The habitus, the durably installed generative principle of regulated improvisations, produces practices which tend to reproduce the regularities immanent in the objective conditions of the production of their generative principle, while adjusting to the demand inscribed as objective potentialities in the situation, as defined by the cognitive and motivating structures making up the habitus.[8]

By identifying *habitus* as applied language, or speech event, we enter into the practice of a 'fantasy that works'. It works by and through speech that investigates, expresses and communicates its findings. A 'grand Fantasy that Works' is 'the durably installed principle'. This fantasy can live only by the centripetal forces of *langage*; these are the practices that operate within a scope of 'regulated improvisations'. Part II, *Praxis*, examines these practices that make up the Tamil speech artefact. The 'reproduction of these regularities' that are 'immanent in the objective conditions of production' will be discussed in Part III, *Representation*, while the 'demands' that are 'inscribed as objective potentialities in the situation' as 'defined by the cognitive and motivating structures' are the subject of this chapter, World.

This progression of generative principle, communicative

praxis, communicative occasion and cognitive structures is basically a cyclical one. The Tamil progression is remarkable in the sense that it is totally circular, marked by internal consistency and harmonisation. The generative principle is the world, the large, live canvas, the primal First that precedes its markers. Its apparent coherence is termed *Dharma*. Derived from the Sanskrit root dhṛ-, this means something like 'to hold, contain, hold-for; possess, live in, beget; to possess certain qualities'. The latin *habeo* indicates a similar combination of concepts. Therefore it is very attractive to equate Bourdieu's habitus with the Sanskrit *dharma*.[9] It is a metaphysical habitus, though, marked by its quality of 'ongoing, eternal': the *sanatana dharma* 'the ongoing coherence' is the *ilakkiyam* that precedes all human attribution. *Dharma* has often been translated as 'law' or 'code'. These terms carry a strong load of standardisation and codification that appeal to the Western mind as fixed and prescriptive. This is not so: the *Sanatana Dharma* is believed to represent cosmological order, but in practice the decrees in which that order is expressed are first and foremost spoken.[10] It is on the one hand exactly that same quality of applied wisdom that is found in the persistent question *enta prayogam* 'What's the use?' and that conceptualises 'truth' as *mey* 'body' (Ta.) or as *satyam* 'the existing' (Skt.). On the other hand, application guarantees the concreteness of such codification. This type of standardisation is highly flexible, because it is set in the communicative speech event, in a doubly interactive situation with shared coordinates of time and place. Such codes are as flexible as the changing world: they can improvise freely within the magic circle of the 'feel' of the generative principle. A similar logic holds for the linguistic practices that express the communicative event.

At this point we can extend the succinct equation that was suggested above with *dharma*: *langage is praxis is habitus is dharma in practice*. Any representation of these practices other than the actual performance produces a kind of reified structure. The Tamilians themselves have come up with such static representations. Further on, in Part III, we will discuss similar 'objectifications'; here, it suffices to mention the fact that such objects of knowledge need to be understood from an interactive performative point of view. Diagrams, icons, manuscripts are telling only when employed in a, let us call it, 'epistemic' event. The ambition to erect a conclusive systematic structure of grammatical laws is bound to be frustrated, if only by the many which are said to be 'also there'. It is hard to follow the inner logic of such improvisation without having internalised its praxis. Memory plays a dominant role throughout the entire process of acquiring the skills, appropriating the praxis, applying its practices and improvising in accord with the propriety of the moment. The main aim of the speech artefact, or, the communicative event is that it works, not the 'so-called authenticity' of what it is supposed to mean.

This type of memorisation is not random: it presupposes physical commitment, as the recall is largely somatic. To remember means to make the body work out the memory, speaking it, sounding it, dancing or miming it out into the world. This physical nature of expression and of the reception of 'meaning' point at the physical nature of meaning itself. The ancient grammarian Tolkappiyanar (date not settled: between second century BC and third century AD)[11] expresses very powerfully the circular argument that the world is the Primal Sign, an 'ongoing marked canvas' sign, the *ilakkiyam* as perennial habitus as well as the *ilakkiyam* as actual habitus. The paradigm of performance as the concretisation of meaning rooted in the belief that word and world are one, is to be found in the chapter on 'utterance' (*col*)[12]

> elläccollum poruḷ kuṟittaṉave // 152
> poruṇmaiteritalum coṉmai terintalum/
> colliṉ ākum eṉmaṉār pulavar// 153

> Each utterance expresses reference matter // 152
> The knowing of the thingness (/referentiality) and the knowing of the
> utteranceness become in the speaking, say the experts // 153

In terms of Foucault, Tamil could not plead more eloquently for its status of 'ancient sign'. This has two consequences: Tamil as a language is not only the generative principle of regulated improvisations, it is also its very ground: it is *Tamilnatu*, the Tamil country, the Tamil people. It is mother Tamil, it is God. Tamil is sweetness, melodiousness, refinement, it is proximity through word sound and image, Tamil is love. Tamil is water, Tamil is the good, auspicious world in which Tamil is spoken.[13] 'Meaning', therefore, is the kinship of the Tamil utterance and the Tamil world. As these two are one, the meaning of the words dwells in the things that constitute the Tamil universe. In this context, Bourdieu's cognitive and motivating structures of the habitus are to be understood as the referential entities that form the Tamil universe. The Tamil textus displays the Tamil world as motif, with existence as loom, with the primal *ilakkiyam* as warp and the momentous *ilakkiyam* as woof. These motifs form 'the cognitive and motivating structures that make up the habitus' in Bourdieu's terms, 'the theory in the head' in terms of Smith and the *ilakkanam* 'markers' in terms of Tamil thought.

From the earliest 'grammarians' onwards[14] we hear about a 'theory of the world'; it postulates three analytic categories: *mutal, karu* and *uri*.[15] *Mutal*, 'the first', comprises the two coordinates time (*kalam*) and space (*nilam*); the second category *karu*, 'embryo', includes the entire creation; and, finally, *uri*, meaning 'peel, skin, bark' or 'propriety, quality', indicates the perspective, the 'point of viewing' from which the world is experienced.[16]

The old grammars distinguish two such human perspectives: the world as experienced from 'the inside' or as experienced from 'the outside'. The first is termed *akam*, meaning 'heart', the home, the private sphere of life; the other perspective is called *puram*, meaning 'exterior, public'. This dichotomy results in a long tradition of poetry of love and heroism. Both spheres were meticulously subdivided into five situations of love or war.

Lyrical poetry imagined the interior world of *akam* as spread out over the five regions, all to be found in the Tamil country.[17] The jungle was considered the typical setting for irregular, clandestine meetings and for love affairs that were hidden from the public eye. The pasture-lands were the scene for patient waiting, the town the seat of unfaithfulness, the seashore signified anxious waiting, and the desert a last resource in the plight of love, namely, elopement. It is striking that four out of five love situations are concerned with waiting, while only the jungles show lovers in happy union. The listing of attributes specifying time, space and nature took an immense flight. Each particular situation could be diagnosed by its inhabitants, their occupations and pastimes, the tunes and the musical instruments of the region, its flora and fauna as well as the gods ruling and residing there.[18] To utter these in poetic composition meant to make them flourish and come true, to instil their contextual power into the reality of a king, queen or other noble members of Tamil society. *Varnam* is mentioned in the oldest layers of Tamil poetry. The performance by courtesans (*viralis*) then seems to have been as rich and effective as the impact of *varnams* in our times.

What, actually, remains today of this oldest stratum of Tamil lyricism is, as was noted before, manuscripts. The rediscovery of its palmleaves forms a long and interesting story which is particularly telling in the light of nineteenth-century 'Orientalism'.[19] What does matter for our discussion is the difference in exegesis of the palmleaf and of the live performance of a twentieth-century descendant. Our poem is not a static datum, but a highly dynamic exploration by the brain. In its thirty minutes or more it allows the mind to wander through the realm of the world as perceived, conceived of and lived. This sign is not a still, like the words on paper: it emerges unfolding layer upon layer, sketching and painting meaning in deeper and more expressive relief. Thus the woven textus of the *varnam* becomes indeed a live, coloured Sign, marked by the markers of Tamil life.

How can we get hold of this dynamism of the sign, the process of 'marking meaning' that can be called *semiosis*? According to Roman Jakobson the semiotic sign-system of Charles Sanders Peirce[20] touches upon the most essential and fertile question of the relationship between language and time.[21] Jakobson's reading of Peirce allows an analysis of the concerted layers of time that maintains the basic dynamism of the Sign without collapsing all data into a linear, cumulative record. In his system of three aspects of signs, Peirce distinguishes on the one hand the *index* and the *icon*, both of which he considers to operate as definite facts, and on the other hand the *symbol*, which he identifies not as a definite fact but rather as a functional framework of convention: 'À l'opposition de l'indice comme l'icone, suivant la théorie de Peirce, le symbole n'est past un objet, mais seulement une loi-cadre qui donne lieu à differentes applications contextuelles de fait, les occurrences.'[22]

Jakobson holds that this 'loi-cadre' is nothing else than a condition for all future replicas to take shape. In this reflection upon the relationship between *index*, *icon*, *symbol* and time, Peirce regards the icon as a completed image of past experience, whereas the index is involved in the actual moment of experiencing. The symbol – which is rooted in a generally accepted meaning – belongs to the realm of the so-called *futurum indefinitum*, an *esse in futuro*, a 'law' which can never be achieved fully, but remains more of a *potentialis*. The symbol gives us the impression that we can experience this *potentialis* in the present, and thereby predict or even manipulate it. The dynamism of the sign created by these aspects of time is visualised by Peirce and Jakobson as shown in Fig.3.

The Tamil sign, too, is woven out of three tenses: a happening, focal present; an expired past; and an 'opposite' that functions rather as a *generalis* or *potentialis*. Tamil syntax allots two of these three tenses a definite status: the happening, experiential present *nikal* (literally 'happening'), and the past *iranta* (literally 'expired'). The future tense *etir* (literally 'opposite'), however, never achieved a definite, absolute or predictive status.[23] Whorf holds that concepts of 'time' and 'matter' are not given in substantially the same form by experience to all men, but depend upon the nature of the language or languages through the use of which they have been developed. The three-tense system of what he calls Standard Average European (SAE) distinguishes three definite tenses: a past, a present and a future; this colours our Western thinking about time to a great extent. Dravidian

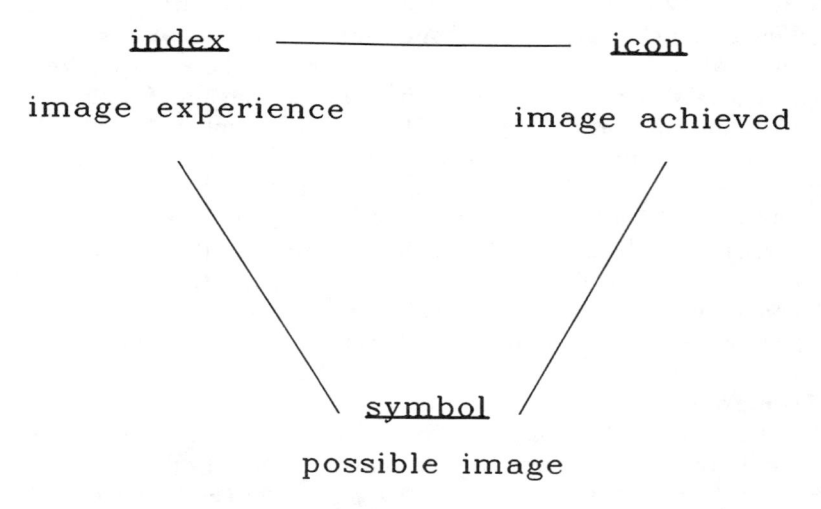

Figure 3 – the Peircean sign

languages, and Tamil here in particular, measured time originally according to two categories: achieved and non-achieved. Imagination of time as a row harmonizes with a system of THREE tenses; whereas a system of TWO, an earlier and a later, would seem to correspond better to the feeling of duration as it is experienced. For if we inspect consciousness we find no past, present, or future, but a unity embracing complexity. Everything is in consciousness, and everything in consciousness IS, and is together: there is in it a sensuous and a non-sensuous. We may call the sensuous – what we are seeing, hearing, touching – the *present*; while in the non-sensuous the vast image-world is being labelled the *past*, and another realm, of belief, intuition and certainty, the future.[24]

This more or less describes the Tamil situation that distinguishes between two definite tenses, that is, the past and the present, and a tense that never attained a syntactically definite nature; it is termed *etir*, meaning 'opposite', 'similitude', 'comparison', indicating a *generalis* or *potentialis*. This different tense system, plus the curious fact that the verb knows two inflexions: a positive one and a negative one, brings us closer to an understanding of the importance of the prevalence of the marked over the markers. The positive inflexion of the verb is recognisable by its particle of tense betraying its position in time. The negative inflexion lacks such a particle; it is therefore absent, non-sensuous and thus not experiential – it simply is not there. The marked *speech artefact* is very much there: it is a process which is sensuous and thereby accessible to understanding. According to the Tamil view, markers cannot even form a structure without their base in a process. Structure needs to be embedded *in materia*, otherwise it is indeed non-existent, and can therefore never function either as the aim of knowledge or as a culmination of understanding. The performance of the Tamil text prevails over any form of notation, firstly, because it stands in an ontological equation with the perennial 'marked', and, secondly, because it holds the entire universe and all times – past, present and *potentialis* – in its conscious focus. 'Everything is in consciousness, and everything in consciousness IS together', Whorf remarked. This may well be the aim of Tamil 'literature': to stand out as a sign that encompasses everything in its communicative expressivity.

This seems to have been a long detour before we get to analyse the 'meaning' of the *bhairavi varnam*. But, without such critical reflection, the entire concept 'meaning' could not be applied to Tamil literature. Summing up, we took the following steps to arrive at a new perspective on Tamil texts:

1. replace the idea of the brain as a database by the idea of the brain as an *artist*.
2. broaden the scope of language from *langue* to *langage*;
3. envisage the application of *langage* as *speech-artefact*;
4. situate the speech-artefact in *interactive* communication between senders and receivers that share the coordinates of time and space;
5. conceptualise such situatedness as the practices that make up a *habitus*;
6. identify the speech-artefact as an 'ancient-sign' in an *umbilical tie* with its world;
7. root the Tamil text in the *existential process* of its world;
8. identify the *media* that carry the expression of the text;[25]
9. examine the *'message in the medium'* in terms of cognition; and
10. *locate* the *conceptualisation* of time, of matter and of the litmus test true/untrue in the Tamil utterance.

After this ten-stop tour, the meaning of the Tamil text, the *ilakkiyam*, or marked process, emerges as a 'real reference' in the Tamil world; its reality is in the fact that it is 'achieved' or can be 'potentially achieved'. The performer makes such meaning experientially present by employing the senses of sight and hearing through his media of expression (word, sound and image), as well as probably those of touch, taste and smell that are rooted in shared physical proximity.[26] On such 'occasion of the text' the brain searches and experiments just as an artist does when testing his creation, its theory and understanding of the world. Therefore, the text is ever active, ever flexible, depending upon the varying conditions of the performance. What counts as true or untrue is the 'tasting' of the text, the experiencing or not experiencing. The Tamil Sign, the *ilakkiyam*, or, for that matter, Tamil 'literature', is firmly rooted in shared presence. The experience experienced in the NOW is the only experience that can be affected by and through the senses. The Tamil Sign brings alive the 'stills' of the past and potentialities of the perennial *ilakkiyam* by drawing their echoes and intimations within the orbit of the process of the performance. The dynamism of the Tamil text as an expressive sign should be conceived of as a loop: from the position of an experiential present, past and *potentialis* are drawn into an enlarged NOW, a 'happening' (*nikal*) that makes all accessible to understanding. Because of the epistemological predominance of the sensuous presence of the Sign, powerfully expressing its resemblance[27] to the primal sign, we propose to adjust the Peircean triad as shown in Fig.4.

3.1 Vaiyam – the Tamil World

In the chapter on *porul*, 'reference matter', Tolkappiyanar sets out what the 'auspicious Tamil' (*cem tamil, centamil*) is about. He is quite outspoken in demarcating the 'auspicious conditions' from the ordinary, banal conditions. Not unlike the distinction between 'bent, crooked' Tamil (*kotum tamil*) and 'beautiful, red, auspicious' Tamil (*cem tamil*), the poetry of love (*akam*) distinguishes between the marginal settings (such as *kaikkilai*, 'unrequited love' and *peruntinai*, 'majority, banal love') and the ideal settings that occupy the centre of attention. The subject of *akam* (*akattinaiyiyal*) in the chapter on *porul* (*Porulatikaram* of *Tolkappiyam*) opens with this statement. Having removed the

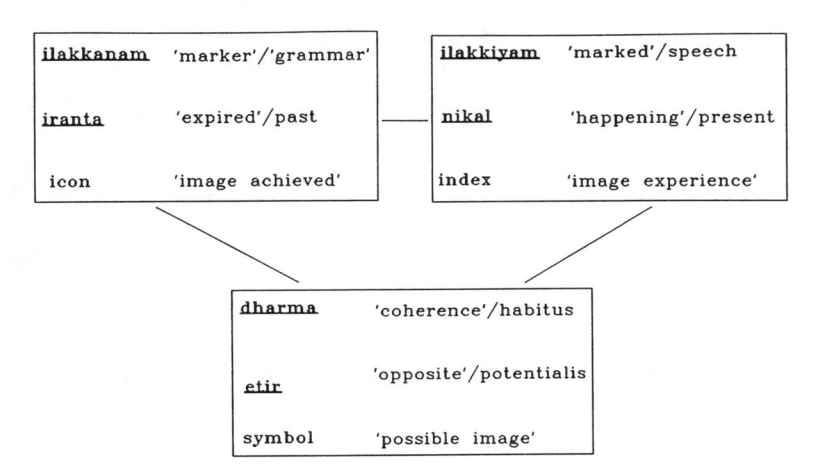

ilakkanam	'marker'/'grammar'	ilakkiyam	'marked'/speech
iranta	'expired'/past	nikal	'happening'/present
icon	'image achieved'	index	'image experience'

dharma	'coherence'/habitus
etir	'opposite'/potentialis
symbol	'possible image'

Figure 4 – the Tamil sign and its dynamics

mismatched and the banal to the periphery, Tolkappiyanar continues with positioning the central topics of lyrical poetry. These are five scenes of love that spread out over the Tamil world (*vaiyam*) as five regions; each of these is characterised by a type of activity that suits the situation of the lovers.[28] Oral wisdom holds that there is an order of three categories of reference. These three create excellence when they are aimed at in the practice of songs. These categories are *mutal* 'first', *karu* 'embryo' and *uri* 'peel, skin, propriety'.[29] In our search for the 'theory in the Tamil head', or, the 'cognitive and motivating structures that make up the Tamil habitus', we will follow these categories in their objects, actions and qualities.[30]

3.1a *Mutal*

'Those who have seen' the nature (of existence) say that *mutal* the 'first, primal' is two: *nilam* (space) and *polutu* (time).[31] These two subcategories are not surprising, and figure today as well. In the course of their twenty centuries of application they have remained remarkably constant and well integrated in the larger discourses on love poetry. In this broader context, which involves Sanskrit conventions as well, it is striking that both the categories of space and of time know a tripartition: the Tamil *nilam* occurs too as *ulakam* (cf. Skt. *loka*), and is known as the triple world (*triloka*), encompassing the world of the gods, of human beings and of the lower creatures. Time is understood as triple, more or less in its aspect of tense: *trikala* (Skt.) or *mukkalam* (Ta.) refers to knowledge of the present (*nikal* 'happening'), the past (*iranta* 'expired') and the *potentialis* (*etir* 'opposite').

In order not to slip into seemingly endless lists that sum up the particulars of the above categories, we will examine the *varnam* from this angle of three worlds and three times. The *varnam* stands out as a sign expressing the categories of *mutal*, *karu* and *uri* in a symphonic orchestration. In our explanation we will try to maintain that coherence of impression and that concerted effort towards excellence. Both the hero, that is the god *Shri Tyagarajasvami*, and the heroine, that is the devotee, excel in their involvement in love, and so does everything that goes into the situation. *Bhairavi varnam* is a vital sign of distinction. It demarcates the grandeur of the god, of devotion and of love in this world, and, at the same time, it brings alive the fame and excellence of the past. It remembers that past so that it becomes a present and sets it off against the backdrop of an eternal *potentialis*, all to be realised in the process of performance.

In using the term 'distinction', Bourdieu's social analysis of 'taste' among the French comes to mind. And correctly so; his charts that map the different tastes, occupations, and material settings of the French worker, middle class and intellectual share a classificatory zest with the Tamil mapping of the world.[32] However, the two differ significantly in their appreciation of the map. Whereas Bourdieu's map is descriptive and carries the weight of a socio-cultural conclusion, the Tamil map is an inventory that is 'true': not only does it reveal reality to those who did not 'see' it, like sages do, it also works. By 'aiming at' the particulars of the categories in the process of performance one brings them about; their excellence gets established for all to see and hear. In this way the past continues to live and shine in actual presence. Distinction, or excellence, *cirappu* in Tamil terms, not only has a temporal relevance, but reaches metaphysical heights as well. Just as the Tamil 'habitus' turns out to be an entire cosmos of metaphysical coherence, the Tamil 'distinction' shares this trait. In consequence, application is of critical importance, and makes the dictum 'demo(nstrate) or die' of the Media Lab ring true.[33]

3.1a.i Space

The triple world emerges in sight in *bhairavi varnam*. At the outset we are confronted with the heroine, her body afflicted by the pangs of love. All her senses smart, as Kaman ('Cupid') has inflamed them with the fever of infatuation. The entire creation seems to breathe with her: the five elements of earth, water, fire, air and ether invade her being through smell, taste, sight, touch and sound. It is as if her body, the locus of her suffering, is tossed in the sea of a larger body, encompassing the entire universe, with nowhere to hide. Her sensory perception is soaked in *moha*, 'infatuation, intoxication': the nose, tongue, eyes and skin register nothing but love, and can express nothing but love. Her helplessness is set in *marutam*: a region that the ancient experts characterised as the site of waiting

According to the commentators on Tolkappiyanar's *Porulatikaram* ('chapter on reference matter of lyrical poetry'), the names of these five regions are *katu* (jungle), *malai* (mountain), *natu* (countryside), *katal karai* (seashore) and *palai* (desert). The activities that the lovers go through in these landscapes are 'meeting', 'joining and waiting', 'waiting and weeping', 'quarrelling', 'separating'. These regions are often referred to by the name of a flower that is associated with it. The jungle area is recognised by its *kurinci*, the mountains by the fragrant *mullai*, the countryside by *marutam*, the seashore by the *neytal* water-lily and the desert by the silvery-leaved ape flower *palai*.[34]

These poetic *topoi* form the 'theory in the head' couched in terms of truly 'interiorised landscapes'.[35] *Marutam* as the cultivated countryside is green with rice-fields and abounds in ponds and rivers; it is dotted with old and large towns that resound with festivals, learning and worship. It is an apt description of *Colanatu*, one of the most ancient culture hearths of South India. Here, in the town of Tiruvarur, lives the hero, the beloved of the girl. Her ardent declaration of love is followed by her dismay at his seeming indifference.[36] She realises her situation of separation and tries to draw close and plead for union with her love. She situates him outside their intimacy, in society, in the sophisticated holy town *Arur*.

> The beginnings of this holy site go back to the worship of its trumpet-flower tree (*Bigonia chelonoides*) and its snakes. The central shrine on the temple-grounds is dedicated to the 'Lord of the ant-hill' Shri Valmikinatha. The earliest Tamil sources speak of the worship of snakes that live under the *marutam* tree.[37] Legend holds that the great god Vishnu chased the other gods, the *devas*, round the world, proud as he was of his great bow. The *devas* prayed to the great Shiva who curbed Vishnu's pride as they reached Tiruvarur. While Vishnu rested his head on his bow and stood dismayed, the *devas*, in the meantime, built an ant-hill at one end of the bow and cut its string; by the sudden straightening of the bow Vishnu's head was cut off and flung to the earth. Vishnu fell dead. However, Shiva restored his life, and, granting the wish of the *devas*, he took his abode in the ant-hill.[38]

Snakes are believed to inhabit their own subterranean world, the *nagaloka*; it is from here that Shiva moved to the central shrine. Even today, there is a separate shrine in the second courtyard, known as *Atakesvaram*.³⁹ No deity resides there, but it leads to a subterranean passage at least six or seven feet deep and closed by a slab of stone. Shiva is worshipped in the shrine in the form of the *marakata linga*, the 'emerald index' of Shiva's presence.⁴⁰ The earliest mystical poet-saints, such as Appar and Cuntarar (seventh century AD) sing about *Aruran*, the Lord of Arur, as the 'one who resides in the ant-hill'.⁴¹ They mention as well two of the great festivals that are celebrated even today in the temple of *Tiruvarur*.⁴²

The Lord of the holy city of Arur is no ordinary lover. He has all the splendour, honour, fame and excellence that go with the aristocratic norms of ancient Tamil poetry. He is full of beatitude (*bhoga*), and to be in his presence results in a similar experience of transcendental bliss. Our girl in love therefore requests him: 'Bhogatyagesha come to my side, to bestow bliss on me too' (anubhōga ceyya vā kiṭṭa). At this point we are confronted with flashes of the manifold images of Shri Tyagaraja as they are sung about in ancient legends (*sthalapuranas*) and as they appear to the eye of the beholder when confronted with the idol of Shiva as Tyagarajasvami in the inner sanctum of the temple.

The working of the temple architecture is quite mysterious: to proceed from the first sight of the great temple-towers (*gopuram*) through the gates into the inner courtyard, through another gate, another courtyard, all dotted with shrines to local and subsidiary gods, builds up an expectation. Finally, one enters through the inner gates, into the dark sanctum. Immediately one is hit by the smells of sandstone, heavy layers of oil, camphor and butter-lamps, incense and flowers. The sounds of the temple drums and long oboes (*nagasvaram*, literally 'sound of the snake') are overwhelming. Deeply hidden in the sanctum is the womb-house (*garbha-grha*), where we stand face to face with god, Shri Tyagarajasvami. His graceful smile that hides and reveals at the same time, has an irresistible attraction:⁴³

> The ancient legends tell of king Muchukunda. Originally, he was a monkey, living on mount Kailasa. Even as a lesser primate he managed to please Shiva through his devotion and was consequently blessed to be born as a Chola king on earth. His prowess and valour were such that he impressed gods (*devas*) and anti-gods (*asuras*) alike. At one point, when the *asuras* were again causing trouble to the gods, king Muchukunda was called for, and in no time

he saw the backs of the fleeing anti-gods. Indra, the chief of the *devas*, granted him any wish he would express. Now, Muchukunda's love for Shiva was unsurpassed and he knew of a most beautiful form (*murti*) of Shiva, namely Tyagaraja. Indra possessed this wondrous image, having received it from Vishnu himself. Vishnu had made this image composed of Shiva, Uma (Shiva's wife) and Subrahmanya (their son) in order to attone for an offence to the goddess Parvati (another name for the wife of Shiva): one unlucky day, he had failed to salute her and, immediately, she had cursed him. Vishnu now effaced the curse by offering worship to the Shri Tyagaraja image. He took to his task earnestly: while resting on his snake couch that floats on the primordial waters, he placed the image on his chest in order to have it close to his heart. Thus, Shri Tyagaraja moved steadily up and down with the regular inhalation and exhalation of Vishnu's breath. Naturally, Indra was very proud of this rare gift and did not anticipate that king Muchukunda would ask for exactly this treasure. But he did. Indra was angry, but could not refuse and, Tyagaraja was hurt, accusing Indra: "You did not remember me therefore you will descend once a year to the earth, to Tiruvarur, and as a low-caste devotee you will offer worship to me."[44] Indra tried to save the situation and had six other images made that were exactly similar to the original form. But Muchukunda was not to be fooled: the ardour of his devotion made him recognize the real Tyagaraja among the seven identical images. With such a devotee, the god Shri Tyagarajasvami was happy to depart from the world of the gods, down to earth, to the great temple of Tiruvarur. There he lives even now in full splendour as the famous processual image. During the great festivals this image is carried on the shoulders of the devotees to the pavilion (*mandapa*) where he holds court or to the huge temple chariot (Skt. *ratha*, Ta. *ter*). As they carry their precious burden, the god seems to dance his primordial dance, the *ajapa natanam* ('the dance of meditative breathing') that resembles the original rhythmic movement on Vishnu's chest.[45] As he holds court he watches temple courtesans performing compositions like our *bhairavi varnam*.[46] The fame of the first Tyagaraja image spreads far and wide. Many poets, musicians and dancers flocked to Tiruvarur to stand face to face with this mysterious image.[47]

The silence of Shri Tyagarajasvami drops her into a recollection of the past. Previously he embraced her, holding her as his very own. Now, she trembles all over and her restlessness drives her out into the world. Her passion no longer interacts with her imagination or with the past, but searches for reality set in the present tense. The third line fans out into a confrontation with that reality. The total of five lines displays the interaction between her senses that are intoxicated by love and the world that seems to have no mercy. Her five senses almost 'hammer' the suffering of separation from the beloved, revealed by the acute immediacy of his absence. The god of Love takes on the shape of Death (*Maran* meaning both), pouring his arrows on her like a shower of rain; thus, he suggests the taste of love without actually offering it. The birds in the mango-grove sting her ears by the sound of their love-play; the cool wind of the mountains touches her, suggesting that the evening is young and awaits the arrival of the beloved; the rays of the moon shine like brilliant cinders, and she cannot bear its sight. The entire nature of *marutam tinai*, the rich, cultivated countryside, speaks to her in signs of happy lovers enjoying each other's company, but he . . . is not there. The earth itself is testimony to her plight and, its smell reminds her of her limited, temporal form. But, this is not a static fact: all worlds and all existences are connected as if in a flux, a continuum that can move through the three times as well as through the three worlds. Compassion, fulfilment and grace are possible even now! Though Shri Tyagaraja is a god, Lord of the world (*jagat isa*), the playful, entire expanse breathing its cosmic breath,[48] settled in the realm of mount Kailasa in the Himalayas, however metaphysical and transcendent he may be, he must come down to earth, to embrace her *now*. Her body is, in the end, the experiential site of his reality. That reality is understood in terms of 'taste', hence his ultimate epithet of *sa-rasa* 'with taste', as if tasting his presence, collapsing all worlds into the most interior of bodily senses.

When we examine the trajectory that the *varnam* traversed in terms of the dimension *space*, we are confronted with a loop that started with the declaration of love 'in me' and ends with the pressing demand 'me, indeed, you must embrace'. In its movement this 'loop-of-love' has travelled through the inner world of the girl, depicting the town Tiruvarur and the grandeur of her beloved, through her memory of their union in an ideal setting for lovers, through her search for him in the outer world, entering into a dialogue with nature, and, finally, through the metaphysical realms of the gods and eternity, committing their existential truth to the sensory test of her own body. The journey begins and ends with the *body*, incorporating on its way the entire *universe*.

Plate 5 Shri Tyagarajasvami on Vishnu's chest[49]

3.1a.ii Time

Bhairavi varnam sets out in a dream-like state that is free of any limitations of space or time.[50] The four (half) lines that make up the *pallavi* and the *anupallavi* are one string of nouns and adverbs, without verbs. Only at the end of the *anupallavi* do we find a verb, namely the imperative *va kitta* 'come close'; before that there is no indication of any action that is set in a particular tense. The initial statement says literally 'infatuation-wise you me-in this moment-in'; that moment lasts for two-thirds of the time it takes to perform the *varnam*. So, it seems that the dream is very persistent. Still, it does not have enduring power: at the end of the four lines that are rendered in mimetic improvisation, reality pounds on the door of consciousness to state its existential demands: she yearns for his presence, close to her, now. It is memory that urges her to a union: 'the bliss of bygone embrace (holding) me as your very own' causes a continuous past affecting the present 'daily thinking of it daily withering away, going over it in my mind, searching you, deeply attached to you'. This state of being is unbearable and demands mutual reciprocation: 'inside I am all trembling', losing all notion of time 'half a minute becomes an aeon', 'the sweetness of your lips, that you must give, this is the right moment, oh Sarasa, Satgunane!'[51]

In the terms of the Tamil experts this line of the *varnam* refers to the earlier meeting of lovers in a pleasure garden and their amorous union. In terms of more philosophical conventions this flash of memory is a flash of the so-called 'yogic memory', remembering a situation of absolute, existential unity. In that view, the fragmentation of life and the innumerable forms it seems to take, conditioned by equally innumerable names and shapes, bring about an acute sense of duality, of separation of Self and Other, of alienation between individual existence (Skt. *aham*) and Being (Skt. *sat*). This impression is strong but not existentially predominant: it is only a phase that Life cyclically goes through.

This cyclical pattern develops basically in two movements: evolution (one day of Brahma) and involution (one night of Brahma).[52] In the involuted state Brahma has no qualities: it is unconditioned existence, dwelling in the mystical sound *AUM*, filled with unboundedness, potentiality, blissful freedom. In its evolved movement it goes through several stages of bipolar fragmentation, such as the opposition dynamic–inert, cooling–

heating, male–female, until it reaches a stage where the power of conditioning (*maya sakti*) takes over. Hereafter, the bipolar tension between form and breath, or, space and time, in other words: physical and psychical realities, causes a rapid multiplication of Life, fragmenting it in ever further-divergent forms.

It is hard to arrest this force of evolution; once it has been set into motion, it accelerates by its own force of desire. The power of desire, of thirst for life, of the yearning for possession and enjoyment of all its variants propels existence into a furious pace of multiplication. Therefore the god of Desire (Kaman) is also the god of Death (Maran). Each thirst results in another physical shape with its own psychic temperament, each lasting but one lifetime. Each leaves behind a residuum of thirst and desire that forces Life to incarnate again, and so on, forming a seemingly endless chain of rebirths.

This power, however, does not stand supreme; first of all, because it is part of a cycle of one day and one night of Brahma;[53] second, because it is possible to effect involution into the unbounded and unconditioned state of being, individually: by reuniting one's own life force to that of the transcendent realm. The memory of that primordial union is the yogic memory that may come true, once again by the individual effort of uniting (*yuj-* 'to bind, unite') the two forces.

The method of doing so is primarily the traditional method of physical meditation exercises and breath control that aim to redirect one's life force back to its spring via the spinal cord. Seven nerve centres (*cakras*) are situated along the spine; five of these are interconnected with the five sensory organs, the five sensory perceptions and the five elements that constitute evolved life; two nerve centres are connected to the realm of non-conditioned life, opening the floodgates of 'release', 'enlightenment', 'bliss', at the topmost centre that is situated at the end of the fontanelle.[54] Thus, the body is not only a form and temporary seat of life, it is also an instrument in overcoming the very conditions space and time. Apart from the traditional physical exercises, called *asanas* (sitting postures), and breath control, called *pranayama*, that characterise the practice of *yoga*, other forms of performance training are considered to be *yoga* as well. Therefore, dance and music carry quite a heavy metaphysical, and even mystical, load.

In the case of *bhairavi varnam* it creates a tension of a multi-layered message. In terms of space we saw how the heroine enters the world, in search of her beloved, interacting with the natural phenomena of the landscape of *marutam*. In terms of time, we see her trying to overcome the natural workings of time: she throws her body into combat with the elements, trying to cleanse it of its natural thirst. The arrows of Desire that force life to attach itself to creation, pour down on her like showers of rain. This taste of water carries the connotation of the taste of love, but is transformed into a taste of Being as 'bliss' (Skt. *ananda*): the vocative *sat-gunane* means 'O, One whose quality is Being'. This lover does not cause a further clinging and fragmentation of life, instead he receives her in an eternal embrace, that abates all thirst by the sweetness of his lips. In his embrace eternity is actual and real, here and now. To be ready for such an embrace she has to 'fold up' the pulling forces of the elements and their interaction with the senses: the sound of the birds (i.e. ether, mouth and ears), the touch of the wind (i.e. the air, hands and skin), the sight of the brilliant moon (i.e. fire, bowels and eyes), the smell of the soil (i.e. the earth, feet and nose). All are transcended in the sweet kiss (i.e. water, genitals, tongue) of her lover, who is *sa-rasa* 'with juice, with tasting', who is *akanta purana vilasan* 'the unfragmented, all-encompassing cosmos that evolutes and involutes as if playing', who is Shiva praised daily as Time itself: Time that encapsulates the movement of the sprouting, maintenance and collapse of creation that punctuate his cosmic dance.

This timeless lover comes when the evening is young (*iravinil*) and all lovers meet to quench their passion. His embrace erases all conditions of space, form, time, limitation and separation. Duality is transcended once and for all in bliss (Skt. *ananda*). His kiss is his grace (Ta. *arul*) and makes his devotees tremble with emotion.[55] When we examine the movement of time that the *varnam* has followed, another loop emerges. Starting off with the 'this moment' of her declaration of love, we experienced her dreams (*potentialis*), her past recollection, her present plight and the eternity of the gods, all to come true in his embrace of her NOW. In this example love has indeed 'taken up more space in the mind than it takes in the bed' (Brodsky 1986: 150): it swallows the entire cosmos, transforming it into the taste of Being, *ippo*, now!, as the last word of the composition. The transformatory character of both dimensions, space and time, is remarkable. Both enjoy their status of 'real' only by their commitment to the happening, actual present, concretised in a physical, shared, sensory presence.

3.1b *Karu*

The second analytic category stated by Tolkappiyanar is *karu* 'embryo', 'creation'. *Porulatikaram* 18 lists the particles that form such a category: 'Oral transmission holds that a summary and specification of the nature of god, food, great tree, bird, drum, behaviour, lute, this, that way etc. is *karu*.' Earlier in *TP*5 he refers to the world of sweet water (*marutam*) as inhabited by the god *Ventan*, 'king'. And indeed, Tyagesha is a king known as *Tyagaraja* ('king of sacrifice, of letting go, lord of the gods'), *Vara Isa* ('lord of the excellent ones'), *Jagat Isa* ('lord of the world'), not to be fathomed by *Hari* (Vishnu) and *Aiyan* (Brahma):[56]

> Once upon a time Vishnu and Brahma quarrelled about the question 'which of us is the greatest?' As they were piling argument upon argument, cumulating their evidence, a fiery pillar steadily arose in front of them. It was not possible to see from where it arose nor where it would stop as it continued to rise beyond their sight. Vishnu and Brahma fell silent for a moment: what or who could that be? Temporarily they even forgot about their own contest and decided to find out what this apparition might be. Brahma took the shape of a goose (Skt. *hamsa*, usually translated as 'swan' and identified as Brahma's vehicle) and soared up into the sky; Vishnu took his incarnation of boar (Skt. *varaha*) and dug into the earth. Both travelled far, but could not detect either the beginning or the end of this awesome pillar of fire. Finally, Shiva showed compassion and told the two gods to stop their efforts: the pillar was nothing and no one but Shiva, who had decided to teach them a lesson by demonstrating that he alone is the greatest of gods. This fiery pillar is to be seen on top of the holy, red mountain *Arunacalam* behind the great Shiva temple of Tiruvannamalai on the night of *Karttikai*.[57]

The royal, superior status of Tyagaraja as Shiva is evident and unquestionable. Shri Tyagaraja of Tiruvarur holds a number of weapons and insignia that are characteristic for royalty: the sceptre (*manittantu*), the sword (*virakantayam*), the garland (*cenkal unirmalai*), the throne (*ratnasimhasanam*), the elephant (*ayiravatam*) and the chariot (*alitter*).⁵⁸ The mere sight of the god inspires awe and the sense of being in the presence of cosmic royalty. A *prabandham* set in the temple of Tiruvarur describes the regal appearance of Shri Tyagarajasvami:⁵⁹

> snakes as bracelets adorn his arms turning to the four directions of the sky; he wears ornaments studded with rubies; with the moon on his head, the deer in his right hand, he is truly the Supreme Lord (Skt. *Paramesvara*). Superior jewels, closely set jewels in his rings, bracelets on his upper arm cast in the form of snakes, his face exuding the good, auspicious and generous nature of the goddess Shri Lakshmi, bedecked with the skin of the tiger, holding the trident, he is truly the Supreme Shiva (Skt. *Paramasiva*). Adorned with flowers of exquisite scent, the resplendent one, peacefully seated on the lion-throne, he is the Supreme Shiva, the family god of the great king Shahaji who belongs to the Bhoshala line.⁶⁰

The *varnam* states that the 'sages worship him daily',⁶¹ and indeed, not a single day's worship is omitted in Tiruvarur.⁶² On festival days special worship is offered; one of the most favourite offers is the recitation of the 1010 names of Shri Tyagaraja, called *Mucukunda sahasra nama*. Another is the *sri Sundaramurti stotra*, that enumerates 114 qualities of the Lord; and a similar litany, named *Tyagarajanamavali* voices another 100 qualities of the god.⁶³ Going through these lists the supreme, divine, royal character of this king of Tyaga (Skt. 'sacrifice', 'letting go') is overwhelmingly clear. His authority is an established fact, even among the gods. They, too, serve in Tyagaraja's court. *Pallaki seva prabandham* depicts, in a vivid manner, the divine services to Tyagarajasvami:

> the god Kubera (the divine treasurer) gives betel-leaves, and camphor, Vayudeva (god of wind) causes a fragrant breeze, Brahma (the supreme, most abstracted god) utters praise, Yama (god of death and time) moves the fan, holds a sword and shield, Candra (the moon) holds the royal umbrella and banner, the Garudas, Kinnaras and Gandharvas (celestial beings) sing in beautiful, soprano voices while celestial dancers like Rambha and Urvasi please the Lord by their performance.⁶⁴

The auspicious, peaceful and superior character of the divine king is a matter of temperament. This, to an extent, is dependent on the type of food that he receives. Shri Tyagaraja is emphatically a vegetarian god. In the course of the second part of the *pallavi* the heroine offers her beloved fresh cow's milk mixed with delicious spices.[65] In the temple of Tiruvarur Tyagarajasvami receives a great variety of vegetarian delicacies: an inscription of Kulottunga II (1178–1218 AD) registers large provisions for food-offerings as well as the names of various dishes prepared in the temple: *puri aval amutu, appamutu, kariyamutu* (side dishes), *tayir amutu* (rice with curd), *pal amutu* (rice with milk), *mankay varral* (mango condiment), *uppinci* (seasoned ginger), *milakamutu* (rice with pepper), *neyyamutu* (rice with *ghi*, i.e. clarified butter), *porikkariyamutu* (rice with fried vegetables) and *ataikayammutu* (betel leaves and nuts); sometimes such dishes were prepared on the basis of *ponakappalam* ('fruit of the golden home'), a specially fine variety of rice.[66]

Five centuries later Lord Tyagaraja has not yet tired of this choice: in song 17, *Jayamangalam* ('victorious auspiciousness'), of *Pallaki seva prabandham* many of these dishes are announced.[67] Even today, during the great festivals the menu is almost the same. The huge quantity of food that is being offered to the god is displayed before him. It is believed that the great god enjoys 'the essence of the food' while he dines with the curtain drawn between him and the crowd of devotees. Other types of food offerings are in fact food-oblations: the image is bathed in raw food, such as: milk, curd, fruit-mixture, but also in non-eatables such as rose-water, sandal paste, holy ashes and holy water. Afterwards, all these substances are distributed among the devotees, who are eager to receive them, swallow them, smear them on their bodies, or eat them seated in long rows in the temple pavilion.

What makes these substances so precious, in the first place, is the mediated touch and contact with the living, material manifestation of the god. By absorbing substances touched by him the devotee absorbs the potentiality of his divine equilibrium and brings himself closer to his grace. Secondly, the eating of the food of the region is a reaffirmation of belonging to that countryside and all the temperaments that go with it. Valentine Daniel draws several 'concentric circles of belonging' in his work *Fluid Signs, being a person the Tamil way*.[68] *Tolkappiyam*'s 'check list' in assessing a poetic situation turns out to be a very pragmatic one, even today. One of the first questions Tamilians ask each other in the domestic sphere, is *enta ur* 'which place', or, in other words, 'which roots', with all the gods, customs of worship and food (vegetarian or non-vegetarian, 'hot or cool', cooked or uncooked) that go with that place.[69]

The next feature that is distinctive for the regional situation is the 'great tree'. On the level of the text we find the 'mango-grove with cuckoos calling'; on the level of Tiruvarur temple we find the temple garden with its sacred, local tree (Skt. *sthalavrksa*), the *patiri*, or trumpet flower tree (*Bigonia chelonoides*).[70] The cuckoo (Ta *kuyil*) is the love-bird *par excellence*, accompanying or recalling the meeting of lovers. The parrot or parakeet is another such bird; its function is slightly different, since it figures mostly as a pet animal, seated on the shoulder of a lovelorn lady, or it serves as a love messenger informing the hero of her plight, and begging him to come soon. The male peacock is an outspoken herald of a love situation; its sexual prowess reflects the male initiative. On the other hand, the peacock announces the rainy season, which is a happy time for united lovers but a reason for despair for lovers in separation.

Next on the list of situational diagnosis is the type of drum that is beaten. *Parai*, the drum, is an extremely important feature in South Indian life. It heralds life-giving events as well as death. Everything in between has its own drum, professional drummers and occasion of drumming. No rite of passage can take place without sounding the drum, no temple festival or procession will be successful without an introductory circumambulation of the drummer drumming his drum. The great temple of Tiruvarur has a rich culture of drums and of drumming. The most spectacular specimen is the so-called 'five-faced-drum', the *pancamukha vadyam*. The *suddha maddalam*, a drum with a loud, dry and 'clean' sound, as well as the little, penetrating double drum, called *kotukkoti*, are famous accoutrements, too, of the Tyagarajasvami temple. It is said that, on the day of the grand procession of the temple chariot, a specific tune, *mallari*, must be played by the large oboe and the *kotukkotti*. The melody is in *nattai* and the rhythm in *kanta natai* (cluster of five beats). This combination evokes the slow, supple vigour of wrestlers challenging each other at the beginning of a match. In a similar way Lord Tyagaraja likes to be challenged by the *mallari*, and will refuse to set out for his journey without hearing the impudent sound of the little double drum.[71] All drums in Tiruvarur are 'auspicious instruments' (*mangalavadyam*) and are played in combination with the highly auspicious large oboe called *nagasvaram* ('sound of the snake'). Within this group the *pari nayanam*, an ivory oboe, is unique to Tamilnadu.

The chief occupations of the inhabitants of the region of sweet water reigned over by the divine king Ventan are clearly those that depend upon the rural wealth of the region. From the earliest records onwards we hear about the clear, sweet, fertile waters of the Kaveri river. Large rice-fields and long stretches of sugar-cane prosper in this part of the country. There are plenty of palm and mango-trees, yielding auspicious fruit. The flourishing of life is very much connected with the availability of flowing, sweet water. All human existence, activity and well-being is dependent on it. Therefore it is no wonder that one of the etymologies of the term tamil refers to water.[72] All cultivation that characterises Cholanadu, all worship that goes on in the temples and all life in the cities revolves around water.

Apart from the ever-present agriculture, the cities are marked by great wealth, artisanship, the casting of bronze, the making of jewellery, weaving, and most of all by erudition, music and dance. Tamil, Sanskrit and Telugu: all these languages settled successfully or were born in Tamilnadu. Tiruvarur figured as a cultural centre from the beginning of the first millennium. The great poet-saints such as Appar, Cuntarar and Nanacampantar (*c.* seventh century AD) sing of Tiruvarur in their verses. This situation continued for one full millennium, in fact, without a break: the three most famous classical composers of South Indian ('Karnatic') music were all born in Tiruvarur – the first, Tyagaraja (1767–1847 AD) was even named after the great deity. The second was Shyama Sastri (1762–1827 AD), whose descendants still live in Tiruvarur and teach there; and, finally, there was Muttuswami Dikshitar (1775–1835 AD), who composed several cycles of songs on deities who reside in Tiruvarur temple that are still played there as part of the ritual offerings.[73]

Within that tradition of musical erudition we encounter the classical lute, the *vina* that is characteristic of South Indian music. The old lute, the *yal*, evolved through a number of stages into a fretted instrument that sets the standard and codification for the system of tonal scales of Karnatic music.[74] This later instrument is considered highly auspicious, as it is played by the goddess

Sarasvati, the wife of Brahma, and, in fact, is synonymous with her presence.[75]

3.1c *Uri*

The third parameter of existence is termed *uri* 'peel, skin, bark'.[76] In contemporary terms we might translate *uri* by 'perspective',[77] the 'point-of-viewing' of the world. In our perception of 'reality' we may choose innumerable viewpoints but we can only choose one 'point-of-viewing' at any one time.[78] This is the case for the very simple reason that our body can position itself in only one spot and in only one moment at any one time. This physical reality is simple; its mental variants are innumerable. To gloss 'reality' as body (Ta *mey*) has therefore irreversible consequences. Tolkappiyanar explains the reference matter of *uri* (*uripporul*) as fairly simple. Within the category of *akam*, the private, intimate sphere of life, he diagnoses five occurrences of specific emotional–somatic states that colour the experience of human existence. *Porulatikaram* 14 lists 'joining' (*punartal*), 'separating' (*pirital*), 'waiting' (*iruttal*), 'weeping' (*irankal*) and 'quarrelling' (*utal*). These belong to the five landscapes that have been mentioned before.[79]

The rich imagery of the ancient poetry between man, woman and nature evokes the dynamic, transformatory character of the term *uri*. *Kuruntokai* 40 depicts two lovers merging their hearts into one fertile ground of love, just as the red (read also 'auspicious') soil soaked with fresh rain prepares itself for gestation:[80]

> yāyum ñāyum yārā kiyarō /
> entaiyum nuntaiyum emmuraik kēḷir /
> yānum nīyum evvaḷi yaritum /
> cempulap peyyanīr pōla /
> anputai neñcan tāṅkalantanavē //

> My father and your father who may they be
> My mother and your mother in which way are they related
> I and you how did we get to know each other
> red earth and gushing rain
> just like that our loving hearts merged into one.[81]

Two human hearts as humid earth. This resemblance suggests a dynamism and processual transformation that allows the type of 'loop' that we discovered in the dimensions of space (*nilam*) and time (*kalam*). Creation (*karu*) is not a static fact: god, man, beast and nature transform, too. All are embedded in a continuum that is ever in flux. Whether on the macro level of evolution–involution or on a micro-level of human existence: the three realms and the three times are ever active and mobile. Thus one human existence is 'incremental' of all times and all places, it may contain and develop all past and potential forms. Evolution can unfold all stages of conditioned, fragmented, manifest Being and retrace its steps as soon as it is cast into a human mould. *Uri* 'peel, skin, bark' resembles the skin of a snake, ever renewing itself, shedding its old worn 'peel' for a new, vital one.

The gradual shedding of old skins until one leaves behind the last conditioning layer equals the metaphysical journey back into evolution. The magic power that works this way is the power of love; right from the inner, intimate world of *akam* it permeates the entire universe. Ardent love melts away inner and outer obstacles, it strengthens the king and thereby the entire country. It transforms the rough quality of existence into sweetness (Ta. *inpam*). The early 'secular' lyrical poetry shares with the later openly mystical songs a deeply transformatory and even metaphysical character. These songs carry the transformatory process much further than a happy, prosperous life, the sweetness of love and the excellence of lovers. By the sixth century AD the hero and heroine are god and devotee. The love emotion is one of intense longing and vulnerable yearning, an opening up until the borders of the Ego melt and merge with the divine. This type of situation is called *bhakti* (Skt. 'share, partake, enjoy, experience, undergo, feel') and can accommodate all situations that belonged to the sphere of *akam*. The old *akam* poetry was voiced directly by the *dramatis personae* of the love situation and recognisable by small indications such as 'What she said', 'What he said', 'What her friend said', 'What her mother said'. In the sphere of devotion (*bhakti*) we find a similar, more implicit situation:

> 'What he (the lover–devotee) said'
> As grass, as plant, as worm, as tree,
> as many a wild beast;

as bird, as snake, as stone, as man,
as devil and as demons;
as unbending celestial, as sage, and as god:
in a hurry,
having taken birth upon birth, in ever different crowds,
having grown so tired –
I came home, today,
seeing
the golden feet in the very substance of our Lord!

Manikkavacakar,
Civapuranam 26–32

The love between god and man is consummated in the moment of 'grace' (Ta. *arul*). This experience redescribes – in fact, reshapes – reality. It is not merely a mental surplus emerging from the act of interpretation as hinted at by Ricoeur. This type of appropriation is deeply and openly devotional. It is believed to be two-sided: god appropriates man, and man appropriates god; god becomes man and man becomes god. This is not a recovery of 'meaning', but a recovery of 'Being'. The divine, equilibrated condition of Being is immanent in all manifest life, space and time. The moment of realisation of their sameness is the moment of grace (*arul*). The mystical poet Arunakirinatar (*c*. fifteenth century AD) sings about this experience in *Kantaranuputi* 51:[82]

uruvāy aruvāy uḷatāy ilatāy
maruvāy malarāy maṇiyāy oḷiyāyk
karuvāy uyirāy katiyāy vitiyāy
kuruvāy varuvāy aruḷvāy kukaṉē

As form, as formless, as being, as not-being,
as fragrance, as blossom, as jewel, as lustre,
as embryo, as breath,
as walk of life, as precept,
as teacher,
you may come,
and bestow your grace,
O Mysterious One.

The ever present immanence of the Lord, of the beloved, and his potential, sudden appearance, renders the whole of human existence pregnant with expectation and longing.[83] The concept of 'future' as a continuous *potentialis* is crucial to this mode of perception. In this context, the loop that we depicted earlier as a graphic representation of the dynamism of the living sign becomes relevant again. We saw that the dimensions space and time could be experienced only by their commitment to the present tense and to physical presence; the here and now proved to be the vital touchstone for 'reality'. Through the workings of *uri*, 'perspective', the second category, 'creation', is rendered meaningful in a similar loop-like fashion. The *uri* of *akam* or *bhakti* commits the three worlds, the three times and the entire universe to an experiential presence of grace. The relationship between god as lover and man as the beloved has the power to transform present, past and *potentialis* into an 'enlarged', all-encompassing present. It opens up the continuum of the three worlds and makes bliss, the ultimate locus of Being, accessible here and now. It can unveil the divine in the entire creation and transform its temporary condition of living into its metaphysical, equilibrated reality.

The relationship between lover and beloved is crucial in this transformation and is couched in terms of the Lord (Skt. *pati*), his cattle (Skt. *pasu* 'cow') and the tie between them (Skt. *pasa*).[84] This first relationship is the 'general facts', while the individual existence, set in this life, on local, contemporary space–time coordinates, is the particular. Their tie is the ground from which the loop soars away and returns embodying eternity along its trajectory. Thus the individual *pasu* stands in a present-tense relationship to the Lord (*pati*), who is an eternal *potentialis*. The tie between the two is known as *pasa* (Skt. 'tie', 'bond') and becomes direct through god's act of grace (*arul*). For a long time it is mediated by the acts of worship. Worship, as we saw before, is basically the dedication to memorising the proofs of excellence: excellence in love, in beauty, in goodness, in empathy and in grace. Many proofs of such excellence (Ta. *cirappu*) have preceded the individual devotee, and the memorisation of these examples in loving dedication by worship brings him closer to the quality of Life-in-Grace. The past, therefore, does not exist as a fact of history; it exists as an example to the present. The Tamil term used for 'History' is *varalaru*; it means 'example', and is interchangeable with *cirappu* 'excellence' and the Sanskrit *purana* 'old'. To tell or perform the old examples of excellence is an act of love, of devotion, and instils the quality of grace into life. The living sign of lyrical, devotional poetry can be depicted as shown in Fig.5.

On the level of *bhairavi varnam*, the transformatory character of the 'perspective' of love, *akam* as *uripporul*, is reflected by the gradual change of the affliction of *moha* ('infatuation'), into the quality of *bhoga* ('delight') induced by the thought of Tyagarajasvami as Bhogatyagesha,[85] and finally into the sweetness of his grace (*arul*). From the erotic thirsting for fulfilment (*moha*) that would lead to further clinging, fragmentation and incarnation, the force of *akam* is connected to the equilibrated *potentialis* of the god. The five lines of the *caranam* depict the combat of the body with the forces of the elements and the senses; what is at stake is the direction of transformation: either back into further evolution and dispersion, or, back 'home' into the involuted, concentrated, bundled state in which all dualism has ceased to be active. This type of experience of love is the saturation of Being with 'Bliss'; in Hindu terms: *sat-*

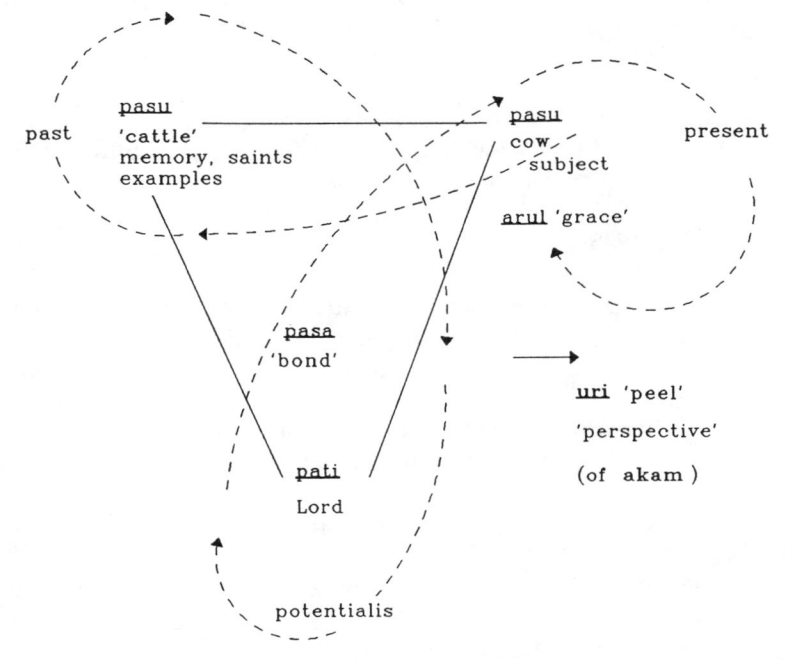

Figure 5 – the sign of Tamil bhakti

cit-ananda 'Being-Awareness-Bliss'. This is not a mental state, an immersion in understanding; it is a 'state of being' that is experienced by and effected through the body. Physical presence, the working of the senses and the double interaction of devotee, world and god as lover are an absolute prerequisite. Once submitted to incarnation in a physical, manifest shape, there can be no 'meaning' whatsoever outside or away from bodily experiencing. Thus the universe, the gods, the world and all that is manifest in it are caught in an ongoing transformational flux that affects the three realms, the three times, and the entire creation. Continuum and flux converge in the perspective of love, falling into place in the body 'in love', and are transcended there in the occurrence of grace. The performance of the text weaves itself into the world in order to transcend it.

Notes

1. Smith, Frank, 1985, 'Literacy: inventing worlds or shunting information', in: *Literacy, Language and Learning, The Nature and Consequences of Reading and Writing*, pp. 195–213.
2. Smith, 1985, p. 198.
3. Such grounding can be provided by schemata of memory, of thought, of scenarios or plans that 'are the possibilities that enable us to interact with the world . . .', Smith, 1985, p. 200.
4. Smith, 1985, p. 206.
5. Smith, 1985, p. 212.
6. See Praxis, Form, pp. 154–5.
7. Kristeva poses the classical question concerning the function of language 'Celle de produire une pensée ou celle de la communiquer' in the introduction of *Le langage cet inconnu*, 1981, pp. 9–17.
8. Bourdieu, Pierre, 1990, *Outline of a Theory of Practice*, p. 78.
9. In a personal communication with Bourdieu as early as June 1991, I proposed to him the equation of *habitus* and *dharma*. He was quite delighted about this suggestion, as it agreed with the equation he had made a few weeks ago in Japan.
10. It is this quality of spoken, that is applied, grammar that guarantees flexibility. Even on the cosmological level the coherence is flexible; naturally, this is hard to understand or

accept within the parameters of Western modernity, codification and ambition to generalise.
11. Cf. also *Praxis*, pp. 145–6.
12. Cf. also *Praxis*, pp. 134–5.
13. Pulavar R. Kannan, my teacher of Tamil prosody, pointed out the passage tamiḻ kūṟu nallulakam 'the auspicious world where Tamil is spoken' in the preface to *Tolkappiyam*. The *Pinkalanikantu* (c. 850–900 AD) refers in stanza 10.580 to the quality of Tamil: iṉimaiyu(m) nīrmaiyum tamiḻeṉal *ākum* 'sweetness and wateriness become if you say Tamil'. Cf. also K. V. Zvelebil, 1992, pp. ix–xviii.
14. That is in *Tolkappiyam*, in *Akattiyam* and *Akapporul*.
15. *Tolkappiyam, Akattinaiyiyal* 3.
16. The term *uri* 'skin, peel', seems to express a natural conceptualisation of the phenomenological position.
17. Cf. CD-i Content-Word-Space-World.
18. For an abbreviated version of this inventory see A. K. Ramanujan, 1970, *The Interior Landscape*.
19. The 'rediscovery' of Tamil literature has been described in detail by K. V. Zvelebil, 1992, pp. 144–227. Compare his account with Said, 1978, *Orientalism*, Chapter 2, III 'Oriental Residence and Scholarship: The Requirements of Lexicography and Imagination', pp. 149–66.
20. American founder of semiotics (1839–1914).
21. Roman Jakobson and Krystyna Pomorska in *Dialogues*, pp. 91–2.
22. Jakobson and Pomorska in *Dialogues*, pp. 91–2.
23. K.V. Zvelebil, 1971, 'The Present Tense Morph in Tamil', in *Journal of the American Oriental Society*, Vol. 91, No. 3, pp. 442–7.
24. Benjamin L. Whorf, quoted by P. Adams, 1972, *Language in Thinking*, p. 133.
25. The *dictum* the 'medium is the message is the massage' was introduced by Marshall McLuhan in his *The Gutenberg Galaxy*.
26. The Sanskrit term *sannidhi* indicates both 'temple' and 'presence'. The actual presence of the Divine is ensured by daily offerings that please the five senses: flowers, food, incense, light, coolness, song and dance.
27. Cf. the relationship between this sign and its world with the ancient sign of Foucault in his 1970, *The Order of Things*, pp. 17–45: 'The Four Similitudes' and 'The Prose of the World'.

28. See *TP Akattinaiyiyal* 2 and CD-i Content-Word-Space-World.
29. See *TP Akattinaiyiyal* 3: mutal karuvuripporuḷ eṉ ṟa muṉ ṟē/ nuvalum kālai muṟai ciṟantanavē / pātaluṭpayiṉ ṟavai nā ṭukālai/
30. 'Objects, actions and qualities' are deliberate translations from the Tamil *peyar*, *viṉai* and *uriccol* listed by Tolkappiyanar.
31. *TP Akattinaiyiyal* 4: mutaleṉappaṭuvatu nilam poḻutu iraṇṭin iyaleṉa moḻipa iyalpu uṇarntōrē.
32. Cf. Bourdieu, 1979, *La distinction. Critique sociale du jugement*, Paris, éd. de Minuit.
33. Cf. Preface, p. xvi.
34. *Kurinci*: conehead, *Strobilanthes*, bluish, grows at an altitude of 6000 ft. and flowers only once in twelve years; *mullai*: *Jasminum sambac*, Arabian jasmine; *marutam*: *Terminalia tomentosa*; *neytal*: *Nymphaea lotus alba*, water lily, white and blue; *palai*: *Mimusops kauki*, silvery-leaved ape-flower that grows in barren tracts; its evergreen blossoms are small and white.
35. See CD-i: Content-Word-Space-World.
36. See CD-i: Content-Image-Space-Text.
37. See S. Ponnusvamy, 1972, *Sri Thyagaraja temple, Tiruvarur*, p. 7, quoting *Perumpanarrupatai* 11.232–3.
38. S. Ponnusvamy, 1972, p. 7.
39. S. Ponnusvamy, 1972, p. 7.
40. Note the significant fact that the presence of Shiva is addressed as *linga*, Sanskrit for 'index', 'sign'.
41. S. Ponnusvamy, 1972, p. 24, quoting Appar *Tevaram* 5:7:8 . . . ārūraṉ eṉum pavaṉi vītivitaṅkanai. . .
42. That is the feast of Tiruvatirai and Pankuni Uttiram. On both occasions the Lord is taken out in a grand procession and offered a 'royal court' in one of the pavilions. The high moment of the festival occurs when Shri Tyagarajasvami denudes one foot for the devotees to see and thus to receive his blessings.
43. See CD-i Content-Word-Space-Performer.
44. Cf. Kersenboom-Story, S., 1987, *Nityasumangali, Devadasi Tradition in South India*, p. 145.
45. *Ajapa* is a technical term for a form of meditation that consists of the movement of inhalation–exhalation. The other images of Tyagaraja also took their abode in Tamilnadu and dance different dances at different shrines; see S. Ponnusvamy, p.

27.
46. See CD-i Content-Image-Space-World.
47. The great composer Tyagaraja (1759–1874) was born in Tiruvarur and named after its famous god.
48. The entire universe is imagined as evolving in the movements of inhalation and exhalation; periods of 'sprouting' (Skt. *srsti*) and 'involution' (Skt. *pralaya*) alternate.
49. This painting is to be found in Tiruvarur temple on the ceiling of the *sabhapati mandapa*.
50. I am grateful to René Devisch for this characterisation of a state that is free of 'space' and 'time'.
51. The terms *sa-rasa* 'with juice', 'with taste' and *sat-gunane* 'he whose quality is being' have been translated as literally as possible in order to bring out their experiential nature.
52. For the reckoning of one day and one night of Brahma, see H. Zimmer, 1974, *Myths and Symbols in Indian Art and Civilization*, pp. 13–16.
53. This macrocosmic perspective is reflected in the cycles of rebirths on the microcosmic level.
54. The yogic path results in a gradual bundling of the force of life, away and out of fragmentation into the undivided, unconditioned Absolute. This journey is located along the five nerve centres that radiate from the spine. Its trajectory correlates sense organs, action organs of the body with subtle elements and gross elements of creation. Consciousness ascends from the nose-feet-smell-earth to ears-mouth-sound-ether; it proceeds while leaving behind the force of physical–mental conditioning to undivided consciousness, and blossoms into the seed-*mantra AUM*. Thus the highest philosophical entity is the unbounded presence of the sound *AUM*.
55. Nandini remembers how her father, Dr V. Raghavan, used to be deeply moved at the words *umai teti*, 'having searched you' as a metaphor for the 'human condition'.
56. All epithets that mark his metaphysical nature occur in the last *caranam*. This enables the poet and the dancer to collapse the metaphysical and the physical into one instantaneous experience *ippo*, 'NOW'.
57. The embodiment of this event is to be seen every year during the month of Karttikai (November) in Tiruvannamalai: on top of its sacred mountain Arunacalam a huge fire is lit, piercing

the dark sky. See CD-i Content-Image-Space-World for mountain and temple.
58. S. Ponnusvamy, 1972, p. 75.
59. This song occurs in the 'processional opera' *Pallaki Seva Prabandham* composed by king Shahaji of Tanjore (1684–1710), and was performed in Tiruvarur until recently. The Indian musicologist P. Sambamoorthy notated the version that was known to the *devadasis* of his time. In 1955 he edited the entire opera; the passage quoted comprises three *caranams* of the first song.
60. King Shahaji belonged to the Bhosala line; in this way he leaves his mark as composer and patron in the song.
61. See the last *caranam* of the *bhairavi varnam* 'anutiṇam paṇiya'.
62. The commencement of worship stipulates the obligation to light a lamp and sprinkle water at least once a day for the image. The number of ritual attendances may vary from one to eight services.
63. These two litanies are recited even today in the great temple of Tiruvarur. The full text was published in 1959 by the Liberty Press in Madras, but the priests do not seem to use that edition. While one *gurukkal* ('priest') sings the names of the god, others place flowers and flower petals at the conclusion of each name. In the course of more than two hours the god and goddess have almost disappeared under the load of rose petals and chrysanthemums. The 'service' of 1008 names is embedded in a larger offering of the signs of royalty, such as the mirror, the royal umbrella, the banner, the sound of the large drum, several auspicious instruments and the singing of praise (Ta. *porri*), to Shri Tyagarajasvami. In 1977 I was allowed to act as *yajamani* ('sacrificer') because I donated the singing of *Tevaram* (Ta. *Tevarakosti*); two extra singers (Ta. *otuvar*) were invited, plus a violinist and a drummer, to perform *Tevaram* while the names of the god were being recited. In 1989 I accompanied Nandini and her mother when they offered a *Sri Tyagaraja Mucukunda Sahasra Namavali*. Such an event involves all the other gods and goddesses on the templeground: they, too, received special worship and the gift of a new dress. During the three days that we spent in the temple, Nandini was encouraged to offer a song to the god: she sang the *padam* 'Mukattai kāṭṭi' for Shri Tyagarajasvami – a beautiful song in *raga bhairavi* that

describes the wondrous face of the god characterised by his intoxicating smile. The *padam* demands an answer from the god as to why he does not reveal his full form to the devotees, but only his face. The secret is ancient and well-protected. Cf. also CD-i Content-Word-Space-Performer.

64. P. Sambamoorthy, 1955, *Pallaki Seva Prabandham*, Telugu Opera of Shahaji Maharajah (1684–1710), Song 3.
65. Cf. CD-i: Content-Image-Space-Performer.
66. S. Ponnusvamy, 1972, p. 66.
67. P. Sambamoorthy, 1955, pp. 17–61.
68. E. Valentine Daniel, 1984, *Fluid Signs, Being a Person the Tamil Way*, pp. 59–225; Valentine Daniel develops the argument of compatibility in human relations. Effective success is the result of concentric circles of compatibility, from the inner chemistry of physical–mental qualities to sexual 'matching', to one's house, its horoscope and site, to the village, one's native place or 'roots', the region and their mutal *rapport*.
69. South Indian shrines are inhabited by various types of gods, with equally varying temperaments. One of the great divides between them is the vegetarian versus non-vegetarian distinction. This became most clear when I was confronted with a temple under construction that was to provide shelter to both types of gods. The inner part of the temple had been assigned to the vegetarian gods; their shrines were well protected by three walls and a roof and surrounded by another high wall, whereas the non-vegetarian gods were situated in the open, outer circumambulatory. The images of the non-vegetarian gods were almost finished but for an essential detail: in their chest a niche had been carved out where a lasting offering should be placed compatible with their temperament before the closing of the image. This essential offering marks the crucial difference. According to my informant, non-vegetarian gods receive and keep there a bottle of whiskey. It corresponds with their dynamic, volatile temperament and goes well with the animal sacrifices that are performed for them. All this energetic fuel is left behind in the interior of the temple: different priests officiate here, offering fruit, rose-water, milk, yoghurt and sandalpaste. These ingredients safeguard the 'cool' nature of the vegetarian gods, whereas the whiskey and meat keep the outer gods 'hot', energetic and ready for action.

70. Tiruvarur has a temple garden with a sacred tree; unfortunately, my memory is not clear as to the birds that are kept here although I vaguely seem to remember a few peacocks.
71. Cf. CD-i: Content-Image-Space-World.
72. Cf. CD-i: Content-Word-Space-World.
73. Cf. CD-i: Content-Sound-Time-World, where Nandini is heard singing the *dhyanakirtana* in *raga todi, tala rupaka* of the *Kamalambika Navavarana* Cycle; cf. also E. te Nijenhuis and S. Gupta, 1987, *Sacred Songs of India, Diksitar's Cycle of Hymns to the Goddess Kamala*, Part I, pp. 142–5 and Part II, pp. 57–8.
74. Cf. CD-i: Content-Sound-Time-Text.
75. Cf. CD-i: Content-Sound-Time-World.
76. DED 561 Ta. *verb*: to peel; strip off, flay; *noun*: rind, peel, skin stripped off, bark.
77. Cf. Merleau Ponty 'I am not tied to any one perspective but can change my point of view, being under compulsion only in that I must always have one and can have only one at once', in his *Phenomenology of Perception*, Trans. C. Smith, London, Routledge and Kegan Paul, 1962, p. 407. Cf. also Gail Weiss 'Context and Perspective' in *Merleau Ponty, Hermeneutics and Postmodernism*, ed. Thomas W. Busch and Shaun Gallagher, 1992, New York, State University of New York Press, pp. 13–25.
78. Cf. also six year-old Anna in *Mister God, this is Anna*, 1974, Ballantine Books, New York, p. 28, assessing the crucial difference between the human condition and God: '"You see, everybody has got a point of view, but Mister God hasn't. Mister God has only points *to* view". (. . .) What about this difference between a *point of view* and *points to view*? This stumped me, but a little further questioning cleared up the mystery. *Points to view* was a clumsy term. She meant *viewing points*. (. . .) When I put it to her this way and asked if that was what she meant, she nodded her agreement and then waited to see if I enjoyed the taste. Let me see now. Humanity has an infinite number of points of view. God has an infinite number of viewing points. That means that – God is everywhere. I jumped.'
79. Cf. CD-i: Content-Word-Space-World.
80. *Kuruntokai*, lit. 'collection of short (poems)' dates back to 100 AD–250 AD

81. Tamil conventions distinguish between 'hidden' love (Ta. *kalavu*) and 'acclaimed' love (*karpu*). The first means literally 'theft', 'robbery', the second 'propriety', 'learning', 'destiny', 'a surrounding wall', and 'chastity'. My teacher of prosody, Pulavar R. Kannan, explained *karpu* as 'application', 'use', 'purposefulness', 'fruition'. In Western scholarship this distinction was translated into premarital versus marital love, or 'free' versus 'bourgeois' love.
82. Cf. CD-i Content-Word-Time-World.
83. Cf. Foucault, 1970, pp. 17–25, 'The four similitudes'.
84. This terminology belongs to the South Indian Shaivism that is associated with the saint Tirumular (probably seventh century AD) and is known as *Saiva Siddhanta*.
85. The demarcation in mime of such epithets is not a light, improvisatory, random interpretation. Visualisation is particularly sensitive to the nuances of indigenous, natural associations. Years ago I suggested to Nandini, by way of experiment, a variant of mime to this line; it portrayed the theme Bhogatyagesha as the exchange of flower-garlands between the god and his devotee, followed by their circumambulation of the ritual fire that serves as a witness to the wedding ceremony. The first part of the variant was accepted, the second was rejected quite vehemently. 'In this line the sublime character of Lord Tyagaraja is portrayed, not such mundane details as going around the wedding fire, holding hands, looking at the Rohini star, etc. These are too narrow for the theme. 'Bhogatyagesha' triggers here images of divine splendour and magnitude, such as Shri Tyagaraja on Vishnu's chest, resting on the primordial waters, slaying the elephant in the Daruvana episode among the ascetic sages, approaching as a saviour of mankind at the end of times, etc. – all sublime deeds are suitable, but not the fumbling over a wedding-necklace.'

Chapter 4

Performer

On the previous pages we have discussed at length the text as sign, as a 'marked', a mark marking the world by which it is marked. However, none of these qualifications can come true without an actual base for the mark. The palmleaf manuscript cannot serve that purpose, on account of its very nature of static reduction. The sign that signals the world has to be an analogue that is as vibrant, colourful and complex as its world. Such a base has to share the organic and synthetic process of life; in fact, the sign has to live in order to bring the signal alive. The performer is such a sign.

When speaking about the text as *ilakkiyam*, the 'marked', we speak, really, about the performer who performs the text. The text is nothing but the person who performs it. Away from its performance there simply is no text and no way of involving oneself in its content. The performer and the occasion of performance stand supreme in the life of the text. It is they who are marked in a significantly telling way. The story they tell is the 'theory of the world' that is necessary to interpret the 'material and immaterial signs of the world'. The concept of culture as a combination of the two, results in 'culture as a performing art'.

In this way culture is characterised by the same mechanisms that Bourdieu ascribes to *habitus*: generative principles, rules, strategies that result ultimately in a 'feel' or 'sense' of the art. The art of performing the story of 'culture', or of the *habitus*, can be understood easily by the image of *homo ludens*, the play element in culture.[1] Huizinga distinguished five characteristics of play that may help us to understand the communicative power of the performer as a sign of his culture: (1) Play is *voluntary* activity, it is free, rooted in freedom. (2) Play is *not banal*, it is serious, a *sacer ludus* that is played with utmost devotion. When the event of playing comes to an end, an atmosphere of *beatitudo*, 'bliss, well-being', lingers on. (3) Play is played out within certain limits of *time* and *space*. This limiting condition gives rise to intentional repetition that develops into 'tradition', as well as to the peculiar order of the 'playground'. This is a characteristic side-effect of play: it creates order; in fact, it *is order*. (4) As a consequence, each game has its *rules*. The principles that underlie the game are unshakeable truths. The overt trespasser and cynic are unacceptable to the play-community, since their withdrawal from the rules of the game reveals the relativity and fragility of the play-world. (5) Therefore play-*communities* establish themselves and their customs firmly, so that their *sacer ludus* can be played out optimally. These five features help us to understand the composite workings of the cultural sign, perhaps the most important of these characteristics being 'voluntary activity'. This may well be the *uri*, the 'skin' or 'perspective' that we discussed before. This 'skin' should be a natural one, otherwise the sign will not work.[2] In the light of the diagnosis of the nature of play, the 'cultural sign' takes the values illustrated in Fig.6.

The cultural sign is committed to real-time and real-place performance. The limitations caused by this condition can be overcome only by regular repetition of the event. The cyclical character of the performance, of telling the story of culture, makes the sign a truly 'incremental sign': the past as well as the future and potential eternity are waxing in the moment of the presence of the performance. The sign is pregnant with all past occasions, performers, rules and blessings as much as it holds in embryo all future occasions or potential occasions to come.[3] In its performance it is highly fertile and fertilising; it substantiates the past and the *generalis–potentialis* in the present. This process can be called *semiosis*, the 'significant signalling of the sign'. The confrontation with the text appeals to two levels of analysis: an analysis of the static sign – the *semeion*: the performer herself as sign; and an analysis of the dynamic sign – the *semiosis*: the performer in performance. Both belong to the sphere of the 'marked' *ilakkiyam*, although the performer herself is understood as *patra*, 'vessel', and the performance as *prayoga*, 'application'. Under these two headings we will investigate the performer as the physical base of the text, and the locus from where the world 'in the head' comes to life.

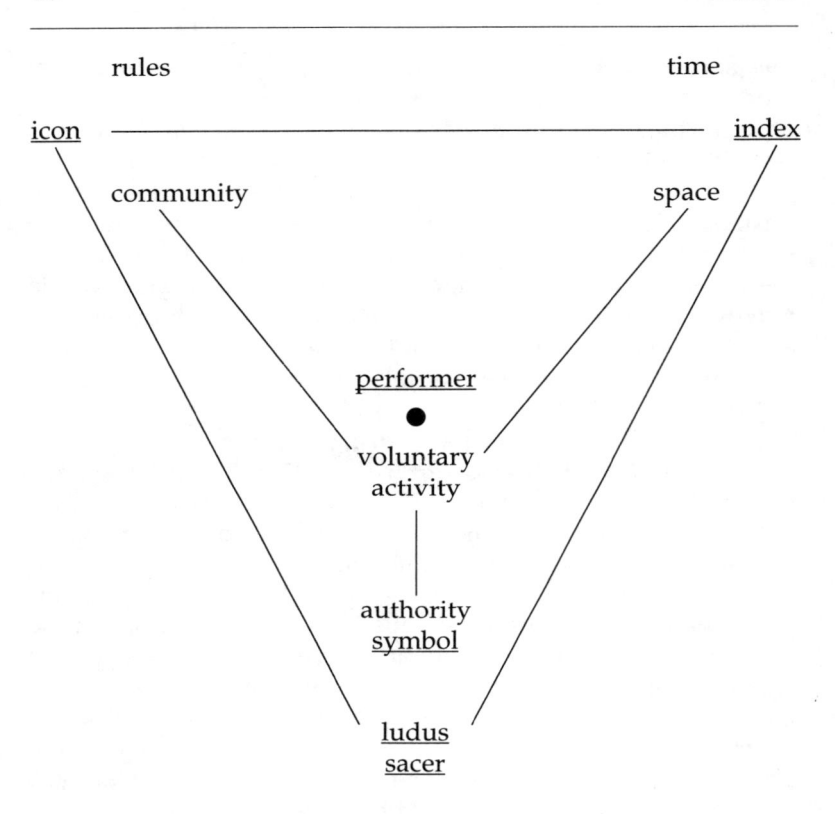

```
                rules                          time
    icon ─────────────────────────────────── index
              \  community              space  /
               \                              /
                \                            /
                 \                          /
                  \     performer          /
                   \       ●              /
                    \  voluntary         /
                     \  activity        /
                      \    |           /
                       \   |          /
                        \ authority  /
                         \ symbol   /
                          \        /
                           \ ludus/
                            sacer
```

Figure 6 – the sign of culture

4.1 *Patra* 'Vessel'

> kalāvatī kamalāsanayuvatī kalyāṇam kalayatu Sarasvatī
>
> Receptacle of the arts,
> Young lady on the lotus,
> Incite auspiciousness,
> Sarasvati!

This refrain of a Sanskrit hymn by the great composer Muttusvami Dikshitar depicts Sarasvati, one of the goddesses of the Hindu pantheon.[4] In the analysis of the sign constituted by the performer, Sarasvati emerges as the symbol and model that the performer should bring alive by her presence. Sarasvati means literally 'the one who abounds in water'. Already in the earliest sources, some 3,500 years ago, she is invoked for fertility and safe pregnancy.[5] Even today, in Tamilnadu, women go to a small but exquisite temple to Sarasvati to pray for the birth of a son.[6] The ancient Sarasvati, who was believed to reside on the riverbanks, soon became associated with the rituals that took place there. This led to the identification of Sarasvati with *Vāc*, 'speech', some five hundred years later. Gradually she was credited with the invention of the Sanskrit language and considered the living form of the alphabet. The great epic the *Mahabharata* shows her composing hymns of the Vedas, even as the mother of the entire Veda.[7] Her image reveals a beautiful young lady, holding the large lute (the *vina*), the palmleaf manuscript, and the rosary; she rides the swan (or, rather, 'goose', *hamsa*), which is a theriomorphic representation of the *atma* (the 'life-principle' or 'soul').[8] Sarasvati is the graceful, female form of equilibrium, and as such compatible with Brahma, the most transcendent of all the gods, as his wife.

In the hymn of Muttusvami Dikshitar four main characteristics become clear: (1) fertility through water; (2) well-being through the senses; (3) wisdom through the arts and (4) authority through transcendence.[9] An immanent logic connects these four features and permeates three levels of cognition: the concrete, the abstract and the metaphysical. At the concrete level it is sensory perception that provides the 'data': the sight of Sarasvati is the natural scenery of the Kashmir gardens, is the young women of exquisite beauty, resplendent and playful; the touch of the mild autumnal light is her touch; the sweet smile of the moon is the benign smile on her face; the intoxicating smell of flowers is the smell of her hair – therefore bees are attracted to it.[10] At the abstract level, her presence generates learning, skills, and wisdom as well as their applications: she holds the palmleaf manuscript and the large lute (*vina*). In her presence the Sanskrit alphabet becomes manifest and eloquence spreads its wings. Sarasvati is its basic condition: as *vagvani* she is the 'sound of speech'.[11] The level of metaphysics shows her as the perfect equilibrium, its graceful shape, serenely seated on the white, cool lotus and riding the *hamsa* (the 'goose/swan') that carries the 'soul' (*atma*) to her husband Brahma, the most abstracted of all gods.

According to the hymn she is power incarnate, she is strength and its absence. Sarasvati dispels existential fear, fosters learning and wisdom and grants boons to mortals. This goddess forms the 'role model' for traditional performers of song, instrumental music and dance. In the community of temple and royal courtesans this identification ran deep:

> She [Dhanammal] would play the veena every Friday. This of course known to many. But do you know that during Navaratri, she would have a bower of jasmine made up, sit under it and play the veena. Agarbatti would add to the fragrance of the flowers but more than all of them was my granny's music. During Navaratri, her bed would be strewn with the soft petals of roses and other flowers, her *supari* would be spiced with cloves, cardamom and saffron. She played the role of a goddess then. A goddess she was to the end.[12]

The impact could hardly be stronger: her very appearance was an epiphany of goddess Sarasvati.[13] The necessary prerequisites for such an identification are, above all, a musical talent: to be endowed with good hearing, a good voice and agile fingers, a strong melodic sensitivity and a firm grasp of rhythm. According to the *Sangitaratnakara* (thirteenth century AD) a dancer needs – on top of these – the following qualities:[14]

> Generally in *nrtta* ['abstract dance'], the person fit to perform the dance movements is a female dancer. [Such] persons are well known to be of three types: *mugdha* ('shy'), *madhya* ('middle'), and *pragalbha* ('bold').[15] There is also a fourth type of youthfulness, in which there is little enthusiasm; and in which the lips, the big breasts, cheeks, and hips are weak. A person having this type of youthfulness is called *atipragalbha* ('blasé'). Since it tends towards old age and is devoid of charm, it is not accepted by the learned. A child, being devoid of imagination, does not please the learned, as a suitable person for dance. Beauty of limbs, perfection of form, a charming and full face, large eyes, red lips like the Bimba fruit, attractive teeth, a neck beautiful like the spiral conch, arms straight like moving creepers, slender waist, hips which are not too heavy, thighs resembling the trunk of an elephant, not being too tall, crippled, or too fat, not having prominent veins, being conspicuous in charm, beauty, sweetness, courage, and generosity, and being either fair or dark in colour – these are accepted by the learned as the qualities of the dancer.

The emphasis on physical beauty is very strong in this text. In reality fitness for the task, that is, physical and musical aptitude, were valued more. Smt. T. Balasarasvati, whose family has been singing and dancing as far back as memory can go, was meant to be a singer but longed to be a dancer instead; in fact, she did become the most famous dancer of our times. Her account of this matter follows:

> 'If someone without knowledge of music performs a dance, how can we accept it? A dancer will shine only if she is soaked in music. My mother used to din this into my head even when I was too young to think.' Mother Jayammal started teaching music appreciation to Bala [short for Balasarasvati: SK] when the latter was barely five years old, so much so, that the little girl could understand the language of music long before she could appreciate the import of the songs. Jayammal had learnt dancing, as did her aunt Rupavati. But because she had a wonderful voice she had opted for music. And because she and the others in the family had studied classical music properly and well, they were all able to understand the attributes of classical art and bring a sense of discrimination to Bharatanatyam as well. Bala showed an aptitude for dance from a very early age. If Kamakoti Ammal who lived downstairs in their house egged her on,[16] it was Mylapore Gowri Amma who seems to have given her the greatest inspiration to take up dancing seriously. Gowri Amma was the daughter of a beauty, Doraikannu Ammal, who danced for Siva at the Kapaleeswarar Temple in Mylapore. She had great respect for Dhanammal and used to call on her often. She too was dancing at the Mylapore temple and had achieved considerable fame, especially for her ability to depict various emotions through facial gestures. Jayammal and her older sister Lakshmiratnam used to sing padams during Gowri Amma's performances. (. . .) Bala was fascinated by Gowri Amma. Besides visiting her as often as possible, she would also try to imitate her dance movements. As she recalls those days, she projects a sense of excitement. 'I used to dress up like Gowri Amma in a *jenti* or *thuya* sari, wear her own jewellery and try to dance like her.' She explains that a *jenti* or *thuya* sari was popular among dancers because it wasn't expensive, and was usually white organdy threaded with gold or silver. 'There would be scolding in the family and some raps on the knuckles too, but I couldn't be bothered by them.' Seeing little Bala's efforts to imitate her *abhinaya* ['mime': SK], Gowri Amma suggested she might be taught dancing. 'Oh, no!' was Jayammal's reply. She was apprehensive about Dhanammal's response to her suggestion, and she wouldn't undertake anything without consulting her.[17] 'One day she got up

the courage to ask my grandmother. (. . .) Grandma, whose eyesight had weakened already, peered into space just for a trice and said No. She didn't budge even when Gowri Amma and Kandappa Pillai directly pressed the suggestion on her. But then she asked my mother one day whether her daughter, that's me, was squint-eyed. My mother answered in the negative. Next she asked if I had good, orderly rows of teeth. Yes, said my mother. Next question: Is she good-looking? My mother said that I was not a beauty, but good-looking all right. Finally she asked if I sang well. I had to sing to prove it. The test was over. Grandma finally gave permission for me to study dancing. (. . .).'[18]

From this account the basic qualifications for a girl to become a dancer are clear. The emphasis on music over stunning beauty is remarkable and meaningful in the context of 'reading-as-a-recovery-of-meaning'. Ricoeur employs the metaphor of reading as the reading of a musical score. The sense of the importance of musical interpretation, its flexibility and highly personal enquiry are evident to him. However, in drawing this comparison he misses the crucial point, namely that 'knowing and understanding' the text in this way means 'knowing how to and understanding how to render the text in interpretation'. Tamil verbal art is very much rooted in sound, and thus, in the skilful, imaginative rendering of that sound. Without that skill, which means a practice, and, implicitly, a way of life, no understanding, interpretation or appropriation is possible at all. This active 'indexicality' of the able performer is the real-time and real-place prerequisite for the continuation of the text.

Such indexicality does not stand in a vacuum. Many generations have preceded the contemporary performances. The nature of performance, though, is such that it does not yield to any form of static representation. No dancer of the past can set an example to the present generation by words alone.[19] Her physical proximity is a basic condition for ideal maturation. To live in the house of one's teacher, to imbibe her moods, temperament and inclinations, to see her perform, these are the living examples of the past.[20] Attempts to represent the practice of dance in a static form have resulted in stone sculptures and paintings on the walls of many temples in South India. They depict the so-called *karanas*, usually translated as 'dance poses'; but more probably these stills catch a moment that is characteristic for a sequence of movements.²¹ It is a moot question whether these representations are an archaic attempt at dance notation, or whether they are carved on places where they are supposed to instil their auspiciousness on the spot for a lasting period of time.²²

The icons that continue to live throughout the ages are the images of the goddess; they set an example that is believed to be alive, active and efficacious for all women to follow. For temple and royal courtesans, whose appearance is extra-significantly loaded, these markers of divinity are the markers that they should absorb and make their own, both physically and mentally. The goddess is very much real and alive. She is woken every day, bathed, dressed, and adorned with jewellery and flowers, and is recognisable by her large red mark of auspiciousness, the *kumkumam pottu*, and by having been rubbed with the yellow *mancal* and golden sandal paste.²³ She holds court (Skt. *darsana*) for her devotees, and distributes her blessings in the form of *prasada*, that is by returning the material offerings after having enjoyed their 'essence'.

Such icons may be stills to the Western eye, but to the Tamil, Hindu eye they are presence, an active and vibrant presence that is full of potentiality.²⁴ To be in direct contact with these divine forms sets them up as an example and shapes one's life. This power is attributed also to photographs of the deceased. Relatives, teachers and past saints are worshipped and 'contacted' by endowing them with the red *kumkum* mark on the forehead. To worship them regularly by means of flowers and burning lamps, minimally, affirms the continuation of the past into the present. The past is alive in its examples, which are memorised by worshipping them in our midst. The past is never a datum, a fact to be compiled, studied or have conclusions drawn from it. The past is present, because it is worth remembering. Following this logic we can appreciate now the sign that the performer constitutes: an individual body, endowed with the necessary qualities that make her suitable for the task, is offered as a 'vessel' or 'pot' to be filled by the model of eternity and of the past *patra*'s ('vessels') whose memory is kept alive among the living. The 'ultimate community of interpreters' is always this interaction of the past, eternal and present interpreters. This brings the individual interpretation of the text alive in any performance. As she enters the stage, we see the *patra* in the full splendour of her identification: the red *kumkumam* dot, long braided hair with flowers, a bright *sari* with golden borders, rich jewellery that resembles the jewellery worn by the gods,[25] a charming presence marked by the sound of her ankle-bells. 'Stating her point' merely by 'being there', she is ready to begin the application of her sign in performance.

4.2 *Prayoga* 'Application'

> As the worlds mightily clash
> And crash in resounding thunder,
> As blood-dripping demon spirits
> Sing in glee amid the general ruin,
> To the beat and the tune leapst thou,
> Mother, in dance ecstatic
> Dread Mahakali! Chamundi! Gangali!
> Mother, Mother, Thou hast drawn me
> To see thee dance! . . ..
> When time and the three worlds
> Have been cast in a ruinous heap,
> When the frenzy has ceased
> And a lone splendour has wakened,
> Then auspicious Siva appears
> To quench thy terrible thirst.
> Now thou smilest and treadst with him
> The blissful Dance of Life !
> S. Bharati[26]

The ambivalent nature of the goddess is powerfully expressed in this modern poem by one of the almost 'national' poets of Tamilnadu. Subrahmanya Bharati was a great devotee of the goddess and of the language Tamil, often referring to it as 'mother Tamil' (*Tamil tay*). The dynamic power of the goddess encompasses the two extremes of existence: violent destruction and death as well as benevolent support and growth. Thus the dynamic principle that is associated with the goddess as *Sakti* (Skt. lit. 'power', 'force') can be both destructive and protective. An excess of dynamism destroys; however, when properly harmonised,[27] it creates, nourishes and protects. A method was devised for controlling that dynamism from within: the creation of a female ritualist whose power (*sakti*) could be ritually merged with that of the great goddess (*Sakti*). As we shall see further on,[28] the temple courtesan, called *devadasi* (Skt. lit. 'slave of god'), was such a ritualist.

The traditional view holds that all women share, by their very nature, the power of the goddess. A regular progress is imagined in the degrees of auspiciousness according to the varying status of women: at the top of the scale is the married woman whose husband is alive and who has borne several children; she is called *su-mangali* 'auspicious female'. On the lowest rung of the ladder is the widow, who is considered highly inauspicious. As a ritual person, the temple courtesan (*devadasi*) exceeds even the *sumangali* in auspiciousness. Firstly, because her individual female powers are ritually merged with those of the goddess; and secondly, because she is dedicated to a divine husband, i.e., a husband who can never die. In consequence, she can never lose her (double) auspiciousness, and is therefore called *nitya-su-mangali*, the 'ever-auspicious-female'.[29]

According to temple manuals the temple courtesans are born from Sakti; they should be employed and protected by the temple because they bring luck, and protect the king and the country; in short, they are said to be the 'sprouting of Sakti'.[30] This derivation from the great goddess must take concrete forms in order to be efficacious. Earlier we described Sarasvati as *vagvani*, 'the sound of speech': and, indeed, it is in the act of speaking that the temple courtesans (*devadasis*) and royal courtesans (*rajadasis*) made their power felt. Sarasvati's being the sound of speech implies the necessity of her presence. This holds for the courtesans as well. Smt. P. Ranganayaki (1914), who was dedicated at the age of seventeen to the god *Sri Subrahmanyasvami* of Tiruttani (Tamilnadu, Chengalput district), earned the right to a house, some lands, and food and clothes from the temple by attending and participating in the temple services. This right was attributed to nine families. The members of these nine families were given nine houses in 'Upper Tiruttani' (*Mele Tiruttani*), a small settlement behind the temple inhabited by the families of *devadasis* and temple priests (*gurukkal*). Goddess Sarasvati has a temple at the end of the *devadasi* street, while the elephant-headed god Vinayaka guards the *brahmana* street.[31]

The task of the *devadasi* to exert her auspicious influence took several forms, such as communication with the divine through regular service at the temple, 'nourishing' the living proofs of vitality and prosperity in the form of service to the king, and ubiquitous preventive, propitiating and purifying measures taken at every step in daily life as well in public life during important events. Ritual attendance in the temple can be subdivided into two basic categories, as shown in Fig.7.

The traditional repertoire of *devadasis* provides songs and dances for both categories and for their subcategories. The richest offering is to be found in the temple tradition, which includes compositions that serve all these aims. The court of the king requires more sophistication and entertainment than is usually found in the temple. In the private, social sphere, however, the emphasis is usually on the warding off of the 'inauspicious'. This is mostly translated in terms of the *drsti*, the 'evil', envious eye that drains the energy from the object of its desire. All songs and dances, without distinction of category or milieu, are set to very specific coordinates in time and space. This orchestration of auspiciousness as a ubiquitous and permanent presence is too complex to be offered here. In earlier and forthcoming publications the heritage of the *devadasis* of Tiruttani has received detailed attention.[32] In this context we must limit our focus to the life of *bhairavi varnam*.

This text and similar *varnams* were performed for the king and his court in front of a sophisticated, learned audience,[33] or, during a procession of the processional image of the god, in the pavilions of the outer courtyard. Processions (*utsava*) may take very different lengths of time and elaboration of detail and grandeur. The grandest procession in Tiruvarur is that of the huge temple

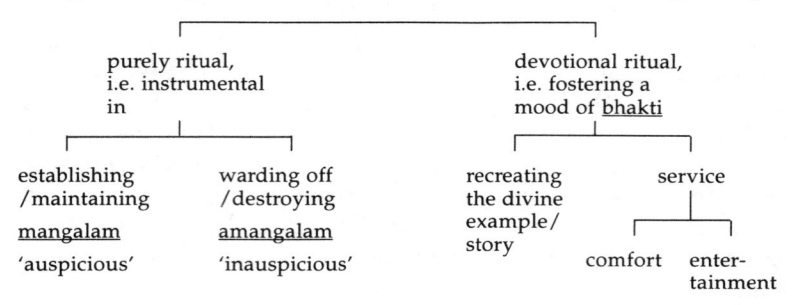

	purely ritual, i.e. instrumental in		devotional ritual, i.e. fostering a mood of <u>bhakti</u>	
establishing /maintaining <u>mangalam</u> 'auspicious'	warding off /destroying <u>amangalam</u> 'inauspicious'	recreating the divine example/ story	service	
			comfort	entertainment

Figure 7 – the character of ritual service

chariot inside which Tyagaraja is seated. This circumambulation of the chariot is the highlight of a processional feast that takes twenty-seven days to be performed in full. During a stop at one of the many resting-places, the god is imagined as a king holding court. The offering of devotional story-telling and poetry formed part of such a setting. On such occasions *bhairavi varnam* used to be performed, facing the divine pair in the midst of a tumultuous crowd, eager to see the god.

It will be clear from the differences between the two settings that the style and elaboration of a *varnam* was influenced by the relative space, opportunity and attention for the performance. While ritual art was straightforward and simple, the royal court encouraged finesse and sophistication. The iconic layer of the sign of *prayoga* is formed by memory. *Smara*, 'memory', 'love', 'worship' constitute 'tradition', that which is handed down from one generation to the next (Skt. *parampara*). The heritage one

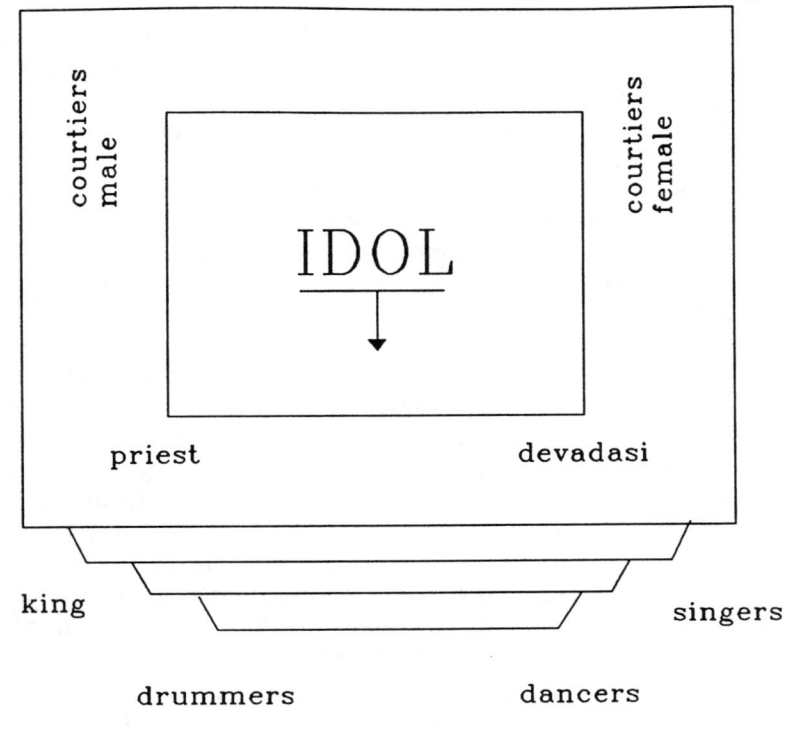

Figure 8 – the Divine Court[34]

receives from the elders is kept alive and fostered in love for its beauty, value and concrete 'indexicality'. 'Tradition serves as the mode of orientation toward present and future, as the way of interpreting existence, not because it tells us where we have been, but because it explains who we are, where we are and should be.'[35] The concept of *smara* as a loving memory that bestows a sound sense of identity eloquently argues the depravity of its absence.

The image of the dancing Shiva is quite well-known: in this dance the 'pulse of Being' is set to his triple aspect of 'sprouting, maintaining, dissolving'.[36] The sculpture shows Shiva dancing in a burning circle of fire, expressing with his right hand the message 'do not fear' and with the left 'my feet are here to grant release from the chain of births'. One foot is lifted gracefully, while the other rests on a little dwarf-like figure. Shiva's dance crushes his spinal cord, and as a result his power is broken. Who is this dwarf? His name reveals his deep confusion: *apa-smara-purusa* 'man-away-from-memory'. It seems hard to me to find an image that is more evocative of alienation than Shiva Nataraja dancing his cosmic dance, breaking Ignorance; ignorance of one's 'roots' as an individual in the categories of time and space, and as a created being of one's metaphysical origin.

Where is tradition located, from where does memory build this precious store-house of belonging? According to Indian, Tamil tradition, memory is nourished by living exponents, by the live transmission of knowledge, not by reading books or visiting museums. In every case, the presence of the living *guru* ('teacher') is assumed to be the final arbiter of tradition. *Guru* literally means 'heavy'; and one might say that it is the *guru* who has 'critical mass', who knows how to weigh the relative importance of all the facets that make up the tradition and to decide what should be chosen in each individual instance. Reading and private study pile up data, but not discrimination. This can be acquired only in practice – practice that must be guided by an adept first. In this way, knowledge attains 'objectivity', through the hardships of individual training at the mercy of one or more individuals. Although the sentiment concerning 'tradition' attributes a neutral status to its content and teachings, Western epistemology would classify this type of knowledge-transmission as 'subjective'. The ambition for Western 'objectivity' is not at all at work in this setting, as 'knowledge' is always applied, 'embodied' knowledge. The category that comes closest to the quality 'objective' is 'propriety, aptness' (*aucitya*). But this, too, is acquired only in practice and by familiarity, and is to be gained from living examples. As a result, the following account will be an account of personal, oral histories that shape a 'body of knowledge'.

> My own teacher of *bhairavi varnam* is Smt. Nandini Ramani. Born in 1950, she belongs, together with her elder sister Smt. Priyamvada Sankar, to the first students of Smt. T. Balasarasvati that did not belong directly to Bala's own family or community. Nandini is a daughter of the famous Sanskrit *savant* Dr V. Raghavan. He was born in an orthodox brahmin community in Tiruvarur. As a research scholar in Sanskrit he worked as the curator of the Tanjore Sarasvati Mahal library.[37] Later he became the head of the Sanskrit department of Madras University, and earned international renown by his numerous Indological publications. In addition he was a fine, creative poet in Sanskrit, and a composer of Karnatic music, earning the title '*kavikokila*' from the saint Sankaracarya of Kanchipuram.[38] Nandini's mother, Smt. Sarada Raghavan, is fluent in Telugu, was trained in vocal music and has an unfailing sense of aesthetics.
>
> Smt. Balasarasvati and her family were very close to the work of Dr V. Raghavan. He was one of the great advocates of her art; and when the Music Academy built a small hall behind the main auditorium, it was Dr V. Raghavan, secretary of the Music Academy for over four decades, who arranged that Bala should be invited to teach there. Under these conditions, within the prestigious framework of the Music Academy, my teacher and her elder sister started to learn dance with Smt. T. Balasarasvati and Shri K. Ganesan, in the 1950s.
>
> These two giants, their family and their musicians are very much alive in the family of my teacher. Staying in the house of Smt. Nandini Ramani for most of the period of my schooling, their names were always around: whether during class or in daily life, there would always be some anecdote or other as an argument, an illustration or a fond memory. In this way Balasarasvati and her family became alive for me too, to the extent that she was kind to me and blessed me.[39] Her brother T. Visvanathan invited me to teach at Wesleyan University, where he is professor of Karnatic music.[40] These events made me share that mesmerising quality of 'Bala's memory' that is to be found in Madras, in Canada, in America, and in Europe.[41]
>
> The choreographer and teacher of dance Shri K(andappa) Ganeshan was nursed by Nandini in his last years. When he was

afflicted by a severe lung condition Nandini had him hospitalised. After a little more than a week he passed away, on 10 December 1987. Two days before that he had told me in simple but firm terms to select this *bhairavi varnam 'mohamana'* for my *Muttamil* project: 'Take *mohamana*.' This work is its result. As he had no relatives or children, Nandini took care of the funeral arrangements, providing new silk garments, and garlands of flowers. Because of the highly inauspicious nature of the rite of cremation women are not allowed to come close even. Just in time she was able to contact his student, the *nattuvanar* Shri K. Ramaiah, who lit the funeral pyre.[42] Next morning, when we came to the funeral ground with fresh cow's milk to pour over the hot ashes, Ramaiah collected the remains in a small earthen pot.[43] He held the pot on his lap as we drove to the seaside. There, at the sea shore he returned the remains of Kandappa Ganesha to nature, to the waves of the sea. As a last parting we sprinkled some sea-water on our heads in order to receive his blessings. His memory is fully alive with us.

The training format, the repertoire and especially the element of 'style' of interpretative rendering, called *pani* ('stores, provisions', or 'word, speech') are very jealously guarded by families and their professional interest groups. To be part of such a transmission is no small or light matter. It brings riches and privileges, but also strong restrictions and responsibilities to entire geneaologies.[44]

How far can human memory go back ? Within my own experience of almost twenty years (1975 onwards) there is first and foremost Nandini; her training forms one huge example of her tradition. This pertains closely to everything that is involved in rendering a composition: the firm, clear placement of the feet, the long elegant lines of the arms, the deep sitting, the still centre, the restrained use of the torso and, in mime, the subtle suggestiveness that never exaggerates or tries to please for its own sake. She has still experienced the old traditional setting of this art both as a student and as a performer. Some twenty years ago she danced in the palace of the *maharaja* and *maharani* of Trivandrum (Kerala) during *Navaratri*.[45] She held the audience spellbound by her rendering of the *varnam 'Dani Samajendra'* for one full hour. This *varnam* in the *raga todi* and *tala adi* was composed by Svati Tirunal who was Maharaja of Trivandrum during the first half of the nineteenth century.[46]

Shri K. Ganeshan was a great example of stylistic 'hygiene'. He was very firm in his demand for clarity in the footwork and beauty of the arms and torso. He used to give subtle hints for holding a hand 'like a bird on a tree' or placing a gesture in a diagonal line downwards not 'like a sword' but 'like a child'. All these comments were made in a very dry, matter-of-fact way. His sense of humour was equally dry: once when I tried to look up a choreographic phrase in my notes, he said: 'Ha, you know it in the book!' Another great example is set by 'music-master' Shri B. Krishnamoorthy. He is all music: as he approaches the house, his humming announces his arrival. The tenderness with which he reveals the musical phrases, the rapture on his face that attends his singing of them and his anecdotes and examples of melodic beauty and thrilling rhythm speak volumes for his tradition.

Almost one generation further back in time were the teachings, reminiscences and outspoken opinions of Dr V. Raghavan, and the rare encounters with Smt. Balasarasvati herself. Professor Raghavan recounted an anecdote of a performance by Balasarasvati of our *bhairavi varnam 'Mohamana'*. When she got to the first half of the *anupallavi*, suddenly at the words *'nakarikamana tirunakaril vacare'* 'in the elegant holy town you live indeed', the skin of one side of the drum split. As we will see in Part II, the double-sided drum (*mrdangam*) is necessary to mark the passage of one line of mime into the next. Another drum was an absolute must. It took half an hour to fetch a new *mrdangam*. During these thirty minutes Kuppusvami Mudaliar managed to maintain the drumming part on only one side of the instrument, while Bala improvised, without repeating herself, mimetic imagery (*abhinaya*) on the words 'in the elegant town you live'. By the time that the new drum arrived, the audience was spellbound by so much poetic virtuosity. Nandini remembers how her father could not control his enthusiasm, saying 'She did it! She did it!', 'as if Bala had just earned an Olympic gold medal'. Similar anecdotes are told abroad: in America, where a number of Bala's students keep her memory alive;[47] in Paris, where my teacher of *vina*, the late Shri Nageswara Rao, lived after having taught at Wesleyan University; and even in Holland, in Eindhoven, where Smt. Vinita Venkataraman remembers her *vina* lessons with the cousin of Smt. T. Balasarasvati, Smt. T. Brinda. In this way all classes are permeated with the memory of Bala or Bala's family, with the finesses of their style and their artistic ethos.

At the summit of the historical family journey stands Shri T. Sankaran, the cousin of Balasarasvati. In his nineties now, he is able to give eyewitness accounts of dancers who are otherwise known to us only from written sources. In a veritable cascade of anecdotes we hear about the legendary Gowri Ammal, a *devadasi* at the Mylapore Kapalishvara temple; how she sang Tamil *padams* herself while she mimed the words with facial expressions and hand gestures. He tells us, too, about the dancers Jeevaratnammal and Kannammal, who were famous in the times of Vina Dhanammal for their excellent footwork. We hear about the many famous musicians who crowded the house of Vina Dhanammal and her daughter Jayammal; about the perfect silence that Dhanammal would require when playing the *vina*: 'In the kitchen, seasoning wouldn't be prepared because the popping of mustard seed would disturb grandmother. The washing of clothes – entailing their beating on a stone – would stop. We would even stop walking around. The people of the street would also become quiet, without any of us asking cooperation. (. . .) If someone talked and disturbed her, grandmother would ask if anyone had noticed the culprit's great *jnanam* ('knowledge': SK). That would silence the person for a long time again.'[48]

Through the family lore we can reach back one more generation, revealing a similar work ethos of complete commitment to the task.

There was this lady called Udayarpalayam Gowri Amma. She was a veena player. I've heard it said that when she played on the instrument, even stone would melt. She lived during the time of my grandmother's uncle. She had become quite ill. She was therefore placed in a hammock made of net. Uncle Appakannu went to see her. She asked for her veena and started playing a Saveri padam '*Bamaro napai*'. Apparently she was too weak to play properly and as she struck the notes, they sounded slightly out of pitch. She handed down the veena immediately, saying that there was no cause for her to play the instrument again. She died the same night. My grandmother told me about this incident.[49]

In this way, through oral history, a great deal of the gigantic repertoire of Balasarasvati can be traced.[50] The artistic milieu lives on in the very vivid memory of those who have inherited this tradition.

The changing social circumstances are remembered with great pain. As in the case of Smt. P. Ranganayaki, *devadasi* at the Sri Subrahmanyasvami temple in Tiruttani, who remembers from her grandmother Smt. Subburatnamma how highly *devadasis* were respected by society. Her grandmother was invited very often to assist at weddings and other rites of passage (Skt. *samskaras*) to 'spread her auspicious influence' by preparing the *tali*, i.e. the wedding necklace for the bride, and the flower decorations of the pavilion and by singing several songs to mark the occasion. Grandmother was so popular that she composed and presented her own songs.[51]

Smt. P. Ranganayaki was unfortunate enough to witness the decline of public respect until it reached a low point in 1947, when the newly independent state of India decided to abolish the *devadasi* 'office' by law.[52] Smt. P. Ranganayaki says that a few months before the decree there was a rush on the dedication ceremony by members of traditional *devadasi* families to solemnise that generation-old rite. The art changed considerably owing to the removal from the temple of the tradition of song and dance by temple courtesans as part of the ritual, and as a result of the disappearance of the royal or aristocratic patron by the end of the nineteenth century. What is to be seen today in proscenium theatres or in films is no longer representative of this old milieu. However, the traditional milieu does continue in a few members who share its oral history. This live, oral history forms the iconic layer of the 'dynamic sign' of the performer. What lies beyond this direct transmission either in place or time does not really count for this group of inheritors.[53] What lies before it is 'lumped into one', a single great example, without taking its divergent time-depths into consideration. It is *varalaru* (Ta. 'example'), *cirappu* (Ta. 'excellence') or *purana* (Skt. 'old'): stories told to illustrate a significant point.

For instance, there is a steady flow of stories around *devadasis* from Tiruvarur. The oldest is from the *Periyapuranam* (twelfth century AD), and speaks about the temple dancer Paravai who was the beloved of the poet-saint Cuntaramurtti Nayanar (end of the eighth century AD). The saint held the great god Shiva himself responsible for their amorous discord, and, on finding the door of his beloved Paravai closed he blamed Shiva and prompted him to speak to her on his behalf. This mission of Shiva as *postillon d'amour* is remembered in the name of a street in Tiruvarur, 'the street which gave out the fragrance of the feet of the Lord'.[54] Ten centuries later we hear of the *devadasi* Kamalam, who was a student of the great musician Muttusvami Dikshitar. For her debut, he composed an entire suite, from which a *padavarnam* on Shri Tyagaraja and a *daru* survive.[55] The financial situation of the famous composer was not always congruent with his fame. Times of prosperity alternated with dire poverty.

There was an occasion when the provisions at home had touched bottom level, so much that there was little left for consumption even for that day. The ladies in the kitchen were in dire straits. At the time Dikshitar was engaged in teaching his songs to his sishyas ['students': SK]. One of them was Dasi Kamalam, who had the *mirasi* rights [i.e. the right to dance before the deity: SK] in the temple. The wife of Dikshitar called Kamalam inside and said 'Kamalam, there is no rice to cook and we are all facing starvation. Can you help us?' Kamalam said 'Madam, why should you worry yourself, when I am here? I shall pledge these gold bangles of mine and with the funds purchase all that you want.' These words fell on the ears of Dikshitar. Has it come to this, he thought, that instead of my maintaining my sishyas they have to maintain me? He felt inexpressibly sad, and when Kamalam came out he said 'Kamalam, what are you doing? Your bangles can feed us for a few days. What about the future? What will be left of your jewels, if you are to maintain us all our lifetime? It is God who gives food for all of us, and, if I am a real Bhakta of Shri Tyagesha, he will not desert me in my hour of need. Do not pledge the jewels and do not give anyone any occasion to say that I am making a living out of my teaching music to my sishyas.' With that Dikshitar left, as usual, for worship in the temple. That very day he had composed a song on Shri Tyagaraja in Yadukulakambodi, beginning with the words 'Tyagarajam Bhaja Re Re Chitta'. He sang that piece with *bhakti* and with emotion before the shrine and returned home. An agreeable surprise awaited him. What had happened was that a high-ranking Government official of the Tanjore king had planned to visit Tiruvarur on that date, and the local Officer had collected provisions on a large scale for him. But that very morning an official communication had been received from the inspecting Officer that his trip had been cancelled, and the local official thought that the provisions for which there was no use in the office might properly be sent to the saintly composer. When Dikshitar came to know of this, he gratefully observed, 'Tyagarajaswami has saved me', and composed the kriti 'Tyagarajena Samrakshitoham' in raga Salaka Bhairavi.[56]

The devotional attitude of the composer, the relationship between teacher and student, and the wealth of the *devadasi* are important facets of this anecdote.

The relative wealth of the temple and royal courtesans is attested by numerous inscriptions on the walls of temples. In particular the great temples, such as the Brihadishvara temple of Tanjore (completed in 1009 AD), Gangaikondacholapuram (completed between 1012 and 1044 AD) and Chidambaram (enlarged during those times) yield rich epigraphic data concerning the occurrence, tasks and wealth of *devadasis*. Inscriptions on the walls of the Tyagarajasvami temple in Tiruvarur tell of Anukkiyar Paravai Nankaiyar, who made large donations to the temple: not only jewels and lamps, but also funds to rebuild its constructions in stone. Large quantities of gold were used for plating and gilding parts of the shrine of Shri Vitivitankar. Copper was used to plate the doors and corbels of the pillars of the pavilion in front of the shrine. An inscription of the twentieth regnal year of Rajendra I (1012–1044 AD) says that the emperor arrived at the shrine of the god Vitivitankar with Anukkiyar Paravai Nankaiyar at his side in his chariot. A brass lamp was set up at the place where the ruler and Anukkiyar Paravai Nankaiyar stood while offering worship to the deity. The affection of Rajendra I for his favourite courtesan (*anukki*, 'one who is intimate') seems to have been so great that a village was named after her as Paravaipuram and a temple as Paravai Ishvaram. During the reign of Rajadiraja I (1018–1054 AD) provisions were made for continued offerings to the images of Rajendra and Paravai Nankaiyar that were set up in Tiruvarur temple.[57] The wealth of the courtesans must have been a hard fact, since it is attested by data from a period of over two thousand years.

The oldest sources go back to the centuries before and immediately after the beginning of our era. The poetry that has been handed down to us from these times makes frequent mention of a great variety of bards. They were of vital importance to the well-being of the king: their praise supported his very life-essence, his prowess and fame – even after his death – and his emotional love life. The bards and the king share an official tie of 'duty' (Ta. *katan*, 'duty', 'debt'), and the king is well advised to keep this in mind.[58] Two bards that surround the king can be considered 'early *devadasis*'; they are called *patini* 'songstress' and *virali* 'strong, brave, victorious one'. We find several fine descriptions of the *virali* in *Cankam* literature.[59] The aspect of their wealth comes out in the fact that special poems, the so-called 'guidance poems' (Ta. *arrupatai*), must direct the bards to munificent patrons, with whom they will enjoy great wealth and prosperity.

A few centuries later, according to the Tamil epic

Cilappatikaram, 'The Lay of the Anklet', the situation does not seem to have changed very much. We receive very detailed information about the dancer Madhavi, her training, her debut and dedication to the king, and about the rewards and life-style that follow. After her debut, the honour of a garland of green leaves plus 1008 golden coins was bestowed on her by the king. This amount should be equalled by a future patron. Madhavi sends her maid outside with the message that this green garland is for sale for another 1008 golden coins; its purchase allows the buyer to become her patron.[60]

In her plea for adherence to traditional practice Bala points out that the dance master of the same Madhavi was a great expert who

> knew when one hand had to be used (*pindi*) and when both the hands had to be used (*pinaiyal*). He also knew when the hand had to be used for exhibiting action (*tolirkai*) and when for graceful effect (*elirkai*). Knowing as he did the conventions of dancing, he did not mix up the single-handed demonstration (*kutai*) with the double-handed (*varam*) and vice versa, nor indeed pure gesture with gesticulatory movement and vice versa. In the movement of the feet also he did not mix the *kuravai* with the *vari*. He was such an expert.[61]

This description makes one point clearly: what novelty can be 'thought up' individually, when almost twenty centuries of this art has been handed down, tested and refined in a continuous line? The new adepts came to this complex of arts only by the middle of the twentieth century, and, from totally different, non-related backgrounds; from their perspective they imagined that this tradition had to be 're-styled'. It did not suffice to change its name from 'Dasi Attam' or 'Sadir' to the socio-historically more prestigious and newly coined 'Bharata Natyam'. The tradition had to re-dress its aesthetics as well.[62] The 'new taste' was grounded mainly in the study of ancient texts, in the so-called 'Hindu renaissance' and in Orientalist expectations.[63] Bala's answer to this new, more 'spiritual' refinement is the advice: work hard, practise first before you speak and innovate. She invokes the Sanskrit poet Kalidasa,[64] who notes that the best of *abhinaya* (Skt. 'mime') was shown by the dancer Malavika when she stands tired and perspiring after her dance. Bala admits that at first it will be difficult to conform to the demands and discipline of rhythm and melody and to the norms and codes of tradition. But if a student humbly submits to the greatness of this art, she will soon enough find joy in that discipline; and she will realise that discipline makes her free in the joyful realm of the art.

According to Balasarasvati the greatest quality of Bharata Natyam is its ability to control the mind. Most of us are incapable of single-minded contemplation even when actions are abandoned. In this context her view on the position of 'theory' versus 'practice' is telling: *'prayogapredhanam kalu natyasastram'*, which Nandini explains as 'theoretical knowledge becomes assimilable through practical application in the art of learning and performing'.[65] In Bharata Natyam practice is central; there is much to do, but it is the harmony of various actions that results in the concentration that is sought. The burden of action is forgotten in the pleasant charm of the art. The feet keeping to time, hands expressing gesture, the eye following the hand with expression, the ear listening to the dance-master's music, and the dancer's own singing – by harmonising these five elements the mind achieves concentration and attains clarity in the very richness of participation. The inner feeling of the dancer is the sixth sense that harnesses these five mental and mechanical elements to create the experience and enjoyment of beauty.[66]

This aspect of 'inner feeling' recalls the analytic category *uri* 'peel, skin', 'perspective', 'own'. The inner feeling of this tradition that the dancer should share and develop inside is the 'perspective', the 'feel' of *akam*, of the emotional inner world that revolves around 'love' as *eros*. The rich Tamil tradition of *eros, love* and *devotion* may have been startling to the Western, Christian and Victorian norms; but within its own realm of culture it is deeply rooted and widely spread. The Tamil world of *akam* is temperamentally very close to the Sanskrit world of *srngara* ('love', *eros*).[67]

Balasarasvati remarks that the innovators try to purify the dance from elements that are considered 'not very spiritual'. According to her it is not *srngara rasa*, the 'erotic love mood' that is vulgar, but the way of portraying it. *Cilappatikaram* and *Manimekalai* list dance, music and the personal beauty of the dancer in that order. Yet unfortunately the last and least of them has come to the forefront at the present time. When so much importance is attached to the looks of the dancer, it is but natural that dancing is considered carnal and *srngara* vulgar. The truth is precisely the opposite: it is her dance and music alone that make a dancer beautiful. If the new dancers hold firm to the tradition, which like the great Banyan tree strikes deep roots and spreads wide branches, they will gain for themselves and for those who watch them, the dignity and joy of Bharata Natyam.[68]

The image of the great Banyan tree is the image of continuous growth from the past into the present and the *potentialis* of tomorrow. Its fruit is the performer who shares the very 'life-juices' of the tree, its form and fragrance, growing the seeds for new life inside its peel. For Bharata Natyam this means an innate understanding of the lyrical beauty of love and its capacity to travel and transform. The three loops that we followed earlier take the senses and physical shape as the point of departure as well as the final point of return. Space, Time and Creation are transcended, and ultimately committed to sensory experience 'here and now'. The last words of the *varnam* state this very clearly: *entanai anaiya ippo* 'me indeed to embrace now!' This is not vulgar, carnal eroticism, but poetry propelled by man's deepest and perhaps strongest longing: to be reunited, non-fragmented, unconditionally 'whole' again.

To travel this distance, the interpreter dances the text and even becomes the text as an ultimate act of interpretation. She is the 'marked', the Sign signed by and signalling her culture. It can do so only because it is embedded and nourished by its context, which is the world. That world is cherished and remembered by its praxes that are practised in performance, and represented in their 'becoming'. The dancer is the interpreter, is the text, is its context and is its representation in time and space, transcending both in performance.

> This is a day in 1961. In Udipi (Karnataka), the sky is a pale blue, hanging over the shrine of the dark god below like a canopy reflecting the radiance of his personality. Within the temple, it is dark; but, lit by the mellow light of oil lamps, the figure of Krishna manifests itself with a smile that tugs at the heart of the worshipper. The air is heavy with fragrance of sandal paste, tulasi leaves and burning incense, and the worshipper breathes it and feels the fragrant presence of the Lord. Chanting accents the musings of devotees; when within, suddenly: *'Krishna nee begane baro. . .'* – the singing is exquisite. A few devotees turn slowly to see a dancer

singing and miming the song in the more brightly lit hall in front of the sanctum. There has been no prior announcement of the event. The dance is spontaneous, a spur-of-the-moment offering to Krishna. She stirs the imagination. 'Come hither, Krishna', she portrays mother Yashoda calling her beloved. A second voice joins in calling out the invitation: that of Gnanasundaram, a working colleague of Balasarasvati's. Unconsciously, the pilgrims turn towards the sanctum, to see if the god-child is answering the call. *Kasi peetambara* . . . The mind's eye sees Krishna dressed in the finest brocaded silk from Varanasi, a diamond-studded flute in his hands, fragrantly anointed with sandal paste, wearing a beautifully strung garland of vyjayanti flowers. *Jagado dharaka namma, Udipi Sri Krishna* . . . mother Yashoda calls to Krishna and the child comes to her. She chides him for eating dirt and asks him to open his little mouth to find proof. Krishna laughs and opens his mouth . . . and, lo, it is not dirt that the mother beholds, but the three worlds. In a moment laden with magic, Balasarasvati, now as Yashoda, now as Krishna, makes the awestruck worshippers see the Blue God transform himself into the very Universe, his ten incarnations, the hero of the *Mahabharata* and then become a playful child again. She portrays Krishna as conceived in a pair of other famous songs, *Jagado dharana* in Kapi and *Naninne dhayana* in Kannada. She is possessed, it seems, by the idea that Krishna is indeed responding to her offering. Back in Madras, entering her home she recounts her 'experience' to her mother Jayammal. She exclaims: 'Amma, why am I still living in this world after this experience? I wish Shri Krishna had taken me away.'[69] Jayammal is deeply moved and responds: 'Yes, I wish He had done it. How extraordinarily fortunate would it have been if He had . . .'.[70]

Notes

1. Huizinga, J., 1955, pp. 5 ff.
2. The praxis of South Indian performing arts dictates such a voluntary dedication to the rigorous training demands: 'Sarasvati does not come with force or to the unwilling.' Grace, both as a physical effort and as a mental attitude is of crucial importance. I remember with shame and amusement my first efforts at mastering the exercises in melody (*raga*) coupled to beating the rhythmical structure (*tala*) back in 1977. As I was preparing to sing the difficult passage, music master B.

Krishnamoorthy stopped me, commenting that I was not preparing for a wrestling-match.
3. Compositions are felt to live their own life as eternal *potentialis*. Nandini had taught me the *varnam Ma mohalakiri* in *raga Kamas, tala rupaka* in 1977–8. In 1980–1 I returned and showed it to her in Madras. She was not pleased: several mistakes had crept in distorting the entire picture. Just like a child I burst out crying: 'but I danced it already there and there like this. I have spoiled the *varnam*!'. At this she became even more annoyed: 'No one can spoil the *varnam*, it is just there, on its own. It is we who have to live up to it, that's all.'
4. The full text is as follows: Kalavatī kamalāsanayuvatī, kalyāṇam kalayatu Sarasvatī. Balābalamantrarūpiṇī bhāratī mātṛkaśārīriṇī malālividāriṇī vāgvāṇī madhukaraveṇī vīṇāpāṇī. śaradjyotsnā subhrākārā śaśivadanā kāśmiravihārā ; varā śāradā parāṅ'kuśadharā varadābhayapāśapustakakarā; surārcitapadāmbujā śobhanā śvetapaṅkajāsanā suradanā: purāri guruguharañjanī murārisnūsa nirañjanī. *Raga: yagapriya; tala: adi*. Translation (mine): Receptacle of the Arts, Young lady, seated on the lotus, Incite auspiciousness, Sarasvati! Manifestation of the syllables of the *bala abala mantra* ('formula apportioning strength and weakness'), Lady Eloquence, embodiment of the Alphabet, You cleave through the accumulated dust (of ignorance), Sarasvati, sound of speech, honeybees seek your braided hair while you hold the lute. Spreading the radiance of autumnal light, Your face resembles the moon, roaming in the Kashmir gardens, exquisite one, Sarada Sarasvati, of graceful bearing, your hands show the bestowal of boons, the absence of fear, the noose and the manuscript. Your lotus-feet are worshipped by the gods, resplendent one, seated on the white lotus, divinely smiling, you delight Purari (Vishnu) and Guruguha (Shiva, also the signature of the composer), daughter-in-law of Murari (Vishnu), pleasing one (to Brahma).
5. *Rigveda* 10.184.2.
6. In 1989 Nandini, her mother and I visited this temple in Cholanadu not far from the Kaveri river.
7. The etymology of Skt. *vid-, veda* implies [mother of] 'all wisdom and knowing'.
8. Cf. CD-i: Content-Sound-Time-World.
9. *Fertility/water*: lotus seat, lotus feet, white lotus seat; *well-being/*

senses: young woman, exquisite beauty, resplendent, delighting, pleasing, playful in Kashmir gardens, moonfaced (i.e. 'cool'), boon-giving, absence of fear, honeybees seek braided hair, radiance of autumnal ('cooling') light; *wisdom/arts*: eloquence, sound of speech, incarnation of the alphabet, *mantra* manifested, receptacle of arts, holds the *vina*, holds the manuscript; *authority/transcendence*: power over strength and weakness, removes fear, holds the noose, delighting and worshipped by gods, daughter-in-law of Vishnu, wife of Brahma.

10. This image hints at the convention of the bee over the fragrant flower in search of pollen, suggesting *srngara*.
11. Cf. Ong, 1982, pp. 72–3.
12. Interview with Balasarasvati in *Sruti, South Indian Classical Music and Dance Monthly*, March, 1984, p. 23.
13. See further in *Representation*, 'translation', pp. 217–21.
14. Sarngadeva, *Sangitaratnakara*, sloka 1224–30. Translation in *The Adyar Library Bulletin*, Vol.XXIII, parts 3–4, 1959.
15. The classification of women is part of both Sanskrit and Tamil poetic conventions. Tamil knows two classifications: one into four stages (*valai, taruni, piravitai* and *viruttai*, that is 'child', 'young', 'middle' and 'old') and one in seven stages: *petai*, an 'ignorant' girl of the age of 5 to 7 years, *petumpai*, a girl of 8 to 11 years, *mankai* an 'auspicious virgin' of 12–13 years old, *matantai* a 'young, artless, natural beauty' of 14–19 years, *arivai* a 'fertile, young woman' of 20 to 25, *terivai* a 'distinguished, discrete' lady of 26–31, and, finally, *perilampen*, a woman 'of great youth' between 32 and 40 years.
16. In the interview with Balasarasvati (*Sruti*, January–February 1984) the relationship between Kamakoti Ammal and Balasarasvati is depicted in a moving anecdote: 'On the ground floor (. . .) lived the house owner (. . .) by the name of Kamakoti Ammal, who was very fond of her "Balakutty" or little Bala. On all the four walls of the *koodam* or main hall of her place were hung a number of paintings rendered on glass, on canvas and so on by the artists of what is today known as the Tanjavur school. A remarkable feature of this gallery was that every one of the paintings depicted Krishna. "I used to look at them with my mouth wide open", recalls Bala. "So many different paintings of Krishna, and many

with semi-precious stones in red, green and other colours encrusted on them!" The sun might fail to rise, but Kamakoti Ammal never failed to call "Balakutty" every morning and ask her if she wouldn't come and wake up Krishna. This was no joking matter for the child and she used to respond, quickly going over to the old lady's place and "waking" Krishna up to the accompaniment of song and dance, much of it her own improvisation. Bala officiated similarly over the "ceremonies" making the noon-time puja, during the evening twilight hour and so on. "You know", she says, "I used to do this six times daily. I still remember it all vividly."'

17. These were the days of the 'Anti-Nautch' campaigns which afflicted the social position of *devadasi* families severely.
18. *Sangeet Natak*, Journal of the Sangeet Natak Akademi 72–3, Special Issue: Balasaraswati, April–September, 1984, pp. 24–5.
19. From *Cankam* poetry onwards we hear about great dancers. Examples set by Madhavi in the *Cilappatikaram* are quoted, and may give their name to 'historically conscious' modern dancers, but do not supply a living model to be followed.
20. My own *gurukulavasa* 'living in the house or family of my teacher', Smt. Nandini Ramani, started in 1975–6 and continued in 1977–8, 1980–1, 1982–3, 1985–6, 1987–8, 1988–9; in 1980, 1985, 1993 and 1995 Nandini lived in my house in Utrecht for a shorter time to teach and perform. During these periods of studying in India I also stayed for short whiles in the house of my teacher Smt. P. Ranganayaki, former *devadasi* at the temple in Tiruttani, and still living there.
21. Cf. CD-i: Content-Image-Time-Text.
22. The issue of *karanas* was 'hot' some years ago in Madras: some turned it into dissertations, theories and intellectual arguments; other dancers took them as models, and started to perform these acrobatic feats.
23. Cf. CD-i: Content-Image-Time-World.
24. See further *Representation*, Reproduction and Translation for the potentiality of their auspiciousness.
25. Cf. CD-i: Performance and Content-Image-Time-World.
26. Translation by Prema Nandakumar, 1968, *Subrahmania Bharati*, National Biography Series, National Book Trust, Delhi.
27. Kersenboom-Story, Saskia, 1987, Conclusion.

28. See Reproduction, pp. 100–9.
29. Kersenboom-Story, Saskia, 1987, Conclusion. Cf. also Holly Baker Reynolds, 'The Auspicious Woman', in *The Powers of Tamil Women*, Susan S. Wadley, 1980, Syracuse University, p. 36 on the various degrees of auspiciousness in women.
30. 'Sakti śrstikai connōm'.
31. See Kersenboom, Saskia, 1991, 'The Traditional Repertoire of the Tiruttani Temple Dancers', in: *Roles and Rituals for Hindu Women*, ed. Julia Leslie, pp. 131–49.
32. Smt. P. Ranganayaki gave me the manuscript written by her grandmother Smt. Subburatnamma that contains all her and her grandmother's songs and dances. She trained me in the songs and dances that were performed in the context of the rituals in the Shri Subrahmanyasvami temple in Tiruttani. Although the songs have been emended and translated the work has not yet been edited. It seems to me that the new technology of CD-i would be eminently suited to represent this tradition, and we await only opportunities to film and record on location and the necessary funds.
33. A full concert used to be offered to the king and his court on the final day of *Navaratri*, called *Vijayadasami* 'the victorious tenth' – when the goddess is revealed in her victorious aspect. On that day the natural tie between the King and the goddess as the essence of his victorious power is emphasised. From the plan of Tiruttani temple this symbiosis is quite clear even in terms of physical space.
34. Cf. Kersenboom-Story, 1987, p. 125.
35. Observation by Jacob Neusner, 1985, 'The Study of Religion and the Study of Tradition: Judaism', in *History of Religions*, 14: 195ff., quoted by Douglas Renfrew Brooks, 1992, *Auspicious Wisdom, The Texts and Traditions of Srividya Sakta Tantrism in South India*, Preface, p. xiii.
36. The image of the Dancing Shiva, *Shri Nataraja*, became well-known and much admired in the West as a result of the inspiring writings of Ananda K. Coomaraswamy in the first half of this century. Cf. also Zvelebil, K. V., 1985, *Ananda Tandava of Siva-Sadanrttamurti*, Institute of Asian Studies, Madras.
37. In 1985, Mrs Raghavan and myself visited the Tanjore Sarasvati Mahal Library. She happened to remember one of the manuscripts Dr V. Raghavan had been working on in his

younger years, and requested to see the manuscript. Apparently nobody had worked on it or perhaps touched it in forty years: his notes were still tucked inside as he had left them.

38. Dr V. Raghavan composed many Sanskrit works, among them a large praise poem on the saint–composer Muttusvami Diksitar; this *mahakavya* was released in 1980, on the occasion of the first anniversary of the author's death. Among his music and dance compositions are included *suprabhatams* and a *sabdam* on goddess *Sri Kalpakamba* of Mylapore temple, Madras, that is still danced in our school.

39. Shri T. Sankaran, one of Balasarasvati's cousins, took me to her house one afternoon for an interview on *devadasis*. She received me with great kindness, and when I offered her some fruit with the customary *namaskaram* ('prostration') she kissed the parting of my hair as I rose. She spoke in detail and with great feeling about her tradition.

40. In 1988 Shri T. Viswnathan invited me to lecture and give master-classes in the temple style of Bharata Natyam in the World Music and Dance Department at Wesleyan University. During that year, the department celebrated the fiftieth anniversary of the death of Vina Dhanammal, Viswa's grandmother. The entire family participated in the form of music and dance concerts. At the concluding function, T. Viswanathan said that my work, commitment and participation at the Wesleyan Navaratri Festival had made me a member of the Dhanammal family!

41. Bala's senior most disciple, Smt. Priyamvada Shankar, elder sister of Smt. Nandini Ramani, celebrated the 25th anniversary of her Bharata Natyam school in Montreal, Canada, on October 22nd, 1994.

42. Shri K. Ganesan died without issue; therefore Shri K. Ramaiah, being his student, acted as his son.

43. Milk is believed to have cooling and soothing effects: it renders the transition peaceful.

44. See CD-i Content-Time-both Sound and Image from the perspective of Performer. Both genealogies are taken from *Balasaraswati*, by Narayana Menon, no date. Published by the Inter-National Cultural Centre, New Delhi, pp. 22–3. Some of the missing dates were taken from *Ponniah Manimala*, 1961, Darpana Publications.

45. Still honouring the age-old custom of offering a music and dance concert to the King on this ritual occasion.
46. The controversy about the authorship of these compositions ascribed to Svati Tirunal are still raging. Some musicians maintain that the king never composed anything, but took the credit for the creative geniuses that he invited from Tanjore to adorn his own court.
47. Among others Kay Poursine, by now a well-known performing artist in this *pani*, who continues to study – after Bala's demise – with Nandini. Luise Scripps, one of Bala's earliest American students, is preparing a richly documented biography on Bala. A major work on the artistic heritage of Smt. T. Balasarasvati and her family was written by the late John Higgins; his PhD thesis *The Music of Bharata Natyam*, Vol. I and II with recorded examples, Ann Arbor, London, 1973 brings back these voices from the past. Another PhD thesis on Bala's *padams* and *javalis* was presented in 1993 By Matthew Allen at Wesleyan University.
48. *Sangeet Natak*, 1984, pp. 15–55, a reprint from the two interviews with Bala by N. Pattabhi Raman and Anandi Ramachandran in *Sruti*, 1984, January–February, March.
49. From 'T. Balasaraswati: The Whole World in her Hands', *Sruti*, 1984.
50. None of the written accounts is complete.
51. For examples see Kersenboom-Story, 1987, pp. 66–7, and Kersenboom, 1991, p. 145.
52. For the full text of the *Devadasi Act*, passed on 26 November 1947, see Kersenboom-Story, 1987, p. xxi.
53. The issue of 'authenticity' as it is pursued in the concert practice of 'Early Music' in the West, is not felt at all, nor would it arouse any professional interest among these traditional performers. What does emerge, today, however, is a 'historical puritanism' on the part of the dance-critics, who seem to formulate and dictate demands that resemble Western literary criticism.
54. Arunachalam, M., 1974, *An Introduction to Tamil Literature*, Tiruchirrambalam, p. 319.
55. The *varnam 'Rupamu Juci'* in *raga todi*, and the *daru 'Ni Sati Ledani'* in *raga sriranjani*.
56. Anecdote in T. L. Venkatarama Aiyar, *Muthuswami Dikshitar*, 1979, National Book Trust, New Delhi, pp. 42–3.

57. Ponnusamy, S., 1972, p. 34.
58. Kersenboom-Story, 1987, pp. 15–16.
59. For example, in *Cirupanarrupatai*, 13–31 (*c*. 250 AD); translation mine: 'Dark hair, which glows with oil resembles pouring rain, bringer of grace; its beauty makes many peacocks hide, each having spread its jewel-studded tail. The feet, wearing shining jewels, move, red in colour, as a tired dog moves its tongue; they carry heavy thighs that are like the trunk of the dark she-elephant whose touch engraves the ground. Resembling the thighs, the plantain tree grows on large hills; its flowers seem to make her hair blossom. The bee, desiring the blossoms of the closely set and freshly opened *venkai* buds, collects the body's beauty spots. The glittering buds of the *konku*, spreading like these spots, resemble cruel breasts, a jewel kept inside. Her sweetness-yielding teeth are like the breast-shaped palmyra fruits that grow in rich clusters; while they seem to be the heavy, opening *mullai* buds in *kullai* tracts; these prove the *karpu* of the *viralis*, who are of sweet nature, with an expression innocent as a deer and with shining brow.'
60. By living up to the financial and auspicious status of the king (mark the number 1008), the aspirant patron qualifies as worthy of the courtesan. Cf. Kersenboom-Story, 1987, pp. 181–2.
61. From Bala's presidential address, read out by her daughter Lakshmi, at the 33rd Annual Conference of the Tamil Isai Sangam, Madras, on 21 December 1975; printed several times for different journals.
62. In the same address, mentioned in fn. 167, Bala remarks (trans. S. Guhan) 'There is a special relationship between Tamil music and Bharata Natyam. (...) ... *sringara*, which was to become the ruling mood of *abhinaya*, was pre-eminent in the Tamil dance right from the beginning. (...) It is this stream of *sringara* that swells into the mighty river of the lover–beloved songs of the Vaishnava and Shaiva saints, the *astapadis* of Jayadeva, and the compositions of Ksetrajna. In Bharata Natyam, too, when it comes to *abhinaya*, *srngara* has been the dominant mood.'
63. On 2 April 1958, Rukmini Devi, founder of the Dance Institute Kalakshetra belonging to the Theosophical Society, Madras, presented a paper 'Bharata Natya Sastra in Practice'; a fiery discussion between herself and T. Balasarasvati

followed.

The clash of background and of outlook was unavoidable and could never be mended. Excerpts from this discussion were noted down by Dr V. Raghavan and given to me by Nandini. At one point the chairman gives a *résumé* of the discussion between the two artistes: 'If I understood Smt. Rukmini Devi aright, she was not trying to lay down any rules or strictures for implementation by everybody. She was merely explaining her own background, which necessarily has a great influence on a dancer's career. She came from an orthodox Sastry's family; at that time dancing was not considered a worthwhile vocation for daughters of families like hers; at the same time she had a burning desire to practise this art; but she already was possessed of certain mental attitudes towards various things in life; in spite of her liking for this art she was unable, so to say, to take kindly to the execution of certain gestures involved in the expression of *sringara rasa* or even some of the *sanchari bhavas*, which according to *Sastras* are particularly important to *abhinaya*. But I do not think that she meant to say that no one should take up these songs or the gestures involved. I have read a good number of *slokas, padams* and *javalis*. Those in the North who are familiar with *Gita Govinda, granthas* like *Rasamanjari*, and even *Kamasutra*, know that they are all written with *laksana*. You do not notice any trace of reservation while expressing *sringara rasa*. And surely these things were composed by very great people, *bhaktas* and even saints. With great respect to Smt. Rukmini Devi, I would like to tell you that as far as these great people were concerned there was no question of any narrow-minded view between *bhakti rasa* and *sringara rasa*. The same poet who composed in *bhakti rasa*, composed things in *sringara rasa* also with equal zest if not more. *Sringara rasa* is only one aspect of the various *rasa bhavas* that are expressed in dance. Again, whether it is *sringara rasa* or any other *rasa*, the compositions were all done not on the lives of ordinary women and ordinary men but on someone whom Hindus regard as God. Nevertheless, if you actually take the contents of the *padam* or *javali*, it really illustrates a particular aspect of the *sringara rasa*, comprises *sankeya, vipralamba* aspects and so on. And there is nothing in them about which to feel reservation. It is more the mental attitude of the person executing. I quite appreciate what Rukmini Devi has been saying. She does not mince matters at all. She fully supports the view that *sringara rasa* is as much a part of dancing as any other *rasa*, and she does not say that because she has not taken to *sringara rasa abhinaya*, it should not continue to have its place in the dance. That is because I think that, as a race, the ancient Hindus were not ashamed of sex, nor were they afraid of sex. That is an aspect which crept into our lives along with the other benefits of the British rule – to conceal things which are probably the most beautiful things in the world, to be ashamed of something handed down to you by your forefathers in all good faith. But it was quite different for our ancestors who lived in this land. That is why you find amorous sculptures on the most famous temples, which are place of spiritual worship, which are of spiritual significance; this is why you find ancient love frescoes of even gods and goddesses, dealing with *sringara rasa* in all its aspects.

Therefore I venture to agree with the view expressed by Smt. Balasarasvati that *sringara rasa* should take its proper place in *abhinaya*, and there is no question of looking down upon those who undertake the expression of it in dancing. If you do not like it you can certainly leave it. But if you do take up a *padam* or a *javali*, you must execute it in full, and you should not exclude from it any portion of *sringara rasa*, for, after all, the great composer intended it to be part of the whole *pada*. It may be that a reference to particular parts of human anatomy is supposed to be vulgar or obscene today, but obviously they were not so looked upon in other times in our country. You have to look at our traditional sculptures, to read our great masters of poetry, to justify my remark, and see for yourself how far the exigencies of modern life and social conditions demand a change in our traditional styles. If modern conditions are supposed to demand exclusion of the exhibition of some of our natural emotions, then it is for the individual artist to discard it.

I quite appreciate the viewpoint put forward by Smt. Rukmini Devi. But at the same time she wants to leave things to individual artists. It is essential for them to choose. Smt. Rukmini Devi did something for which we can never sufficiently thank her; she saved this art from total extinction.

With all respect to her, I am more inclined to agree with Smt. Balasarasvati that *padams*, etc., should continue to exist in the set-up of Bharata Natyam side by side with other things. These have been composed by great and eminent people; some of them were dancers themselves. If particular dance items are not suitable for the temperaments of individuals, or he or she will be unable in his or her temperament to exhibit certain gestures, according to me that is a matter of individual choice. But it should not be laid down as a rule that things should be excluded. I hope I have been understood and not misunderstood.'
64. From Bala's presidential address.
65. *Sruti*, March 1984, 'Bala, my Guru', interview of Smt. Nandini Ramani, and separately with Luise Scripps, p. 39. Question to Nandini: 'Did Bala teach dance theory as part of the training she offered?'; answer: 'Today every dancer begins to study *Abhinaya Darpana* and *Natyasastra* along with adavu learning. But Bala's pragmatic approach excluded theory as a separate and independent branch of study. *Prayoga predhanam kalu natyasastram*. Theoretical knowledge becomes assimilable through practical application in the art of learning and performing. Bala would recall incidents describing minute details of *abhinaya* and would explain why she chose a particular set of themes and *mudras* and their context. She would discuss the scope offered by the sahitya for all possible developments.'
66. From Bala's presidential address.
67. Cf. also Conclusion.
68. From Bala's presidential address.
69. Cf. the 'dangers' of *natya*, in *Representation*: Translation, pp. 219–22.
70. *Sangeet Natak*, 1984, pp. 15–16.

Part II

Praxis

Chapter 5

Speech Artefact

The overcoming of *statics*, the expulsion of the absolute – here is the essential turn for the new era, the burning question of today.

Roman Jakobson

Jakobson quotes this premonition[1] in his first contact with the theory of de Saussure on the antinomy between a state and change of language, that is, between synchrony and diachrony. According to him synchrony is not static, but contains many dynamic elements; it is imperative to take this into account when using a synchronic approach to analysis.[2] The equation of synchrony with stasis and diachrony with change serves a 'hidden agenda', namely, that of the history of language. He recalls:

> I wrote a long, worried letter to Trubetzkoy asking him to react to an idea that had come to fruition in my mind, the idea that linguistic changes were systematic, goal-directed, and that the evolution of language shares its purposefulness with the development of other sociocultural systems. Although more than fifty years have elapsed since I wrote that letter, I can still vividly remember my anxiety as I waited for the reactions of that linguist and associate whom I admired above all others. On December 22, 1926 Trubetzkoy answered me with one of his most significant messages: "I am in perfect agreement with your general considerations (. . .) The general outlines of the history of language, when one reflects upon them with a little attention and logic, never prove to be fortuitous. Consequently, the little details cannot be fortuitous either – their sense must simply be discovered. The rational character of the evolution of language stems from the fact that language is a system. (. . .) If Saussure did not dare to draw the logical conclusion from his own thesis that language is a system, this was due in large measure to the fact that such a conclusion would have contradicted the widely accepted notion of the history of language, and of history in

general. For the only accepted sense of history is the notorious one of 'progress', that queer concept which as a consequence reduces 'sense' to 'nonsense'.[3]

Jakobson searches for 'internal logics' in language and other aspects of culture and national life that are *sui generis*, that implement their own specific laws which have nothing to do with progress. From his angle the synchronic 'slice' of a phenomenon under study is highly active in various simultaneous, dynamic ways. These dynamics are interlocked both in 'coëval time and uneval time', in shared space and in spaces referred to but not shared. According to Jakobson 'the speech community tends to include the temporal axis among the linguistic factors which are directly perceived'.[4]

As an example he quotes the side-by-side use of obsolete elements as 'archaisms' and new elements as the 'latest in fashion'. This use is a fact that can be observed on many levels of language; whereas the temporal interpretation is a metalinguistic fact. This seems to be another way of stating that the 'marked' always prevails over the 'markers': that the *ilakkanam* ('markers') have no existential base without the factual *ilakkiyam* ('marked'). In Jakobson's terminology, it implies that the simultaneous is the ground for succession to make itself known.

The forces at work in synchrony are the interrelated internal logics of simultaneity as well as the vital traces of succession. He quotes the Russian neurologist and psychologist I. M. Secenov (1829–1905), who observes that 'in order for the utterance to be understood, attention to the flow of speech must be combined with moments of "simultaneous synthesis"';[5] this attests to another 'feel' and 'agenda' for history than the purpose of 'progress' and the piling up of 'static slabs'. It reminds us of the image of 'incremental time', in which the past is waning but still active and the future already sprouting, waxing into a possibility – all committed to a present simultaneity. 'Simultaneous synthesis' is a process of combining those elements that have already disappeared from immediate perception with those that belong to coeval, active memory. In retrospect, the Indian concept of *smara* 'memory' as worship and as love becomes clear, as well as its method of remembering and practising worship.

Jakobson continues his quotation 'these elements are then combined into increasingly larger groupings: sounds into words,

words into sentences, and sentences into utterances'.[6] The following subchapter 'Form' outlines the Tamil curriculum in the praxis of the verbal arts, stipulating a similar progression. The training of long- and short-term memory as an underlying logic for the grammars of language and literature explains partly the fact that coexistence and succession are intricately intertwined in the life of language and literature, as well as the fact that language and literature are capable of transporting us across both time and space. What remains is the problem of the nature of time as it is at work within the structure and life of language. Roman Jakobson distinguishes two aspects of time: 'there is on the one hand the time of the speech event and on the other hand the time of the narrated event'. He sees the 'clash of these two as particularly evident in verbal art', and raises doubts as to whether 'it is possible at all to overcome the fact of an uninterrupted temporal flow, which opposes poetry to the stasis of painting'.[7] As early as the middle of the eighteenth century Ephraim Lessing proposed to replace coexistence in space with succession in time in the case of poetic description. The laws of language allow the gradual unfolding of an impression, just as they enable the receiver in his own turn to describe the processes of that impact in a linear, analytic way.

A younger fellow writer of Lessing's, Johann Gottfried Herder (1744–1803), defended poetic imagery in its capacity to evoke simultaneous scenes and thus to transcend an exclusively linear succession of the events it renders.[8] Basically, this discussion revolves around the problem of representation that is at the root, too, of the epistemic blind spot that emerges between Western literary scholarship and Tamil oral expertise. Verbal art, in terms of Tamil solutions, processes the combination of simultaneous flow and past impression, that is the speech event and the narrated event, in a way that is similar to the proposition of Herder. By combining the elements of word, sound and image, the threefold Tamil is capable of expressing both the pictorial impression that belongs to painting and the sequential flow that renders static images flexible to suit the development of the story. Jakobson turns to medieval Easter plays to state a similar point.

> Finally, in the Easter play of the Middle Ages, which combines the mystery of the saints with a conventional farce of grotesque figures, the characters experience simultaneous existence in two temporal

sets. On the one hand they participate in the unfolding of the events of the gospel story that preceded the Resurrection of Christ, while on the other hand they anticipate with pleasure the annual Easter meal. Thus the events of the gospel story appear simultaneously as facts of the distant past and as phenomena that are repeated every year. In short, narrative, especially poetic, time can be unilinear as well as multilinear, direct as well as reversed, continuous as well as discontinuous; it can be even a combination of rectilinearity and circularity, as in the last example. I believe that it would be difficult to find another domain, except perhaps for music, where time is experienced with compatible acuity.[9]

The final comparison of the domain of poetic narrative with the domain of musical expression seems vital to me. The central problem of Time in language and literature is not quite the distinction between the time of the speech event and of the narrated event. This is interesting only from the point of view of the literate scholar who tries to elicit the 'truth' value. He believes, firstly, that he is capable of representing this 'truth' in media and through methods that he is familiar with; and secondly that he can contribute in this way to the mission of history, or offer an 'expert critique' on the surge of 'progress'. In contrast, the expert in an oral tradition tackles the problem of time from a totally different angle: he will try to compose words and images in such a way that the flow of time is capable of carrying and communicating both. His worries and acumen revolve around a technical know-how and a feel that is deeply familiar with the internal logic of human communication. Perhaps, these are the logistics and purposefulness that Jakobson is after, even without mentioning them explicitly. Thus it turns out that the problem of representation is linked up with problems of an ontological, teleological and epistemic nature. In short, poetic narrative, speech events, oral texts do not yield easily to a methodology that is attuned to two-dimensional representation by writing; they feel much more at home with the methodology of the performing arts, in which music reigns supreme. As a result the dimension of Time has been largely neglected in the study of language and language products. Phonology and prosody tend to investigate small-scale objects that can easily be rendered static, and thereby controlled. Pragmatics makes an attempt at the study of the *deixis* of time as a structuring factor in language. Taking for its model purely quantitative, empirical assessment based on the natural sciences, it cannot escape positivist ambitions for stasis, measurement and control:

> Both time and place deixis are greatly complicated by the interaction of deictic co-ordinates with non-deictic conceptualization of time and space. To understand these aspects of deixis in depth it is first necessary to have a good understanding of the semantic organization of space and time in general (. . .). Briefly, though, the bases for systems of reckoning and measuring time in most languages seem to be the natural and prominent cycles of day and night, lunar months, seasons and years. Such units can either be used as *measures*, relative to some fixed point of interest (including, crucially, the deictic centre), or they can be used *calendrically* to locate events in 'absolute' time relative to some absolute *origo*, or at least to some part of each natural cycle designated as the beginning of that cycle (Fillmore 1975). It is with these units, calendrical and non-calendrical, that time deixis interacts.[10]

Up to this point Levinson discusses indeed the points of reference in the 'real', 'outside' world. This particular use of Time is *polutu*, Tamil for 'moment, sun', but plays no significant role in the formation of a Tamil utterance; what does matter there is *kalam*, to be translated here with 'duration'. In musical practice and in prosody this time-unit is measured by a wink of the eye or by a click of two fingers (Skt. *aksara*). Even quarters of the click constitute units of time: preparing the thumb and middle finger, joining them, rubbing them and producing the 'click' as the middle finger descends.[11] Thus letters, syllables, words, lines, verses and larger compositions are measures in larger units or cycles of *aksara*s. This is done with a purposeful know-how, it is a technique that employs *duration* for an expressive, communicative purpose, making the maximum of what Lyons calls (1977a: 685) *deictic simultaneity*:

> Like all aspects of deixis, time deixis makes ultimate reference to participant-role. (. . . .) It is important to distinguish the moment of utterance (or inscription) or *coding time* (or CT) from the moment of reception or *receiving time* (or RT). As we noted, in the canonical situation of utterance, with the assumption of the unmarked deictic centre, RT can be assumed to be identical to CT.[12]

What is at work during this deictic simultaneity, its structure, devices, variables and their effects on understanding and 'meaning' is not discussed anywhere.

Another noteworthy effort to deal with the dimension Time is offered by Tedlock in his *The Spoken Word and the Work of Interpretation* (1983). His argument is laid out in the chapter 'Phonography and the Problem of Time in Oral Narrative Events', and cuts deep in its highlighting of the opposition of sound dominance versus inscription dominance:

> ... phonography (I here apply the term to all sound recording) has had an enormous effect on ethnomusicology, but those who deal with the *spoken* word- whether they be linguists, folklorists, cultural anthropologists still seem to regard phonography as little more than a device for moving the scene of alphabetic notation from the field interview to the solitude of an office with playback facilities. The real analysis begins only after a document of altogether pre-phonographic characteristics has been produced.[13]

The other brand of scholarship is concerned with the *phonè*, the sound of the voice, itself. Its continuity is one of 'gross physicality' – an image that is found in Tamil expertise as well. There, the minimal unit, 'letter' (Ta. *eluttu* 'scratch', 'engraving'), is diagnosed as either *mey* 'body' or *uyir* 'breath': the first indicates consonants, the second vowels. The two become workable units only in syllabic consonance: *acai* meaning 'to move, to stir'. This insight goes well with Tedlock's observation that phonetic research, dealing with the neural organisation, physical production, and sensory perception of speech sounds calls attention to the continuous overlapping of these sounds (as opposed to the particulate and successive nature of the phoneme). In fact no workable smaller unit can be found than the syllable.[14] Tedlock first sets out on a course that is seemingly independent of both, and adopts 'an approach more appropriate to the natural or physical sciences'. He confronts the reader with a part of his fifty-metre-long inscription of a tape-recorded story. The oscillogram shows three tracks: one of amplitude, one of pitch, one of the continuous time-scale. The harvest is rich, and yields pause junctures, intonational markers, stresses, and vowel quantities that are reckoned as para-linguistic features and suprasegmentals. 'It is no wonder', observes Tedlock, 'that such gross acoustical features as those we discovered on our scroll barely enter into discussions of supresegmentals, to say nothing of segmentals, such features seem to be at the border of borders, or even beyond.'[15] The only way out seems to him, just as it seemed to Jakobson and even to Ricoeur (as a method of reading), to be the analogy with music, and in this respect they agree with Umberto Eco. Phonological treatment of the singing voice would lead to an unacceptable, non-workable reduction of the music. The musical score is a reduction supplied with powerful signs for its restoration back to life. 'If musicologists have been slow to adopt the methods and vocabulary of semiotics, as Eco notes, the reason may be that when it comes to temporally complex phenomena, musicology, as Jean-Jacques Nattiez seems to suggest,[16] has more to offer to semiotics than semiotics has to offer musicology.'[17] At this point we get very close to the second 'brand' of scholarship outlined above: the expertise on *phonè*, 'sound'. But first Tedlock still attempts to assign his data to the realm of semiotics. However, he experiences the straightjacket of grammaticalisation as too manipulative to do justice to the collected data, nor does he recognise a fertile treatment of the dimension time in the structuralist work of Lévi-Strauss:

> Duration is entirely absent except when we read what Lévi-Strauss has written and supply our own durations at our own shifting tempo. It has been said that structuralism and the linguistics it is based upon are unable to deal with historical time except as a succession of frozen moments, but we may add here that they are also unable to deal with the time it takes to tell a story. When Lévi-Strauss imports a musical model into the discussion of myths, it is not to restore the lost 'music' of storytelling itself but to construct a new 'music' out of the relationships between differing successions of mythemes. The score has now become an orchestral one, with several staves running along synchronously, but the time signature, tempo marks, note values, rests, and ties are still missing.
>
> Lévi-Strauss, in his review of a book of Zuni narratives which I scored for pauses, changes of amplitude, and other gross acoustical features, calls for the integration of these features in structuralist accounts, though he makes no suggestion as to how this might be done.[18]

Eco has not yet given up the hope that these features might be incorporated in an enlarged grammar of signs. One thing troubles him: these phenomena are encountered at a 'lower threshold, at the point where semiotic phenomena arise from something non-semiotic'. Between their signalling activity and 'the sign' there seems to be a missing link. Tedlock understands this 'missing link' as a necessary result of a theoretical view which sees the relationship between signal and sign analytically, that is as a dual opposition with an excluded middle.[19] Perhaps Tedlock is right in sketching the situation thus, only with one large difference: namely, that in the reality of verbal art, the middle is not excluded but is the ground on which signalling and sign come to fruition. The 'missing link' of Eco is the *praxis* of signalling; the 'codified' training, or live 'grammars' of communicative words, sounds and images. The application of these idioms or 'supplies' acquired by practice takes its full shape in the communicative, interactive setting. Only there, in the midst of the doubly interactive event of the performance, can the sign emerge and be absorbed. This situation may coincide with the second choice that Tedlock offers at the end of the chapter.

> We may, as linguistically modeled semiotics always will, subordinate the questions raised during our exploration of signals, in this case acoustical signals, to the ultimate demand of signs, retreating back inside the hermetic safety of codes. In the present case that will mean leaving Zuni grammar exactly as it is, a presumably integral code, and assigning extra-grammatical features to membership in a separate code whose integrity will continue to be open to question, so long as a way cannot be found to eliminate the last vestiges of temporal continuity (and thus materiality) from its signs. In a semiotics thus constituted, we will hear of "*para*linguistics" and "*supra*segmentals" or of Eco's "*missing* link" or "*lower* threshold" or "*fuzzy* concepts" or "*imprecise* expressive texture" – or the effects of a "*complex* network of subcodes",[20] a network that never quite seems to get unraveled.
>
> If, on the other hand, we are to free semiotics from its subordination to linguistics – a movement which requires a balanced approach to the relationship between signals and signs, one in which the demands of codification are denied any claim to finality – then we may allow ourselves to realize that in exploring the region on and around the "lower threshold" of an established code, we have inadvertently discovered that the code itself does not occupy

quite as remote a layer of heaven as we thought it did and may even be suspected of having inescapable connections to the ground, given that even the semantic field of its morphemes (to say nothing of its lexemes) is inhabited by gross acoustical features that resist final reduction to the status of perfect signs.[21]

This scenario holds true for the Tamil sign, which is largely somatic in its signalling capacity. This signalling is always a shared, bilateral, coeval event that is never exactly the same, even if the performers would like it to be so. It changes according to the needs of the time, place and audience of the performance, but not in a totally arbitrary, random way. The limits for modification are inscribed in trained bodies that have acquired a highly flexible 'grammar' in the course of a long practice and exposure to the public. It is in praxis embodied by performers that we must search for the 'missing link'. The internal logic and specific laws that Jakobson had in mind are physical, gross reality in the live expertise of the artist. By drawing language, language creation such as verbal art, and semiotics within the orbit of the performing arts, we finally seem to have arrived once more at the ubiquitous metaphor of music; this time, however, in order to take its methodology seriously.

Charles Seeger proposes the music event as occurring in both general space–time (as phenomenon) and music space–time (as normenon). Between general space–time and music space–time (. . . .) there should be no postulation of a one-to-one correspondence. General time is a given quantity over which we have no control but to act in it: music time and space is a creation of man, over which he has almost unlimited control. The formation of significant utterances is as much determined by a strategic formation of space – here, the tonal quality and composition of sound – as of time – here, the tonal duration and span of sound. A scholarship that is capable of recording, analysing, codifying, interpreting and anticipating such strategies cannot do without the dual preconditions of space and time. This brings us back to the problem of the form of representation: as an inscription, painting or document or as a live narrative event? Tedlock concludes that the problem of time in oral narrative events exists in the discrepancy between their *matter* and our *manner* of perceiving these events. As confirmed *literati* (or: 'letterati') we are ever reluctant to adjust our 'vision' to the phonographic 'image'.[22] The implications of this drastic adjustment might result in the assignment of linguistics to a specialised area within semiotics. But that story, concludes Tedlock, 'has not yet taken place'.

It is taking place, though, and has taken place, for many centuries in many speech communities that cherish their oral tradition. The basic tenet of Tamil in defining itself as threefold, that is as composed of word, sound and image, subscribes to the principle of dynamic simultaneity; the postulate that literature is a 'marked event' that prevails over 'codified markers' subscribes to Tedlock's position with regard to the relationship of grammar and speech, and of language and sign. Tamil pursues a different type of linguistics; indeed, a linguistics that is subservient to semiotics and that is dynamic, operating through simultaneous synthesis; that is concrete, holding together and synthesising the three worlds, the three times and creation; last but not least, it pursues a language product that is purposeful, because of its capacity to fuse, which is felt as beneficial. The idea quoted earlier that 'linguistic changes were systematic and goal-directed and that the evolution of language shares its purposefulness with the development of other sociocultural systems' is embodied by the Tamil tradition. Indeed, its continuation follows its own internal logic and specific laws that have nothing in common with 'progress', but which have everything to do with human communication. The focus of their intelligence and acumen is geared towards the 'how' of the utterance.

The distinction between *kotum tamil* 'ordinary, bent Tamil' and *cem tamil* 'auspicious, beautiful Tamil' can serve as a conceptual translation of the 'lower' and 'higher' thresholds of semiotics. To take the step from the 'lower' to the 'higher' threshold means to undergo training in the triple skills of *langage*. The *praxis* of *cem tamil* supplies us with concepts, methodology and techniques to study 'Orality' as a conscious effort that takes off from the 'General Oral'. Seeger remarks that the 'general oral' is a given capacity over which we have not much choice but to act in it; 'orality' operates in a time and space that is a creation of man over which he has almost unlimited control.[23] Just like the art of 'chiselled Tamil', Orality is a chiselled effort that evolves according to norms cherished by man, into forms embodied by man. Its 'grammars' are inscribed in human memories and human bodies; the texts that they speak are highly dynamic, composite and concrete. In positioning application over system they fulfil Jakobson's vision of 'the essential turn for the new era, the burning question of today'. The fact that these grammars are embedded in practice and performance turns them into works of art. From this angle we may coin verbal art forms as **SPEECH ARTE FACTS**: products (*factus*) of disciplinary training (*langue*) in the three branches of *langage*, word, sound and image (*artes*) under the basic conditions of time and space, and, finally applied as *speech* (*parôle*) that serves the purpose of doubly interactive communication.

The speech artefact captures *langage, langue, parôle* and thereby its *habitus*, with all its sociocultural, semantic demands. Grammar, application and semantics are joined in one united effort. This effort is both systematic and dynamic; on the simultaneous plane it operates as a flexible composition of earlier stored elements, constantly choosing which of the many variants of the disciplines to employ for maximum communicative effect, while on the diachronic plane it synthesises the three worlds, the three times and the known order of creation. Is the speech artefact a dream come true? It is and it isn't: on the performance level it is

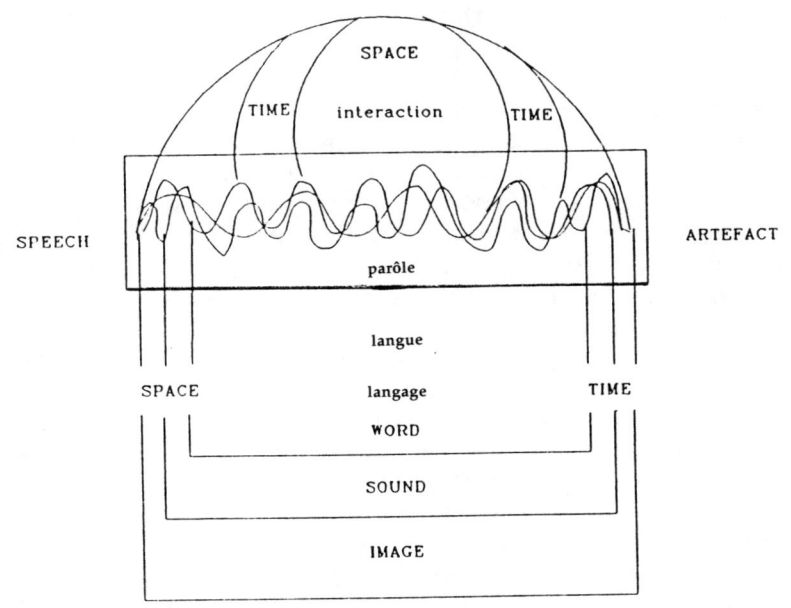

Figure 9 – the speech artefact

an age-old dream that perpetually comes true, each generation; on the level of abstracted representation it is the new multimedia that signal a dream to come true for scholarship. For the first time it is possible to represent word, sound and image in their composite synthesis, true to their existence in the dimensions of time and space, as well as to supply them with an interactive commentary on their origin and formative logistics in addition to their interactive interrelations with the world of application, their referential deixis and the quality of their reception. Apart from the functions of interactive commentary, one could envisage other facilities, such as extensive training circuits and interactive workshops where the user might practise and be corrected in his own attempts. Perhaps the days of this new type of scholarship that Tedlock foresaw have arrived today.

5.1 Speech Occasion

The Speech Artefact *bhairavi varnam* does not stand on its own as an arbitrary activity. It forms the central part in a well-thought-out strategy of a solo performance. As we will see further on, *bhairavi varnam* tries to strike a sensitive balance between abstract and figurative imagery. This is not a small task that can be achieved offhand, without much preparation. Therefore, the traditional concert 'suite' paves the way for the *varnam* to express itself. The term 'concert' *kacceri* is used for both music and dance concerts, which shows once more the importance of sound as a guiding force for human communication. As a result, the key for the strategy of the dance-concert is to be found in musical strategies. Indian music makes a basic distinction between the realm of melody and the realm of rhythm. According to its inner logic rhythm belongs to the world of abstraction, while melody belongs to the world of form, of the body and of figurative imagery. The terms employed mark this difference quite well: *tala* (Skt.), rhythm, is the palm of the hand, the instrument for counting the beat,[24] whereas *raga* (Skt.), melody, is the process of colouring, like paint that gradually spreads in a blank piece of cloth; in a similar way, melody gradually soaks the mind of the listener, colouring it in its own shade.[25] This logic should be kept in mind when examining the occasion of performance of a *varnam.*

The progression of the dance concert is remarkably well structured by a clear communicative strategy: after the tuning of the instruments and the singing of an invocatory stanza, the dancer appears in order to present the following choreographies:

1 *alarippu*: '*alari* flower': an abstract, purely rhythmical piece;
2 *jatisvaram*: abstract choreography (*jati*) on musical notes (*svara*);
3 *sabdam*: 'word', figurative mime of narrative nature interspersed with small abstract choreographic phrases;
4 *varnam*: 'colour', elaborate, improvisatory mime of a highly emotional, lyrical nature, set to an eminently emotive *raga* that is worked out in great detail and variation, interspersed with complex, abstract choreographic salvoes (*tirmanams* 'end').
5 *pada* (Skt.,Ta: *patam*) 'song', delicate, 'pondering' mime around one central feeling in a situation of love, employing again highly emotional *ragas* worked out at length and in a slow tempo without any dominant rhythmic presence.
6 *javali*: 'song', also dealing with a theme of love but usually much lighter – sometimes even humorous and flippant.
7 *tillana*: 'finale'; taking an optimistic *raga* as 'red thread', the intricacies of rhythm spin one figure of abstract dance after the other in a dazzling combination of all three tempi, preferring the fast third tempo.
8 *sloka*: 'verse': mime to a devotional verse.

A complete dance recital is well thought out and based on deeply traditional aesthetic principles. The oldest Sanskrit treatise on performing arts available to us (c 200 AD), the *Natyasastra*, ascribed to the legendary sage Bharata, deals with the dynamics of aesthetics. Sanjukta Gupta explained this chapter by means of a metaphor taken from the work of Abhinava Gupta (ninth century AD).[26] This philosopher–aesthetician holds that meaning cannot be communicated to a mind that is firmly set in its own patterns and private occupation of thought. The wise artist regards the mind of the audience as a seal set in a particular imprint; by means of an apt artistic strategy, the performer is capable of slowly melting the solidified seal into once-again fluid wax. This is the moment where she sets out to communicate her own content of feelings, visions and experience by gently imprinting them into the receptive mind. As she allows the message to settle, communication takes shape and is able in fact to touch the audience that attends the performance.[27]

Obviously a great deal of successful communication depends on the right strategy. The traditional *Bharata Natyam/ Dasi Attam* recital offers such a strategy: by starting with the purely rhythmic joy of *alarippu* the attention of the audience is drawn on an abstract level; gradually the affects of melody and image mellow step by step its mind and focus of attention. When we have arrived at the *varnam*, that is after approximately forty minutes, the audience has loosened up to accompany the performer in her 'emotional research' conducted in the *varnam*. Still, there is a firm explicit structure in its choreography which will be discussed on the following pages, that helps the audience to follow and stay with the dancer. This *'pièce de résistance'* is a change of temperament in the recital: the *varnam* contains all elements of this verbal art, up to a maximum of complexity.

The *pada* ('song') that follows concentrates on one central emotion. It is marked by an almost unobtrusive rhythmic cycle set in a slow tempo and a predominant, elaborate treatment of a *raga* of great emotional affect and scope for improvisation. *Pada*s are in fact the most demanding compositions, both on the dancer and on the audience; they have to merge together and float far up and down with the ways of love and passion. Several *pada*s, in different *raga*s are traditionally contrasted with each other in one recital. In 'modern Bharata Natyam' a weird type of literate attitude has crept in, giving preference to 'thematic' clusters, and having recourse to rhythmical interludes to sustain the attention. After the impact of the *pada*s, the *javali*s, 'love songs', set a lighter mood and prepare the audience for a way 'back' to ordinary life, carrying the imprint of the fragility of the human heart still with them when they leave the site of the performance. The *tillana*, once more a major rhythmical piece, rounds off the emotional journey with an abstract joy of vitality and freedom. This is an account of the communicative strategy of the concert viewed from the side of the receiver. The side of the performer is expressed by Balasarasvati herself:

> The greatness of this traditional concert-pattern will be apparent even from a purely aesthetic point of view. In the beginning, *alarippu*,

which is based on rhythm alone, brings out the special charm of pure dance. The movements of *alarippu* relax the dancer's body and thereby her mind, loosen and coordinate her limbs and prepare her for the dance. Rhythm has a rare capacity to concentrate. *Alarippu* is most valuable in freeing the dancer from distraction and making her single-minded.

The joy of pure rhythm in *alarippu* is followed by *jatiswaram*, where there is the added joy of melody. Melody without word or syllable has a special power to unite us with our being. In *jatiswaram*, melody and movement come together. Then comes *sabdam*. It is here that compositions, with words and meanings, which enable the expression of the myriad moods of Bharata Natyam are introduced.

The Bharatanatyam recital is structured like a Great Temple: we enter through the *gopuram* [outer hall, 'temple-tower': SK] of *alarippu*, cross the *ardhamandapam* [half-way hall] of *jatiswaram*, then the *mandapa* [great hall] of *sabdam*, and enter the holy precinct of the deity in the *varnam*.[28] This is the place, the space, which gives the dancer expansive scope to revel in the rhythm, moods and music of the dance. The *varnam* is the continuum which gives ever-expanding room to the dancer to delight in her self-fulfilment, by providing the fullest scope to her own creativity as well as to the tradition of the art.

The *padams* now follow. In dancing to the *padams*, one experiences the containment, cool and quiet, of entering the sanctum from its external precinct. The expanse and brilliance of the outer corridors disappear in the dark inner sanctum;[29] and the rhythmic virtuosities of the *varnam* yield to the soul-stirring music and *abhinaya* of the *padam*. Dancing to the *padam* is akin to the juncture when the cascading lights of worship are withdrawn and the drumbeats die down to the simple and solemn chanting of sacred verses in the closeness of God.[30] Then the *tillana* breaks into movement, like the final burning of camphor, accompanied by a measure of din and bustle.

In conclusion, the devotee takes to his heart the god he has so far glorified outside; and the dancer completes the traditional order by dancing to a simple devotional verse. At first, mere metre; then, melody and metre; continuing with music, meaning and metre; its expansion in the centrepiece of the *varnam*; thereafter, music and meaning without metre; in variation to this, melody and metre; in contrast to the purely rhythmical beginning a non-metrical song at the end. We see a most wonderful completeness and symmetry in this art. Surely the traditional votaries of our music and dance would not wish us to take any liberties with this sequence.[31]

The old, solo recital, formerly called *Dasi Attam* ('dance of the *devadasis*'), and now known as *Bharata Natyam*, is not meant to make statements, spread messages or teach the norms of good and evil. Other forms of dance are ideally suited to perform this role.[32] Bharata Natyam is more like a meditation, an exploration of the 'interior landscape' of the world of *akam*, of love.[33] The melody and mime roam through its realms sunk in wonder and amazement, guided by a lingering longing for the reciprocation of love. Either anticipating, assessing the situation or looking back, the heart is always vulnerable and mellowed by the urge of love to reach out and transcend the narrow borders of the Ego. It is in this vulnerability that Bharata Natyam prospers, neither in a 'spiritual holier-than-thou' attitude, nor in a calculated desire to charm, but in a meditation of the heart: '*srngara* is the cardinal emotion which gives the fullest scope for artistic improvisation, branching off continually, as it does in the portrayal of innumerable moods full of newness and nuance'.[34] To enter and sustain such a mood and take an audience along requires firm grasp and mastery, clear structure, keen awareness and strategic, sensitive flexibility. How these are employed can be inferred from the example of *Bhairavi Varnam*.

5.2 Speech Example

The speech artefact *varnam* is an example of 'colourful uttering'. Its very name indicates the activity of colouring or painting, gradually taking hold of the receivers' perception. The utterance expresses itself in the threefold Tamil (*Muttamil*), the three performing arts of word (*iyal*), sound (*icai*) and image (*natakam*). Together they form a weave, a *textus*, that is well planned and shaped. As a 'linguistic unit' it transcends the boundary of the sentence that is held as the highest linguistic unit in Western linguistics. Roman Jakobson sees this boundary as a limitation: 'Superior wholes, namely utterances, which may embrace a higher integer of sentences, and the discourse, which normally is an exchange of utterances, remained outside the scope of linguistic analysis'.[35]

Bhairavi varnam is such an utterance that embraces a higher integer of sentences, and that is reckoned as one expressive unit.

In Tamil terminology the highest 'linguistic unit', that is the highest '*Muttamil* unit', is *pa* the 'song-weave', meaning both 'verse', 'singing' and 'weave'. Such weaves, that remind us of the ancient *textus*, are woven out of three strands (word, sound, image) by means of the warp and woof of the conditions *space* and *time*. Without exception, each of the three threads has to commit itself to this double formative logic. The aim of this logic is to chisel the message in a powerfully expressive way. The main ingredient of its expressivity is the contrastive articulation of the figurative and the abstract. The mental, figurative content of the utterance is foregrounded by means of abstract framing. The division of labour assigns the role of abstraction to rhythm and the management of *time* as *duration*, while the role of concrete figuration is played by melody as the management of *space* as *form*. Not unlike the passepartout around a painting, the message is focused because of its abstract surroundings.

The metaphor of painting leads us to examples of painters who have successfully contrasted the figurative and the abstract as well as generated the abstract from the figurative and vice versa. The striking difference in the work of Vassily Kandinsky shows these complementary contrasts. His paintings from the period of the 'Blue Cavalier' give out a 'perfume' of mystery and an ideal synthesis of painting, music, science and – philosophy. The works inspired by the Bauhaus reveal a concept that is essentially dynamic and in progress, expressed in a language that is precise and rigorous, made up out of points and lines, tense or opposed, that form angles, circles and new figures.[36] The Tamil attempt follows a similar trajectory: the combination of word, melody and mime that delve into an ever-deepening mystery, and, on the other hand, the abstract clarity and anticipation created by the combination of sharp onomatopoeic syllables or solfège set to increasingly complex rhythmic patterns. Whereas the lines of the first type of movement resemble the sweep and suggestive power of Kandinsky's figurative 'Impressions', the second type of dance is precise, rigorous, and, like his 'Dessin', formed by straight lines, diagonals, and half and full circles.[37] This inventory of expression is applied as follows in the utterance *bhairavi varnam*:

Strand 1: Word – *iyal*

The contrast between abstract and figurative performance is carried by abstract, nonsense syllables and solfège on the one hand, and by Tamil verbal composition on the other hand, which supplies the mental focus, backbone and point of departure in an improvisatory mime that deepens with each repetition of the Tamil line. An example of the first device of abstraction is the sequence of nonsense syllables that mean nothing but that are a clear onomatopoeic reflection of the sound made by the feet on the floor: the words expressed by the dance-master *tat tun -dike-take tadingine take tu.nga- tunga* signal the (abstract) steps *té té - té té ditdit té tey tey- tey- ta-*, set to a purely rhythmical structure; they are called *col kattu* 'bundle of utterances'. The same principle of abstract steps is followed by combining them to singing the names of the notes of the melody line in its rhythmical phrasing (*solfège*); in technical parlance: to the *svarapaddhati*. The first example has been worked out in the CD-i demo;[38] the second example occurs in the second half of the *varnam*, and therefore cannot be illustrated here. This other, common use of the word (*iyal*) is the figurative, referential function of the Tamil language; in dance and music, this is called *sahitya* (Skt. 'composition'). The words '*mōṭi ceyyalāmō eṉ cāmi metta*' 'ignoring me, is that possible, my lord and beloved?' are repeated sixteen-and-a-half times. In the subchapter 'Content' the ways in which 'meaning' is investigated, etched and coloured into a rich experience are outlined.[39] The strategy of contrasting the abstract and figurative verbal load lies in constantly alternating the two throughout the entire composition.

Strand 2: Music – *icai*

As was pointed out earlier, the sound component is the guiding principle of the performance. The entire *varnam* is moulded in the womb of time. In general, 'time' should be understood here as 'duration'. The long, melodic stretches of the Tamil lines are accentuated by the short impulses of rhythmical fire. The management of the rhythm-cycle is uncomplicated when it forms the backbone of melody, especially in the first part of the *varnam* (that is the *pallavi* and the *anupallavi*), whereas when it stands on its own, in the short rhythmic portions, the opposite holds true. There the complexity of the rhythm-cycle, tempo, clustering of rhythmical phrases within the cycle has been developed to a maximum. The ingredients for this policy of contrasting the abstract to the figurative are, on the one hand, rhythm *tala*, set in a cycle of six beats *rupaka tala*, evolving from the slow first tempo (*kala*) in the *pallavi* and *anupallavi* to the faster second tempo in the middle portion (*muktayisvara sahitya*) and *caranam* (refrain plus elaborations), interspersed with rhythmical explosions that employ all three tempi (slow, middle and fast). These rhythmical salvoes called *tirmanam* ('ending') are marked by an intricate inner structure of the rhythm cycle that subdivides the rotating wheel of six beats into clusters (*natai*, or, *gati*) of 3, 4, 7, 5 or 9 beats. The result of this rhythmical arithmetic can be observed in the example of the third 'salvo' *tirmanam*.[40]

The combination of this tight arithmetical structure and the clear-cut, geometrical beauty of the choreography has a startling effect of abstraction. The figurative, emotive power of the performance is carried to a great extent by the melodic sensitivity and fantasy of both accompanying musicians and dancer. In an ideal case, the dancer is capable of accompanying her mimetic rendering of the Tamil lines by her own singing. It is the melody that fosters the mood (Skt. *bhava*, 'becoming') of a performance. The configuration of notes (*svara*) holds the promise of a 'tonal poem' that is capable of painting the emotional process. Indian classical music has long ago conceived the experiment of expressing tones, feelings and mental states in terms of imagery, painting and the use of colours. The basic course of South Indian vocal and instrumental music starts off with a meditation on the *raga* ('tonal scale') and *tala* ('rhythm cycle') that have been followed since the fifteenth century.[41]

> In the glow of sunset this esteemed prince makes his presence felt in the temple of music. His face is radiant with the kisses of his queen; his emerald and ruby earrings are as pretty as parrots. He wears a beautiful garland, *Malavaraga Raja*. Borne along on the shoulders of six women, he is seated in a swaying palanquin, his lady by his side. A maid in front fans him with a *camara* ('fly-whisk'). He is clad in yellow silk and adorned with flashing ruby earrings. The sacred thread gleams on his shoulder. I worship the lord of *Adi Tala*.[42]

The Indian answer to the 'tonal poems' of Scriabin, the experiments of Kandinsky and Schoenberg in 'Yellow Sonority',[43] is the *ragamala*, the '*raga* painting' that depicts the quintessence of the emotional 'centre of gravity' of a scale and the myriad of melodic possibilities that spring from that well. Each major *raga* has such a situational painting and meditative description that connects the inner experience with exterior representation.[44] According to Kandinsky one cannot separate the two – both grow out of the same roots, that is 'that complex total that constitutes the soul of the artist'. In his search for apt expression the artist-musician does not distinguish between inner experience and outer form.

This conviction is worded very well by the Indian term *manodharma*, which is mostly used to indicate the process of improvisation. To my mind, it rather tries to name the 'artistic research' into the real breadth and depth of feeling. Artistic imagination (*manas*) roams through the realms, the scope (*dharma*) of feeling that inheres in the *raga* – the affective, magic circle. To know the circumference of that circle by singing, dancing, sounding or painting it is what this improvisational interpretation is about; it is fundamental research.[45]

Bhairavai varnam sets off with such a tentative exploration of the *raga bhairavi*. Such an initial search is called *alapana*, which means 'etching', outlining the essential dynamics and shapes of the mood in burin, to be filled in fully in the course of the *varnana* 'colouring'. The musical terminology makes clear, once more, that the metaphor of music with regard to texts is a metaphor in the medieval, practical sense, or, in contemporaneous terms, a metonymy of the text. The essence, the beginning and end of a text are music, musical sensitivity and musical creativity.

Strand 3: Image – *natakam*

The strands of recitation and music share a basic precondition of the fourth dimension, the dimension of time. It is not possible to imagine 'static sound'. As Ong remarks 'All sensation takes place in time, but no other sensory field totally resists a holding action, stabilization in quite this way. (...) There is no equivalent of a still shot for sound. An oscillogram is silent. It lies outside the sound world'.[46] In Physics the reduction of a dimension means that the information that inheres in it is lost. To transform a four-dimensional field to a three-dimensional or even to a two-dimensional one (as is the case with writing) implies an irretrievable loss of particular information which cannot be represented, restored or suggested in any other way than in its natural state.[47] Dance and mime (*natakam*) live a double existence: on the one hand, they must be dynamic in order to narrate, but, on the other, even when frozen into a still, they continue to be expressive. They dwell in the fourth as well as in the third dimension. Ong holds that 'vision can register motion, but it can also register immobility. Indeed, it favours immobility, for to examine something closely by vision, we prefer to have it quiet.'[48]

In the flow of dance, stills are used in this way to heighten the visual impact, especially when portraying an iconic representation of the gods as *dramatis personae*, or in order to underline the rhythmical complexity and *élan*. Image (*natakam*) knows therefore two modes of expression: the abstract imagery can be called 'dance', 'choreography proper' (*nrtta*, Skt. 'dance'), and is composed of geometrical steps called *atavu* (Ta. 'step');[49] the figurative mode is closer to improvisatory mime (*nrtya*, Skt.'mimetic dance'), and makes use of a true lexicon and grammar of expressive use of the body, from minor limbs like fingers and hands (*hasta*, Skt. 'hand') to postures, gaits and sequences (*karana*, Skt. 'doing, making, effecting').

The entire training of the expressive use of the body is geared towards *abhinaya* (literally, 'bringing towards'), which is usually translated as 'expression', but which, in fact, means more than that. In *abhinaya* the concerted effort of word, music and dance culminates into a irresistible affect. Bharata (*c*.200 AD) diagnoses the success of a performance as *siddhi* ('power, force') of two kinds, 'human success' (*manusi siddhi*), that is known by shouts and praise, and 'divine success' (*daiviki siddhi*), that makes itself felt by a high degree of *sattva* ('beingness') through tears and gooseflesh.[50]

This cumulative effect of the event is in its *rasa*, the 'tasting', or 'juice' of shared experience. Its totalising effect is brought about by the ingenious weave of word, sound and image. Of these three, it is image, the solo dancer who concretises the entire load of the performance. Ong states: 'Sight isolates, sound incorporates'; but when image travels on sound, and becomes the corporeal form of sound, the two weld into one crescendo of interiorisation: 'Interiority and harmony are characteristics of human consciousness. The consciousness of each human person is totally interiorized, known to the person from the inside and inaccessible to any other person directly from the inside.'[51]

For this reason the term *abhinaya* is well chosen: it is not the 'expression' of one unique individual, but it is the offering of the affective power of a given content to an audience, gradually preparing their consciousness to receive the impression and turn it into a personalised, subjective interpretation. The meaning and 'success' or 'truth' of the text are not in its concepts but in its gooseflesh. Musicologist Harry Powers once asked Bala what sign she considered the hallmark of success in performance. He remembered her words: 'that you leave the event as a changed person'.[52] In the terms of Frank Smith, 'knowledge' as 'understanding' has been achieved during such an event; the brain has worked, tested, tried out and enjoyed its own creations on the basis of the impact of the performance. Such knowledge is 'not a fractioning but a unifying phenomenon, a striving for harmony'. Without that interior condition, the psyche is said to be in bad health.[53]

The striving of the speech artefact is well expressed in these words. The ultimate aim of Tamil poetry, and thereby of *bhairavi varnam*, is indeed the harmonisation (Ta. *icaintu*) of all three strands (word, sound and image) over the two formative conditions of space and time.

Notes

1. Jakobson, R., 1990, *On Language*, ed. Linda R. Waugh and Monique Monville-Burston, p. 165, quoting his own writings *Iskusstvo* (Art), 1919, p. 30.
2. Jakobson, 1990, p. 165.
3. Jakobson, 1990, p. 170.
4. Jakobson, 1990, p. 167.
5. Jakobson, 1990, p. 171.
6. Jakobson, 1990, p. 171.
7. Jakobson, 1990, p. 173.
8. Jakobson, 1990, p. 173.
9. Jakobson, 1990, pp. 173–4.

10. Levinson, Stephen C., 1987, *Pragmatics*, p. 73.
11. Cf. CD-i-Form-Word-Time-Drill
12. Levinson, 1987, p. 73.
13. Tedlock, Dennis, 1983, *The Spoken Word and the Work of Interpretation*, p. 195.
14. Tedlock, 1983, p. 195; cf. also CD-i: Form-Word-Space-Drill.
15. Tedlock, 1983, p. 204.
16. Tedlock, 1983, p. 205, quoting Jean-Jacquez Nattiez, 'The Contribution to the Semiotic Discussion In General', p. 132.
17. Tedlock, 1983, p. 205.
18. Tedlock, 1983, p. 207.
19. Tedlock, 1983, p. 207.
20. Tedlock, 1983, p. 214, fn.42 quoting Umberto Eco, *A Theory of Semiotics*, pp. 21, 125, 216, 296.
21. Tedlock, 1983, p. 214.
22. Tedlock, 1983, p. 215.
23. Seeger, Introduction, p. 4, in analogy with the 'speech event'.
24. CD-i: Form-Sound-Time-Skills.
25. In this context 'audience' does not indicate 'listener' but *preksaka* (Skt.), 'watcher' or *rasika* (Skt.), 'taster'.
26. Dr Sanjukta Gupta is one of my teachers of Sanskrit; with her I read parts of the *Natyasastra*.
27. Cf. CD-i: Content-Image-Space-Performer.
28. Cf. CD-i: Content-Image-Space-World.
29. Cf. CD-i: Content-Word-Space-Performer.
30. Cf. CD-i: Content-Word-Space-Performer.
31. Entire passage taken from Presidential Address at the 33rd Annual Conference of the Tamil Isai Sangam, Madras, December 1975, by Smt. T. Balasarasvati. Its translation by Shri S. Guhan was published in several journals, among them *Sangeet Natak*, Journal of the Sangeet Natak Akademi, 1972–3, April–September, 1984, pp. 8–14.
32. In traditional South Indian performing arts, a broad distinction can be made between lyrical (mostly solo) forms and epic (mostly group) forms. Examples of powerful epic theatre are *Kattai Kuttu* (also known as *Teru kuttu*), *Yaksagana*, *Kucipudi*, *Bhagavatamela*, *Kutiyattam*, *Kathakali*; see also Vatsyayan, Kapila, *Traditional Indian Theatre, Multiple Streams*, 1980, National Book Trust, New Delhi.
33. Cf. CD-i: Content-Word-Space-Text.
34. See Balasarasvati's Presidential Address.

35. Jakobson, 1990, p. 111.
36. *Wassily Kandinsky*, réimpression de *XXe Siecle* ,1974, by F. Hasan, 1984, Paris.
37. *Wassily Kandinsky*, 1984, pp. 101–9.
38. Cf. CD-i: Form-Image-Time-Competence.
39. Cf. CD-i: Content-Image-Space, see Text, World and Performer.
40. Cf. CD-i: Content-Sound-Time-Competence.
41. A systematic training in vocal music, melody and rhythm was codified by the saint-singer Sri Purandara Dasa (1484–1564 AD); it is still followed in South India.
42. Savithri Rajan and Michael Nixon, 1982, *Shobillu Saptasvara*, Stree Seva Mandir Press, Madras, 1982, pp. 2–3.
43. *Wassily Kandinsky*, 1984, pp. 27–31.
44. Cf. CD-i: Content-Sound-Space-World.
45. Cf. CD-i: Content-Sound-Space/Performer.
46. Ong, 1982, p. 32.
47. Discussion with Vinita Venkataraman, who is not only a student of *vina* in the Dhanammal school through Smt. T. Brinda, but also an M.Sc. Gold Medallist in Theoretical Physics (Madras University) and a Master in Informatics (Technical University, Eindhoven).
48. Ong, 1982, p. 32; cf. also Bourdieu, 1990b, p. 94.
49. Cf. CD-i: Form-Image-Time-Skills and idem-Space-Drills/Skills.
50. *Natyasastra*, XXVII, *sloka* 1, 2 and 3.
51. Ong, 1982, p. 72.
52. Personal communication with Harry Powers, American ethnomusicologist, on our way to Bala's house in 1975.
53. Ong, 1982, p. 72.

Chapter 6

Form

6.1 Grammars

With the advent of the computer not only has a new technology been triggered off, but also a new reflection on knowledge, its nature and how to understand its workings. Cognitivism depends heavily on the metaphor of the brain as an information-processing computer, and on the presumption that by studying computers we might be able to learn something about ourselves as human beings.[1] Earlier Frank Smith made the counter-proposition of the 'brain as an artist'. Both represent an approach to the elusive and enigmatic 'brain' that gives clear evidence of rule-guided behaviour, only to circumvent the same in seemingly unpredictable and numerous 'exceptions'.

> When reality kicks back (...) cognitivism finds itself being chased up a blind alley. At this point a resurgent interest in philosophy, particularly in epistemological matters, is natural. Ludwig Wittgenstein's philosophy of language is now the height of fashion. (...) A central theme (...) is his desire to remind us of the inner relationship between understanding human actions and understanding forms of artistic expression. Art has an ability to portray indirectly the phenomenon of the "unsayable", to use Wittgenstein's own term.[2]

On its way from the four-dimensional human application to the computer application, *any* design of a knowledge-based system has to plead guilty of serious reductionism. The newly formed knowledge, displayed in new technology, is different from the human condition, and lacks the seamless logic of the real-life situation. Where does this 'fluid, flexible logic' reside, and 'how' does it work? As Göranzon and Josefson remark, 'reality kicks back', and does not allow clean reductionism. As a result new concepts have entered the intellectual arena, such as 'tacit knowledge'. What is 'tacit knowledge', and why is it important to us in our attempt to understand a Tamil text? According to Janik 'tacit knowledge' is 'that very familiarity which tends to lead us to overlook its importance when we are dealing with such "deep" issues as what thinking or knowing is all about'.[3]

In the case of *Bhairavi Varnam* 'knowing' is about 'experiencing', understanding through 'harmonisation', 'beauty' and *mangalam*, 'auspiciousness'; in computer technology it means an adequate design and an efficient program that can reason out, explain and predict all possible variants. The way to this result is paved by a clear (computer-) linguistic logic that is capable of forming and recreating earlier formations of 'information', combining and recombining these elements into ever further generative regularities. These two aims, the real-life Tamil aim and the computer-directed aim, bifurcate at a very early stage. On the one hand, they share initially a certain systematicity of 'grammar' that forms the 'expressive units' of speech. The 'programming' of the human memory is achieved with great effort, attention to detail and minute systematicity. After all, in an oral tradition 'you know what you can recall'.[4] The application of the interiorised knowledge, however, shows great flexibility. Without familiarity with the specific milieu in which the expertise is to be applied it may seem as if a 'virus' has entered the 'life-program'. This 'virus' might well be called 'tacit knowledge'; or, in the terms of Frank Smith, it is the 'successful Fantasy'; or, in the terms of Bourdieu, it is the 'generative principles that are embedded in the habitus'; and finally, in Tamil terms, it is the wisdom of *prayoga*, 'application in the world'. This application is another way of referring to the praxis that is practised in the real-life situation. Thus a way to enter that 'blind spot' of 'tacit knowledge' is to enter the praxis of language as *langage*: 'The increase in interest in apprenticeship training and the humanities' position as a force to counterbalance technological change are two themes that require deeper debate.'[5]

It is at this point that the 'know', 'can' and 'recall' meet. Knowledge in an oral tradition is deeply rooted in both skill and familiarity. Therefore the transition to analytic, programmatic and technological thought is not automatic. Göranzon diagnoses a serious hurdle that is hard to take; he distinguishes three categories of knowledge:

(1) propositional or theoretical knowledge;
(2) skills, or practical knowledge; and
(3) knowledge of familiarity;

and observes that there is 'a clear tendency to overemphasize theoretical knowledge', and that we tend to forget completely the knowledge of familiarity when discussing the nature of knowledge in a philosophical context.[6]

The Tamil situation is just the other way around. Practical knowledge reigns supreme: propositional knowledge entirely inheres in the 'skilful utterance', while taking as its vehicle knowledge of familiarity in order to express itself and make itself felt. As a result, Western scholarship might have run the risk of assuming that people who 'lack theoretical knowledge in given areas also lack any knowledge whatsoever of that particular area'.[7] The inversion of dominance between the propositional and the practical, from the propositional over the practical to the practical over the propositional, has been illustrated several times before by quoting the traditional Tamil view *'ilakkanattukku mun ilakkiyam'*: 'before the markers the marked'.

Göranzon follows Wittgenstein's philosophy of language in stating that 'the rule is built into the action' to express the same idea.[8] The advantages of emphasising practical knowledge over propositional knowledge are in the flexibility of concepts as they inhere their usage. In this vein, Wittgenstein perceives a concept as a *set of activities that follow a rule*, in contrast to regarding the concept as a rule.[9] Another advantage is the retrieval of the dimension *time*, which was lost, according to Bourdieu, in science.[10] The focusing on strategies of practice instead of on universal rules brings back values that were lost in the intellectual focus on the universal alone.[11]

The 'grammar *Tolkappiyam*' may be such an example of an intellectual achievement that works on other linguistic principles. Its three chapters, *Eluttatikaram* ('Chapter on graphemes'), *Colatikaram* ('Chapter on utterance') and *Porulatikaram* ('Chapter on reference'), constitute a 'grammar of usage' (*marapu*) and strategies (*iyal*). *Tol kappiyam*, 'the Ancient Telling', expounds:

(1) *Eluttatikaram*: the usage of sound, followed by the strategies on the birth of sound; the usage of collecting and compiling sound, coupled to the strategies of joining and varying such combinations;
(2) *Colatikaram*: the usage of the formation of speech, coupled to the strategies of declension and its variables, usage of the vocative, and strategies of use of noun, verb and their further specifiers; and
(3) *Porulatikaram*: strategies of reference as 'object-oriented' meaning, and strategies of affecting, comparing, artisanal making (*poiesis*) and idiom.[12]

To take *Tolkappiyam* for a grammar in the positivist sense seems to be a serious mistake. The manner of exposition rejects such an intellectual attitude. To understand this work as a 'grammar of strategies' leaves its message much more freedom of interpretation, but grounds its usage in the shared storehouse of contextual knowledge acquired in practice.

Göranzon distinguishes two types of practice: *routine practice* and *development practice*. In a 'routine practice the rules are closed and can be described in a set of essential and sufficient conditions'. Whereas development practice is 'an activity that is characterized by *open rules*, meaning that their expression admits of a variety of meanings'.[13] In this light it is interesting to look once more at the terminology employed by Tolkappiyanar: both the chapter on graphemes (*Eluttatikaram*) and the chapter on utterance (*Colatikaram*) offer a combination of such closed rules (*marapu*, 'usage', 'routine' practice) and open rules or strategies (*iyal*, 'word', 'discourse', 'development practice'). *Porulatikaram*, the chapter on referential meaning, employs only the term *iyal*; and, indeed, this can be regarded as 'development practice'.

As a result Western Tamil scholarship has almost unanimously dated the text of the *Tolkappiyam* as belonging to different strata in time: the oldest portions, *Eluttu* and *Col*, might go back to the fourth or even fifth century BC, while the chapter on 'meaning', *Porul*, would belong to the fourth century AD.[14] In short, Western scholarship holds it possible that there exists a gap over perhaps eight centuries between the exposition on graphemes and utterance (invariably termed 'Phonology' and 'Morphology' in Western scholarship) and that on reference ('Semantics' in Western translation). This has equally persistently irritated Tamil scholars and experts: 'as if our Tolkappiyanar could not have conceived of such a thing as 'meaning', and made Tamil wait for the Sanskrit *Dharmasastra, Arthasastra, Kamasutra* and Bharata's *Natyasastra* to formulate the meaning of Tamil'.[15]

How to reconcile the two views? The combination of the distinction between *closed* rules and *open* rules, its probable reflection in the Tamil *marapu* and *iyal*, that is 'usage' and 'discourse', as 'routine practices' and 'development practices', plus the fact that the formalisation and anthologisation of the Tamil bardic tradition took place around the fifth century AD,[16] may explain a great deal.

We have seen that closed rules, the so-called routine practice, agree well to codification and description. Thus *marapu* does not change much, and its inscription on to palmleaves in the fourth or fifth century AD may well reflect a situation of centuries ago.[17] In contrast to closed rules, open rules change constantly in unison with the world they refer to. *Iyal* 'discourse' on reference (*porul*) is naturally a true 'development practice' that dwells in the needs of human communication, i.e., in speech situated in a specific time–space continuum. If the specific time of inscription happened to be the fifth century AD then it is only natural that *Porulatikaram* reflects the spirit of that time and milieu. Göranzon continues to argue that open rules cannot be entirely expressed in words. The practice of such rules rather than the rules themselves form the prism in this perspective. It goes without saying that such practices cannot operate in a vacuum, and form part of an entire *habitus*.[18]

6.2 Example

How can a student studying a culture, other than his own, become acquainted with this totalising knowledge? On the level of propositional knowledge and closed rules, representation through description, inscribed in writing, carries a long way. But the routine practice and knowledge of familiarity cannot be stored in the two-dimensional medium of the book. Both are as complex and multi-faceted as the real-life situation. An intellectual focus of attention on the particular, the concrete case or example promises a rich epistemic harvest. According to Johannesen 'It is not only a question of the errors in thinking we make when we focus on the universal. It is also a question of values that are lost through this intellectual attitude.'[19] These values dwell in our usage or practice, they show the way in which we understand something; its rules are 'built into the action'. Practice brings out a fundamental relationship between 'rule' and 'action', namely, 'to master and coordinate actions implies an ability to be part of a practice'.[20]

How to acquire such mastery? In his *Philosophical Investigations* Wittgenstein imagines '... if a person has not yet got the concepts, I should teach him to use the words by means of examples and by practice ...'.[21] Much depends upon the quality of the example, its adequacy and expressivity, and on the quality of the practice. Göranzon remarks

> There are good examples which lead our thoughts in the "right" direction and which refresh our minds, and there are examples that make it impossible to understand the sense of a practice. This cannot be made explicit by means of a formal description. It requires the ability to put forward the essence of a practice through examples that are followed by teaching, by practice.[22]

Practice is in fact a 'tool' to achieve maturity. The essence of practice is 'growth', growth of command into mastery and, finally, into freedom of imagination. Wittgenstein holds that 'If language is to be a means of communication there must be an agreement not only in definitions but also (queer as this may sound) in judgements.[23] This grasp is the grasp of *aucitya* which we introduced earlier.[24] On the one hand it encompasses the mastery of actual conventions, but on the other it involves ingenuity, inventiveness and skill. The preparation for such a command of communication is termed 'road' (Skt. *marga*, Ta. *vali*), and aims to lead the apprentice through a systematic, graded course applied to different activities.

Ideally speaking, the trainings in word (*iyal*), music (*icai*) and mime (*natakam*) are followed side by side. The 'simultaneous synthesis' we referred to earlier is the destination of all three roads. It is therefore not surprising that they share, to a great extent, similar 'stations' along the road of growth to mastery, as well as similar strategies to get there. The main trajectories on the road of apprenticeship are

- **drills**: identification and isolation of 'minimal units';
- **skills**: sequences of such units and their mutual affects (such as euphony);
- **competences**: choice; combinations; variants; mixing; setting – in short, composing;
- **performance**: synthesis; rendering; and
- **interpretation**: freedom of imaginative play within the communicative scope of the utterance.

These graded stages mark the 'essence' of practice. However, they are numb when offered in such abstract terms. It is at this point that the concrete example must take over in order to demonstrate and give a 'feel' of the values that make up the complex and multi-faceted logic of actual practice. Mere description will not do; first of all, it never suffices; secondly, it does not attain any eloquence. The two-dimensional character of writing can not process the four-dimensional information, nor can it synthesise the various activities of word, sound and image.

One of the revolutionary assets of interactive multi-media is the fact they can do both; moreover, they are capable of offering the user a concrete, active example of practice. The example that has been given here on the CD-i is one part of five minutes taken out of the total of thirty minutes that make up *bhairavi varnam*. This example is given as one 'whole' – that is the integral recording, transcription and translation of the five minutes – entitled Performance. Jakobson says that 'from a realistic standpoint language cannot be interpreted as a whole, isolated and scientifically sealed, but it must be viewed as a whole and as a part'.[25] Therefore *Performance* is analysed and made interactively accessible in two parts: as *Form* and as *Content*. The eloquence of this example should be such that the user obtains a fair idea of the structure of the whole as well as an opportunity to enter the formative logic that inheres in the technical practices that constitute the artefact and the referential networks of this particular utterance.[26]

6.3 Application

One of the advantages of drawing practice into the focus of attention is the retrieval of the dimension *time*, and through focusing on the strategies of practice Bourdieu foresaw the return of values that were lost in the intellectual focus on the universal alone.[27] This observation, coupled to the insight of Seeger that the 'General Oral' is a given fact, a phenomenon, whereas the human effort 'Orality' is an intentional attempt, a normenon,[28] should allow us entry into those values that had disappeared from our horizon.

In line with these anticipations, the CD-i analyses the *varnam* throughout the entire program in terms of the three arts, namely, of word, of sound and of image.

On a meta-level this complex artefact is approached from the angle of *formative* knowledge and of *referential* knowledge. These two 'sub-menus', termed *Form* and *Content*, are organised along two axes: that of 'space' and that of 'time'. The logic behind the generic growth of Form is the progression from drills to skills to competence. The logic behind the referential Content is the network of the text woven into the world as articulated by the performer, in short, the progression of Part I: *Habitus*. The interactive user who practises himself by means of the 'application', the CD-i *Bhairavi Varnam*, will acquire a fair amount of both practical knowledge and knowledge from familiarity that prepare him for a confrontation with the 'real life' application of *bhairavi varnam* in performance.

6.3a Strategies of Form

A 'good' example in Göranzon's terms is able to put forward the essence of a practice through examples that are followed by teaching.[29] Teaching a practice evolves through didactic strategies that are made concrete in the process of transmission. The concrete materiality of the teaching can be followed in the CD-i program; here, on paper, we can only outline the systematicity of the strategies followed. The realm of purely material form of word, sound and bodily image attains concretisation through a progressive training. The training allows the adept to enter ever deeper into the materiality of the aim to render the body into a medium of epistemic research and expression.

The first degree of training, that is investigation of the bodies' capacity in the world, is the somatic localisation of word, sound and image. The receptive sensory organs, such as the ear and the eye, are made to identify the contrastive qualities of sound and sight. The productive sensory organs, such as the throat, and various limbs, are forced to identify the place and quality of production of these observations. The throat is trained to produce the sound qualities of the language Tamil[30] as well as the right sound qualities of musical tones.[31] The hands are trained to measure the duration of the sound of words[32] and of rhythm;[33] the entire body is trained to become concrete image: in terms of 'space' the smallest expressive unit is the hand,[34] in terms of 'time' it is the beating of the foot.[35] Once these respective qualitative units have been identified, the didactic strategies of quantification may start. Word, sound and image are trained through trajectories of

- adding
- doubling
- splitting:
  - halving
  - quartering
  - doubling halves
  - doubling quarters
- prefixing accents
- postfixing accents
- stringing
- transforming
- mixing

The training of musical notes, rhythm and abstract image make, in addition use of the devices of repetition in three tempi (slow, middle and fast) as well as repetition to and fro. In observing, or, perhaps even practising with, the CD-i program these main strategies and substrategies should be followed with the agglutinative character of the Tamil language in mind.[36]

6.3b Strategies of Mimesis

The importance of the endeavour 'mimesis', or *natya* will be discussed further on. What matters here is the graded training of the body in order to be able to become a sign. The ancient *Natyasastra* (Skt. 'Guidelines for Mimesis') identifies bodily representation (Skt. *angika*) as threefold: that of the limbs (Skt. *sarira*), that of the face (Skt. *mukhaja*) and that of the entire body (Skt. *cestakrta*).[37] A seemingly unending enumeration of subdivisions into major limbs, minor limbs, ways of moving, postures, combinations and various types of gaits are described, with indications of a practice that incorporates all these elements. The nature of this information makes the *Natyasastra* into a text that is almost unreadable; it substantiates the argument, that writing is good only for propositional statements and for codification.

The CD-i demo allows a glimpse into the training of the minor limb (Skt. *upanga*) 'hand',[38] thus underlining the need for media other than writing to represent practice and the values that inhere in its enactment. The basic strategy followed in the training of mimesis is repetition of the patterns of action agreed upon by tradition. Mastery of these patterns does not result in mechanical reproduction: on the contrary, continued practice brings about a type of freedom that is capable of dealing in a creative manner with unforseen circumstances. According to Janik rule-following activity may originate in rote behaviour, but it terminates in creative activity. It is essentially creative.[39] In the words of Balasarasvati:

> ... a dancer has only to submit herself willingly to discipline. It will be difficult in the beginning to conform to the demands and discipline of rhythm and melody and to the norms and codes of the tradition. But if she humbly submits to the greatness of this art, soon enough she will find joy in that discipline and she will realise that discipline makes her free in the joyful realm of the art.
>
> *The greatest authorities on the dance have definitely recognised that it is the orthodoxy of traditional discipline which gives the fullest freedom to the individual creativity of the dancer.*
>
> Young dancers who go in for novelties will find that their razzle-dazzle does not last long. On the other hand, if they hold firm to the tradition, which like the Great Banyan tree strikes deep roots and spreads wide branches, they will gain for themselves and those who

watch them the dignity and joy of Bharata Natyam. I come out with these submissions only because of my anxiety that they should realise this. The young will recognise the greatness of this art if they study it with intense participation, calmly and without haste. One has to begin early and learn it for many years to reach a devout understanding of the immanent greatness of this art. Then comes the recognition of one's great good fortune in being chosen to practise this art; this recognition leads the dancer to surrender herself to her art. Such surrender makes her aware of the divinity and wholeness of Bharata Natyam. And the art will continue to flourish without the aid of new techniques which aim at "purifying" it or changes in dress, ornament, make-up and the interpolation of new items which seek to make it more "complete". This is my prayer.[40]

This much of attention is given to Balasarasvati's feelings on practice because she voices the perennial treasurehouse of values that are surmised in contemporary Western discourse on praxis. However, her *pointe* is that rules inhere in active discipline; they do not exist away from practice.[41] To imagine that 'rules stipulate, and application follows' is to put the cart before the horse.[42] Rules are hardly to be distinguished from the behaviour through which they are constituted. As a result, firstly, there exist no 'abstract rules' and secondly, to propose rules and force a practice accordingly (which is the case of the razzle-dazzle Bala refers to) is an impotent mission.

Janik proposes that, 'basically, rule-following has a peculiar internal order which is determined by our natural history, i.e. by our being the kind of creature we are'.[43] This is again the scope that belongs to the discussion on 'tacit knowledge'. Within this broad horizon we have just discussed the growth of skills into mastery as one centripetal focus of tacit knowledge, stored in the body. The other realm of tacit knowledge is even more intimately embedded in somatic reality, namely the knowledge by acquaintance or familiarity that results from sensuous experience. Western scholarship sets out to describe the knowledge one knows by experience. But 'if we think of the difference between smelling or hearing and describing what we smell or hear, the smell of coffee or the sound of a clarinet we discover that it is not possible to *begin* to describe any such experiences in such a way that people who had not themselves experienced them could recognize them'.[44] Janik states further that 'to have had these experiences and to have reflected upon them – which is what most of us normally, and philosophers *never*, do – is to realize that we do not have to be able to describe them to understand them'.[45] Once more, this type of knowledge, the subtle distinctions between the sound of the oboe and that of a clarinet must be attributed to acquired skill.

The original question *enta prayogam* 'What's the use?' of a scholarship that is fully aimed at description becomes more clear now. According to a contrastive 'episteme of performance'[46] knowledge as understanding is convincing only as a skill that is capable of evoking the original experience. For this reason both *Tolkappiyam* and the *Natyasastra* devote a great amount of attention to the training in affect. The emotive use of the body is a matter of skill and expertise: on the one hand, its know-how and sensitivity are compared with the process of cooking, whereby the resulting understanding is one of *rasa* of 'tasting', or, on the other hand with the process of painting, in which *materia* is affected by the colour of paint. The experienced audience is at one and the same time the canvas that absorbs the colours in the process of painting and the taster (Skt. *rasika*) who savours the delicate combinations and crescendo of taste.[47]

The philosopher Strawson wonders what an epistemology would be like that would not be based upon the comparison between the mind and the eye, but, say, upon that of mind and ear;[48] to stretch this imaginative reflection further, what would an epistemology be like that would be based upon the harmonisation between mind and the senses? This is in fact the task that Indian grammars of performance have posed themselves. By relying on propositional knowledge (Skt. *sastra*, Ta. *nul*) that is embedded in concrete praxis (Skt. *marga*, Ta. *vali* and also *varalaru*) the training in the grammars of word, sound and image ensures a physical base and point of reference for all three types of knowledge: propositional, practical and knowledge of familiarity. Graded application (Skt. *prayoga*) yields command over the implicit 'tacit knowledge' and a mastery that results in the freedom of imagination and creative activity.

Janik sees the idea of an algorithm for a piano sonata as epistemologically absurd as well as aesthetically abhorrent.[49] For him, the ultimate beauty of the attraction of the music must remain hidden to remain attractive. Not so, from'the angle of the 'performance episteme'. It is well known that actors, especially in the school of Stanislavsky, were utterly skilled in portraying and

Form 155

evoking emotions in the audience. The Indian attitude to *rasa* 'taste, tasting' is as pragmatic as it is meticulously systematic. Taking the body for the seat of knowledge and the ground of practice, *Natyasastra* sets out first to analyse the various emotional 'tastes' (Skt. *rasa*) as well as the underlying emotional 'states-of-being' (Skt. *bhava*) and the processes that build up the inescapable affect of 'tasting'. Both epic and lyrical mimesis pay detailed attention to the training of the body to express these different states-of-being and the processes that connect cause and affect. The natural progression that culminates in *rasa* is imagined as shown in Fig.10.

It will be clear that this schematic representation of the processes of affect will need a concrete content in order to become effective. The Tamil term for *rasa* is *meyppatu* 'affecting the body', and it needs a setting of at least one sender and receiver to achieve this 'interactive touch'. The dynamics of the formation of

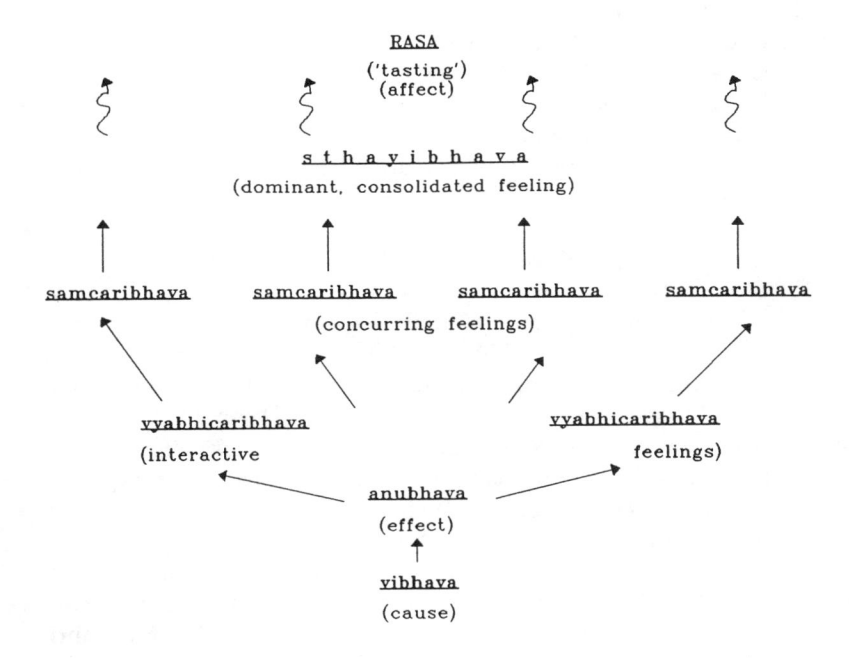

```
                            RASA
                         ('tasting')
                          (affect)

                        sthayibhava
                (dominant, consolidated feeling)


    samcaribhava    samcaribhava    samcaribhava    samcaribhava
                           (concurring feelings)


              vyabhicaribhava         vyabhicaribhava
              (interactive                feelings)
                              anubhava
                              (effect)
                              vibhava
                              (cause)
```

Figure 10 – the process of affect

'meaning' have been outlined now; the next step is a *content* that can supply these dynamics with 'body' and 'critical mass'.

Notes

1. Göranzon, Bo and Josefson, Ingela (eds), 1988, *Knowledge, Skill and Artificial Intelligence*, Springer Verlag, Heidelberg, p. 4.
2. Göranzon and Josefson, 1988, p. 4.
3. A. Janik, 'Tacit Knowledge, Working Life and Scientific Method', in: Göranzon and Josefson, 1988, p. 54.
4. Ong, 1982, pp. 33–7.
5. Göranzon and Josefson, 1988, p. 5.
6. Göranzon, 'The Practice of the Use of Computers. A Paradoxical Encounter between Different Traditions of Knowledge', in: Göranzon and Josefson, 1988, p. 17.
7. Göranzon and Josefson, 1988, p. 17.
8. Göranzon and Josefson, 1988, p. 11.
9. Göranzon and Josefson, 1988, p. 11.
10. Bourdieu, 1990a, p. 9.
11. Göranzon and Josefson. 1988, pp. 15–17.
12. I am *solely* responsible for this somewhat idiosyncratic translation.
13. Göranzon and Josefson, 1988, p. 15.
14. Cf. for example Zvelebil, K. V., 1973, pp. 143–4.
15. This feeling was expressed with great vehemence by my teacher of Tamil prosody, Pulavar R. Kannan.
16. Cf. Zvelebil, K. V., 1974, pp. 28 ff. 'Periodisation of Tamil Literature', 'Problems of Relative and Absolute Chronology'.
17. In 1978 the oldest *nagasvara vidvan* of Tiruvarur (Shri T. Natarajasundara Pillai, then around 90 years old) firmly maintained 'marapu mār ṟalla': '*marapu* does not change'.
18. Göranzon and Josefson, 1988, p. 15, Göranzon: '... it is important to emphasize the intersubjective aspects of following rules in a practice. It is logically impossible to be the only person following a rule. A single practice can therefore not be seen as a logical place for dialogue and shared action.'.
19. Göranzon and Josefson, 1988, p. 11, quoting Kjell Johanessen, 1988, *Tyst Kunskap: om regel och begrepp*. Research Report,

Swedish Centre for Working Life, Stockholm.
20. Göranzon and Josefson, 1988, p. 11.
21. Göranzon and Josefson, 1988, p. 11, quoting Wittgenstein, 1953, *Philosophical Investigations*, Oxford, Blackwell, p. 201.
22. Göranzon and Josefson, 1988, p. 11.
23. Göranzon and Josefson, 1988, quoting Wittgenstein, 1953, *Philosophical Investigations*, p. 242.
24. See Performer, p. 95.
25. Jakobson, 1990, p. 112.
26. For description, cf. CD-i Help function.
27. Bourdieu, 1990a, pp. 5–9.
28. For discussion cf. Seeger, Introduction, p. 4.
29. Göranzon and Josefson, 1988, p. 11; cf. also p. 172.
30. Cf. CD-i: Form-Word-Space-Drill.
31. Cf. CD-i: Form-Sound-Space-Drill.
32. Cf. CD-i: Form-Word-Time-Drill.
33. Cf. CD-i: Form-Sound-Time-Drill. The CD-i WORM ('Write One Read Many') was completed in December 1994. When I showed this disc in Madras during the Music and Dance season (mid December to Mid January) several musicians objected to the way the *anga kakapatam* was demonstrated. This rhythm figure is very rare and personally I have never seen it being used anywhere by anyone, so I took the description from P. Sambamoorthy's *South Indian Music*, Book I, tenth edition p. 40. Sambamoorthy was also considered to be wrong but no consensus was reached about what should have been the correct form of *kakapatam*.
34. Cf. CD-i: Form-Image-Space-Drill.
35. Cf. CD-i: Form-Image-Time-Drill.
36. Cf. Kersenboom, S., 1994, 'Markers and Marked, The Language of Indian Dance', *The Encyclopedia of Language and Linguistics*, Pergamon Press, Oxford, p. 365.
37. *Natyasastra*, Ch.VIII–XIII.
38. Cf. CD-i: Form-Image-Space-Drill/Skill/Competence. On seeing the progression *hasta-mudra-abhinaya* Shri K. Ramiah our present *nattuvanar* commented that the Tamil terms *pinti* for single hand and *pinaiyal* for both hands would have been more correct.
39. Göranzon and Josefson, 1988, p. 57.
40. From Bala's presidential address.
41. Cf. also Conclusion, p. 227.

42. Cf. also Janik, in: Göranzon and Josefson, 1988, p. 57.
43. Göranzon and Josefson, 1988, p. 57.
44. This position is also taken in Indian aesthetics: basically *rasa*, 'tasting' is a process rooted in 'memory'. The 'tasting' of 'existence or beingness' (Skt. *satyam*) draws on a so-called '*yogic* memory', i.e. remembering the source from which one came.
45. Cf. also Chapter Orientation, pp. 175–5.
46. Cf. also Conclusion, pp. 233–4.
47. *Natyasastra*, Ch.XXVII, 50–8, gives an outline of the 'ideal' spectator: 'those of character, high birth, quiet behaviour and learning, desirous of fame, virtue, impartial, advanced in age, proficient in drama in all its six limbs, alert, honest, unaffected by passion, expert in playing the four kinds of musical instruments, very virtuous, acquainted with costumes and make-up, rules of regional languages, the four kinds of histrionic representation, grammar, prosody, and various *Sastras*, experts in different arts and crafts, with a fine sense of *rasa* and *bhava*, they should be made spectators in witnessing drama. Anyone with unruffled senses, honest, expert in the discussion of pro's and con's, detector of faults and appreciating merits, can be a spectator of drama. He who becomes glad when seeing a person glad, sorry when seeing sorrow, miserable on seeing misery, he is fit to be a spectator in drama. All these various qualities are not known to exist in one single spectator. Hence, because the objects of knowledge are so numerous, and the span of life so brief, the inferior, common person in an audience that consists of superior, middling and inferior members, cannot be expected to appreciate the performance of superior ones. Hence anyone who recognises a particular dress, profession, speech and action as his own, is considered fit for appreciating the same.' This very pragmatic outline for 'aesthetics of reception' continues to describe the distinctive features of the superior, middle and inferior types of critics.
48. Göranzon and Josefson, 1988, p. 56.
49. Cf. Fig.10 for the process of affect. Although this process seems to have been made accessible and controllable, it is not. Earlier we discussed two types of success (cf. p. 139), human success (Skt. *manusi*) and divine (Skt. *daiviki*); the first can be manipulated to some extent, the second cannot.

Chapter 7

Content

7.1 Semiosis

The schematic representation of the process of affect can be understood also as the structure of semiosis. The aim of the signalling sign is to create an impact, or, in other terms 'meaning'. How this is achieved is not a one-to-one relationship, but traverses several stages of affectation. Again, these propositions seem meaningless without a clear application in an example. The best example at hand, here, is the *performance* stored in the CD-i demo; the Tamil line 'mōṭi ceyyalāmō eṉ cāmi metta' forms a rich testcase for the above scheme. The fact that these words are repeated sixteen-and-a-half times gives away the complex character of its meaning. The argument gains by analysing the line in full:

> mōhamāṇa eṉmītil nī inta vēḻaiyil /
> mōṭi ceyyalāmō eṉ cāmi metta //

The first half of the *pallavi* sets off immediately with the cause of the utterance: *moha* 'intoxication, confusion' by love is the pressing urgency of the entire event. As a cause (*vibhava*) it effects the inner affliction of the heart, the mind and the body (*anubhava*). Cast in this state, the Subject reaches out into the world searching for an adequate response. The answer is not a response to her plight, but an interaction with her senses of perception: her nose, ears, eyes and skin are touched by signs of infatuation living outside her suffering body. This interaction between her searching body and the sensory perception of outer signs is the question-and-answer movement of *vy-abhi-cari-bhava* ('out-to-moving-feeling'). The signs that function as messenger of love can take many shapes, each telling their own story. This is the realm of seemingly endless associations, almost open semiosis, of the themes of love: the blooming of the lotus, calling to mind the unfolding of love; its strong perfume, attracting the bees humming eagerly and descending into its heart. The twittering of birds evoking the image of their love-play and inseparable faithfulness. The touch of the cool breeze in the rustling leaves echoes the cooling, tender touch of her lover. The brilliant rays of the moon, tormenting her while she tries to sleep, tossing from one side to the other, resemble the fiery arrows of the god of love. The confluence of associations (*sam-cari-bhava* 'together-coming-feeling') is overwhelming.

The poetic strength of an interpreter lies in this 'treasure house' of improvisations; it enabled the dancer T. Balasarasvati to extend the presentation of the first half of the *anupallavi* (*Nagarikamana tirunakaril vacare*) to half an hour. The result of this piling up of emotional impact is the emergence of a dominant feeling that is to stay for some time (*sthayi-bhava* 'standing feeling'). In the case of the first half of the *pallavi*, this dominant feeling is the vulnerability due to the intoxication by love: at the end of the improvisations we see the heroine growing weaker owing to lack of sleep, lack of appetite and lack of concentration: she literally is consumed by love.

The second half of the *pallavi* stands in sharp contrast to the first mood: although afflicted and weakened by love, her heart is full optimism and expectation, singing its love-declaration in the ascendant, major scale of *raga bhairavi*;[1] the words 'mōṭi ceyyalāmō' [[or] *moti ceyyalamo*] strike the ear with their melancholy set in the descending minor scale. And, indeed the same route of cause and effect is followed in her experience of disappointment and deep uncertainty. The dominant feeling that results from this trajectory is one of deep desolation and wondering what to do. Four lines of the *varnam* develop their semiosis along this pattern, while the second half of the *varnam* 'hammers' the message in by various rhythmical emphases which cannot be dealt with here, as a result of lack of space in which to offer concrete examples. The dominant mood throughout the entire *varnam* is *moha* 'love, infatuation, intoxication', that gradually blossoms into the full extent of *srngara rasa*, the 'erotic sentiment'.[2] The lyrical temperament of the *varnam* and its emotive rendering are meant gradually to overwhelm the audience, ineluctably transforming their perception into the actual experiencing of love.

7.2 Suggestion

The technique of opening up the treasure-house of imagination is called *kurippu* (Ta. 'gesture, sign').[3] By means of gesturing, different times and spaces are evoked in the audience by the performer. The evocative power of the gesture depends heavily on recognition, shared memory, shared judgements and shared fantasy; therefore, it is rooted in shared references, and makes familiar objects the vehicle of the message. The 'object-oriented' character of meaning as *porul* can be ascribed to this logic.

The flow of *samcaribhava*'s 'concurring feelings' bestows a real-life presence on images from the past and eternity. In skilful suggestion the icon and symbol come to life. The performer feels free to 'quote' from other texts, other performances, other times, other places, almost without discrimination as long as it works. Her freedom substantiates the 'live-character' of the weave, the *textus* that is woven out of as well as into the world by her action.

Part I *Habitus* was organised according to this logic, and formed the model for the sub-program Content of the CD-i demo. The real confrontation with the challenge of representing 'tacit knowledge' becomes clear in the attempt to program the referential content of a speech event or speech artefact. The two conditions for concretisation of 'meaning', namely, *space* and *time*, reveal their real demand on all three levels of knowledge: the design of the program as well as the 'indexing' of the data-entries[4] requires propositional knowledge; to supply visual and auditory examples is akin to practical knowledge; but the selection of examples, their presentation in word, sound and image, requires intimacy with the original field. As this Compact Disc is a demonstration disc, the time available for each *index* point has been very much limited (mostly to 60 sec.) and has remained uni-layered; one could imagine a situation where the user could open up auditory, visual and textual 'files' behind the various details that make up one *index* point. For the moment, the challenge has proved to be difficult enough.

The condition *space* was analysed and suggested to the user in terms of *Text, World, Performer*, envisaging the 'Text' of 'word', 'sound' and 'image' as a 'given' that takes its full shape in the functional context of its world only through the actual rendering by a performer. The condition *time* was analysed and suggested to the user in terms of the 'temporal quality' of the Sign. The levels *Text, World, Performer* represent here the tenses of *past, potentialis* and *present*. The text level of 'word', 'sound' and 'image' in terms of 'time' is the proof of the effort to 'arrest' time, to preserve a precious moment. Such efforts usually take the shape of 'stills', of 'frozen documents' that help memory to restore its original beauty in a future event. In other words, the text is a monument of the past, and has no present-tense value unless it is committed to the present-tense experience by means of application, that is, performance. This commitment is in alignment with the *generalis*, the *potentialis* of the sign as it exists, existed and will exist in the world. In terms of time the text is a man-made inscription, the world its scope of meaning, whereas the performer is its actual, live articulation. In terms of the Sign, the text is the *icon*, the world the entire *symbol*, and the performer the *index*, absorbing and signalling all three levels, tenses and aspects. Together they form the fertile ground of 'incremental time', putting to use the past and generating the future possibilities.

Suggestion, *kurippu*, tries to do just that: in the form of a corporeal gesture, sharing time and space with its audience, it signals past, *potentialis* and present, making them happen *now*.

7.3 Mime

Applying the icon and symbol to an indexical event means to bring (Skt. *ni-, naya-*) their 'feel' towards (Skt. *abhi-*) the 'other', the audience. This is concrete, mimetic expression termed *abhinaya*, which is not the same as 'translation'; it is the cumulative rendering of a line that allows a central focus of feeling to emerge to the foreground of imagination.[5] This 'pivotal focus' or 'centre of gravity' is also termed *karuttu*, 'genius', and results in the sharing and tasting of the event.[6]

The rendering of a line in *abhinaya* depends on imagination and the capacity to penetrate in the 'genius' of its portent. Therefore the paraphrase of *bhairavi varnam* given below is not a translation of the actual words of the line, nor a translation of one application of mime: it is a free improvisation in prose of possible renderings of the *varnam*.

mōhamāna enmītil nī inta vēḷaiyil[7]

A miracle of love swells in my heart, it carries me away, I am totally absorbed in you; you fill every single minute.

My heart aches, my mind reels, all because of you, day and night.

The lotus of my heart opens to you, like a flower in full bloom, awaiting the honeybees as eager to enjoy the pollen as the love birds cooing and joining with their mate.

A cool breeze touches me gently like the gentle touch of my lover, like his tender kiss on my cheek.

The moon cascades all over me – its fire must be Kama's arrows, they hit me here and there, without mercy; sleep won't come to me now.

Drowning in the intoxication of love my body fades away.

mōṭiceyyalāmō en cāmi metta[8]

Irritation?. Please, do not allow this to yourself; after all, you are the one who is my lord, my very beloved !

Indifferently you turn away from me, not even willing to set your eyes upon me. How can that be, my love, when faced with so much tender affection?

Allow me to take your hand? Oh: you pull away, my heart misses a beat, overflowing with love; what does it mean?

Look, the beautiful moon has risen; this is the time for lovers to meet. But you close your window, shutting me out, alone.[9]

The heavy perfume of the blossoms of jasmine – carefully chosen, strung with affection into a beautiful garland, please accept this. You lay it aside? I cannot believe this.

Sandal perhaps? Putting great effort into grinding sandal into a soft, perfumed paste, mixing it, moulding it, I offer to apply its cooling touch to your skin. You avoid my hand. Why? What is wrong?

Mother cow, your goodness oozes out, taking the form of milk. Fresh milk, mixed with fine herbs poured out to drink: even this purity you refuse? Why, my Lord? I no longer understand; what am I to do?

nākarīkamāṉa tirunakaril vācarē[10]

The holy realm of Tiruvarur is where you reside since time immemorial.

Sophistication is throughout the hallmark of this splendorous town.

In this region dotted with temples, the towers of the grand temple of Tiruvarur – where Shri Tyagaraja dwells with Shri Nilotpalambal at his side – are the largest and reach for the sky.

Kamalalayam, the deep, wide pond of the temple, is ever filled with water dotted with lotuses.[11]

Women of all ages, young and mature, with beautiful large bright eyes, play and live there. They adorn themselves, true to their auspicious marital status.

Hey, my friends, come, let us go and fetch water from the temple tank. Look, there's some moss on the surface of the water;[12] remove it gently and pluck a blossoming lotus (for our *puja* room at home, or to adorn our hair). How crystal-clear is the water and how rich, sufficient surely for all our pots. Take it freely and carry it home.

Those who have mastered the secrets of the four Vedas, who carry the holy thread, flock together in the temple to go through the stories of old.

Full of love for the threefold Tamil, the poet-saints recite, sing and dance the auspicious Tamil.

The famous, huge temple-chariot of Tiruvarur carries Shri Tyagarajasvami and his spouse through the holy town. Innumerable devotees pull, with great effort, the awesome wooden structure; others try to catch a glimpse of the divine pair. The air resounds with the sound of the loud *nagasvaras* and the thunderous drums.[13] What a miracle indeed!

Pōkatyākēcā anupōkam ceyya vā kiṭṭe[14]

Oh Great Lord, Linga, Shiva, I beg you: come here, to me.

Auspicious Shiva seated on the bull, your embrace I humbly request.

Beautiful Lord, resplendent one, adorned by the earrings strung together out of chrysanthemum flowers, resting on a throne covered with flowers, please accept my garland in return for yours.

Mysterious One, carrying the moon and the river Ganga in your hair, didn't you tie your tresses into a knot and set out to roam about in the world, besmeared with dust and sacred ashes as a mendicant?

Great Shiva Nataraja, holding the deer in one hand, and the *damaru* drum in the other, you dance your cosmic dance in the ring of fire, burning out all impurity.[15]

Oh Profound One, when the sages challenged you in the *Daruvana* wood, you silenced them all by conquering the tiger, ripping off its skin and wearing it as your garment.

Oh Pleasing One, Delight of Vishnu's heart, abiding right there, you dance your silent dance, carried by his breathing chest; please, Lord, come to delight me too!

recollection

As your very own you embraced me. That splendour I think of daily, withering away, my mind searching, seeking you, attached greatly. Inside me everything trembles, now half a minute becomes an aeon. The sweetness of your lips, that you must give, now is the right moment, *Sarasa, Satgunane*.

Māraṉ kaṇaikaḷ tūvurāṉ caramāriyāy

The god with bow and arrows aims at me and shoots one arrow after the other; how can I protect myself?

Aiming at me he takes one flowery arrow and another and another, shooting with precision.

As he prepares his bow, arrows start to descend from everywhere like a cloud pouring its rain. My poor body is trembling all over, fever affects my limbs, where can I hide?

ear

In the mango-grove nightingales are singing; they seem to be everywhere, tormenting my poor ears with the sound of their call. Now what am I to do?

skin

The leaves rustle in the cool breeze, the evening is still young; the moon has not even fully set, nor do the stars twinkle at their best. Now you must please come to embrace me, without delay – my strength is ebbing away.

eyes

The bright rays of the moon are as unbearable as cinders I can no longer suffer this: my longing for an amorous union makes my heart swell.[16]

merger

> Lord of Lords
> daily praised,
> Lord of the Excellent,
> praised by the sages,
> Lord of the World,
> Playing in the endless Expanse,
> Bestowing grace on your devotees,
> Unknown to Hari and Aiyan,
> Living in the spotless worlds,
> Fulfilling all wishes,
> Holy Tyagesha,
> Residing in the realm of Kailasa,
> me indeed, to embrace, come,
>   NOW.

Notes

1. Cf. CD-i-Content-Sound-Space-Text.
2. Cf. *Habitus*, fn. 169, as well as Conclusion pp. 231–2.
3. DED 1533, kuṛippu 'intention, gesture, summary, mark, sign'.
4. Each information point was analysed and built up in a quadrilateral compound: Index-title, Information-content, Information-representation, Medial Form (i.e. media) of representation.
5. Note the implication of the term *abhi-ni-*, *abhinaya* 'bringing towards', presuming a receiver, whereas 'expression' does not imply such interactivity.

6. DED 1078, karuttu 'design, purpose, opinion, attention, desire, judgement, mind, will'.
7. Gradual focus on 'mōha'.
8. Gradual focus on 'mōṭi'.
9. This variant was not taught to me by Nandini but taken from the film 'Bala' by the Indian cineast Satyajit Ray.
10. Gradual elaboration of *'tirunakaril'*.
11. The temple tank of Tiruvarur is one of the largest in South India, and famous for its ever-present water.
12. Cf. CD-i: Content-Image-Space-Text.
13. Cf. CD-i: Content-Image-Space-World and CD-i: Content-Time-Performer.
14. Increasing focus on *'Tyakeca'*.
15. In the early morning of the Arudra festival, which is named after its star Arudra (Orion), the image of *Shri Nataraja* is taken out of the sanctum and carried in procession through the temple precincts and around the village or town; cf. CD-i: Content-Image-Space-World. This circumambulation cleanses the entire space of the impurities of the 'dark half' of the year (Skt. *daksinayana*) and clears the way for the 'bright half' of the year that starts a little later (Skt. *uttarayana*).
16. In older times, the word *manam* might have read *sthanam* 'chest, breast' which would make the translation 'makes my breast heave'. Such changes were voluntarily made by traditional dancers and choreographers, in tune with the times they were living in; but the new textual purists claim that the 'authenticity' of the text must be respected at all costs. This issue arose in the latter half of the 1980s; whereas by then the authentic performers had dwindled to a handful of very old experts who are hardly ever consulted!

Part III

Representation

Chapter 8

Orientation

> We have direct experience of reality but indirect knowledge of it. Reality bumps up against us, impinges upon us, yet until we have found a way representing that reality, it remains impervious to thought, only those portions of reality which are capable of being represented can affect us.
> – C. S. Peirce[1]

Part III 'Representation' is concerned with the relationship between the *representation of knowledge* and its world. *Episteme*, use and strategies determine the concrete sign that represents human knowledge. These are deeply rooted in the cultural milieu that they serve and therefore they live crucially different lives, taking strikingly different forms. Without attributing 'superior' or 'inferior' qualities to these different ways of representing knowledge, Part III outlines their mutual incompatibility when interpreted without critical reflection.

Foucault traces the bifurcation of the 'ancient sign' into a 'natural' sign and a 'conventional, man-made' sign from the seventeenth century onwards. 'It is the man-made sign that draws the dividing-line between man and animal; that transforms imagination into voluntary memory, spontaneous attention into reflection, and instinct into rational knowledge.'[2] Brodsky voices this argument even more energetically '. . . by itself reality isn't worth a damn. It is perception that promotes reality to meaning (. . .) Refinement and sensitivity are imparted to such a person by the only source of their supply: by culture, by civilization whose main tool is language.'[3] This is the 'fantasy that works'; because it has been committed to form, to concrete representation it has become accessible to thought.[4] How can we be sure that it does not stay and live only there; how can we assume that there exists an 'organic' relationship between our precious representations of reality and reality itself ? We cannot –

171

there is no guarantee whatsoever but for belief: either belief in 'the pure and simple connection between what signifies and what is signified', or in 'the ideology to serve as its foundation and philosophical justification'. Both beliefs are a matter of culture or custom. Applying the notion of 'culture is a performing art' to the representation of reality we can balance two praxes of 'reality': (1) a 'general, physical' reality (the 'phenomenon') and (2) a 'specialised, cultural' reality (the 'normenon'), on several pairs of 'scales':

1 *Occurrence* – 'general reality' is to our present knowledge, unfathomable existence, by approximation called 'universal'; cultural reality occurs within it.
2 *Provenience* – 'general reality' is, for us, a given fact; cultural reality is man-made.
3 *Identity* – 'general reality' is unique; cultural reality is multiplex: there are as many particular cultural realities as there are distinct structures, since each structure defines its own cultural reality.
4 *Continuity* – 'general reality' is a continuum without known beginning or end; cultural reality is a continuum that varies infinitely among various structures and has as many beginnings and endings as there are instances of it.
6 *Measurability* – 'general reality' cannot be measured by norms of its own that are evident to humans without human attribution; cultural reality is constituted by norms of praxes that are transmitted from one generation to the other.

These scales are derived from the discussion of musical time and 'general, physical' time, but can be extended to the evaluation of 'natural' form and created form, to 'natural' sound and human language and melody, to 'general, physical' reality and man-made, cultural reality. Seeger's postulation that a one-to-one correspondence between the 'general, physical' and the 'man-made, cultural' is not tenable, pertains to all four examples.[5] It demands a thorough reflection on the nature of representation as well as an 'analysis of knowledge itself'.[6]

Indian thought has been deeply concerned with such epistemological questions.[7] Human birth is seen as a condition that is constantly being determined by Form and Concept;[8] it occurs within a physical reality that actively fragments into innumerable lives conditioned by various organic qualities.[9] These processes are propelled by the pulse of its breath, that goes cyclically through the movements of 'sprouting', 'maintaining' and 'dissolving'.[10] Human imagination dwells within this 'pulse' and deploys its energy via five 'armours of cognition':[11]

- *kala* – limiting, manifesting partially;
- *vidya* – imagined knowledge;
- *raga* – affection, interest, discrimination;
- *kala* – coordinates of space and time; and
- *niyati* – 'bent': chance and necessity.

These five take their physical seat in the five senses and instil their logic into the organs of cognition and of action[12] in the interaction of these ten organs with the ten subtle and gross elements of physical reality.[13] Together the physical *materia* and the physical pulse constitute the bipolar process of the evolution and involution of Existence. In the course of evolution Existence enters into ever further fragmenting procreation, whereas the entire fanning out into form is reabsorbed in a concentrated remainder that contains all potentialities.[14] The outward force is imagined as *maya sakti* 'power of conditioning', whereas the inward force is termed *cit sakti* 'power of consciousness'.

How does human knowledge relate to these 'cosmic realities'? In this scheme, the place of human knowledge, objectivity and representation are clear: they are 'illusory', based and coloured by discrimination, subject to space–time coordinates, chance and necessity, and their capacity to reveal is only limited. Nevertheless, they share in 'power', *sakti*, that potent principle that permeates the entire Existence – whether in involution or evolution. Even though human existence is characterised by limitation (and therefore sorrowful), it forms part of a trajectory that encompasses all and that continues to exist even beyond Form and Concept. The signs of knowledge are finite in a similar way, stretching into the infinite. The human shape and its partial signs are a chance, an opportunity to open up the space of 'experiencing' beyond representation. Maybe the Indian tenet *sat-cit-ananda* 'Being-Consciousness-Bliss' that the involutory *cit-sakti* ('power of consciousness') brings about, moving beyond representation, is echoed in the poetic essay *'Las Meninas'* (orig.

'Les Suivantes') that introduces *Les mots et les choses*. Foucault observes in his description of Velasquez's painting

> But there, in the midst of this dispersion which it is simultaneously grouping together and spreading out before us, indicated compellingly from every side, is an essential void: the necessary disappearance of that which is its foundation (. . .). This very subject (. . .) has been elided. And representation, freed finally from the relation that was impeding it, can offer itself as representation in its pure form.[15]

What connects the ancient, circular sign, the arbitrary, conventional signs, and even the open space of the essential void, is not a 'concept' nor a 'form' but a certain 'power'. 'Fantasy that works', 'arbitrariness measured by function', '*Sacer Ludus* that leaves behind *Beatitudo*' and the Indian *ilakkiyam* spreading 'auspiciousness': all these signs share some power, some fascination because they are felt 'to work'. The questions 'how' and 'to what extent' are of less importance than the fact that they work for mankind, that they do have an impact on human existence.

This impact can be studied. A new test of the value of a particular knowledge representation might envisage testing its interaction with its world instead of its empirical relation to 'truth'. Such study is first and foremost a study of how knowledge is acquired, represented and used. Questions regarding the strategies of acquiring knowledge as well as the way in which to represent it, concern the *episteme* and *medium* of knowledge, its *codification* that forms part of an actual *praxis*, and the *form* of the *representation* as it is used in the *habitus* of knowledge. Seen from this perspective each Sign representing human knowledge is a miniature *expert system*, launched into the world to be used in terms of human culture. In terms of expert systems, the program of such a 'Sign' must contain: (1) a knowledge base which contains the representation of domain-specific knowledge; and (2) an inference engine which performs the reasoning.[16]

In terms of the Humanities we may understand immediately data and their analytic presentation as the knowledge base, and theory as the inference engine which performs the reasoning. Ringland and Duce admit that 'deeper representation of the domain (cf. *habitus*: SK) in terms of spatial, causal or temporal models is avoided, but these are problems that a general knowledge representation system cannot side-step'.[17] Which are the criteria for a workable expert system that maintains a fruitful relationship with its users and their world?

DEMANDS for a workable expert-system:

1 **Expressive adequacy**: is a particular knowledge representation scheme sufficiently powerful? What knowledge can and cannot particular schemes represent?
2 **Reasoning Efficiency**: what is the trade-off between expressive adequacy and reasoning efficiency?
3 **Primitives**: What are the primitives (if any) in a knowledge representation? What primitives should be provided in a system and at what level?
4 **Meta-representation**: How do we structure the knowledge in a knowledge-base and how do we represent knowledge about this structure in the knowledge-base?
5 **Incompleteness**: What can be left unsaid about the domain and how do you perform inferencing over complete knowledge and revise earlier inferences in the light of later, more complete knowledge?
6 **Real-world knowledge**: How can we deal with attitudes such as beliefs, desires and intentions? How do we avoid the paradoxes that accompany self-referential propositions?[18]

Originally, the notion of 'knowledge representation' was essentially connected with 'writing down, in some language or communication medium, descriptions or pictures that correspond in some salient way to the world or the state of the world'.[19] As such it served the 'classical episteme' of 'order and measurement by analysis and comparison within a database of exhaustive consensus; measurement by means of the intellectual instruments of probability, analysis and combination.[20] Now, the notion of 'knowledge representation' can be broadened to communication media that can do much more than descriptions 'written down'. With the advent of multimedia that can store script, sound and moving image we get closer than ever to the oldest form of 'knowledge representation', namely the *human body* trained in *oral tradition*. The modern, interactive multimedia are capable of both the 'classical episteme' of 'order and measurement' and also of epistemes that are natural to oral transmission as the preferred 'knowledge representation'. To test the two ways of representing knowledge by means of the criteria that are applied to *expert systems* will yield insight into their respective databases: the human, internalised, somatic system that is reproduced in each generation, and the man-made, exteriorised, objectified systems that are stored and preserved for generations. These different databases will reveal different 'inference-engines', that is, different epistemes, or theories that serve to 'translate' different reasonings in the use of the expert system: 'rewording in writing to be read', or, 'embodiment in performance'.

Notes

1. Peirce in Kaja Silverman, 1983, *The Subject of Semiotics*, pp. 14–25.
2. Foucault, 1970, *The Order of Things*, p. 62, quoting Condillac, *Essay sur l'origine des connaissances humaines*, (*Oeuvres*, Paris, 1798, t.i, pp. 188–208).
3. Brodsky, 1987, *Less than One*, p. 150.
4. Cf. also, Foucault, 1970, *The Order of Things*, p. 67 '... the signifying element and the signified element are linked only in so far as they are (or have been or can be) represented, and in so far as the one actually represents the other'.
5. Seeger, 1977, pp. 6–9.
6. Cf. Foucault, 1970, *The Order of Things*, pp. 67 and p. 75.
7. Cf. M. Hiriyanna, 1978, *Essentials of Indian Philosophy*, especially pp. 106–29 on *Sankhya Yoga*, and A. Mookerjee, 1982, *Kundalini*, p. 99.
8. i.e. *rupa*, 'form' and *nama*, 'name'.
9. i.e. *sattva*, 'essential', *rajas*, 'dynamic' and *tamas*, 'inert'.
10. i.e. *srsti*, 'sprouting', *sthiti*, 'maintaining' and *pralaya*, 'dissolving'.
11. i.e. *kancuka*, 'armour'.
12. i.e. ears–mouth, skin–hands, eyes–bowels, tongue–genitals, nose–feet.
13. i.e. ether, air, fire, water, earth.

14. i.e. *mahabindu*, 'great dot'.
15. Foucault, 1970, *The Order of Things*, p. 16.
16. Ringland and Duce, 1988, *Knowledge Representation, An Introduction*, p. 1.
17. Ringland and Duce, 1988, p. 3.
18. Ringland and Duce, 1988, p. 5.
19. Ringland and Duce, 1988, p. 3.
20. Cf. Foucault, 1970, *The Order of Things*, on *mathesis*, pp. 72–4.

Chapter 9

Reproduction

9.1 The Human Expert

No man-made expert system lives up to the demands listed above except for the transmission from one human carrier of cultural knowledge to another. Out of these six demands, five are met with great ease:

1. Expressive adequacy is maximal in the human 'database' because of the multimedial, interactive quality of the exchange of expertise. Training can be offered by verbal instruction, which makes use of rhetorics, strategies that belong to the verbal arts; by graphic representation; by demonstrating examples; and by practical training interactively instructed and tested.

2. Reasoning efficiency is maximal too, as it corresponds to real-time performance, absorption and grasp.

3. Primitives are a very stable 'given', namely, the body implying the five senses that constitute shared presence.

4. Meta-representation is formed by praxis: its curricula, rites of passage and performance-format.

5. Incompleteness: the incompleteness of the live transmission of knowledge is minimal in the case of a shared background of common-sense and tacit knowledge. If such a background is not shared then the salient point of its importance will become painfully and painstakingly clear: in such a situation the student will have to go through the entire *habitus* by practice to obtain this vital knowledge. This ensures the familiarity necessary to perform inferencing over 'complete' knowledge as well as the practical possibility of revising earlier inferences in the light of recent data, concepts or tastes. This argument for knowledge of familiarity and practical opportunities for knowledge acquisition is obscured in 'objectified' expert systems, but re-enters via the backdoor of context and tacit knowledge.

6. Real-world knowledge in human, live transmission means 'man-made, cultural' knowledge. This is dealt with maximally, provided that the aim is not to prevent beliefs, desires and intentions, but on the contrary, to 'rub them in effectively' in the course of transmission of expertise. As a result, there is no paradox, since all propositions are openly self-referential.

On the whole the human, somatic expert seems to emerge from the test with flying colours; to such an extent that one wonders why we externalise expertise at all. Probably, because two demands for a powerful expert system that result in a crucial third demand have remained implicit in this list, namely:

7. durability
8. precision, resulting in:
9. dependability.

These concerns are at the core of the motivation to exteriorise knowledge in databases outside the human carrier of expertise. Human embodiment of expertise is very vulnerable for several reasons, such as life-span, talent, willingness, and integrity. The dream of externalised, democratically accessible, and lastingly valid knowledge underlies our ideals of egalitarian command over knowledge, of the gradual growth of insight, of chances for self-improvement and for 'progress' at large.

Unfortunately, the dream hardly ever comes true: for, example, when databases are accessible, they may lack adequacy, efficiency, or completeness and be tainted by ideological attitudes; or, when databases are adequate, efficient, and 'complete' they may lack accessibility and will probably be rooted in a highly specialized conceptual–cultural milieu. Imagine both possibilities in the human context of a talented teacher, a talented student, an untalented teacher, and an untalented student, etc. Sometimes human embodiment of expertise may turn out to be a combination of all the worst conditions: untalented, inaccurate, without integrity, inaccessible or, on the contrary, prosytelising and oppressively jealous. All these facets are possible in the live transmission of knowledge. In terms of Bourdieu, they form the seat of 'symbolic violence', oppression and cruelty.[1] A smooth sailing that circumvents all these cliffs of human passions is as unimaginable as it is naïve.

At each step in a training of expertise, one is reminded of

hierarchical asymmetry of status, of dependency, and of wit. From the outset a student becomes 'marked' by a particular stamp of a teacher, of a 'line', or a 'school' which yields privileges of intimacy and natural access on the one hand, but closes the way to any other 'school' or teacher. All traditional ceremonies, general and 'pedagogic', are occasions of affirmation of status, power and indebtedness expressed in the form of services and presents. Knowledge is deeply rooted in identity, status and dignity. This 'sense of belonging' is very precious, and can be gained only through sufficient practice, test and sacrifice. When acquired in this way, knowledge runs deep and is lasting. 'You must take it into your bloodstream' is the advice of Nandini for a durable, precise and dependable 'base of expertise'.[2]

This highly personalised database was never meant to be democratic, free, easy, 'general' or idealistically 'universal'. On the contrary, the transmission from one expert to one student is a very private, protected sometimes even 'secret' process that often takes place while living in the house of one's teacher (Skt. *gurukulavasa*). From 'one to one other' (Skt. *parampara*) the teacher transmits the techniques and conventions of the expertise and along with it an ethos, a style and pride that concern a family, a place, a region, a language or a professional affiliation. All these aspects are highly subjective, and they are meant to be so. After all, the expertise is precious because it works in the world; it can be used there because it knows its home so well. The human expert is in 'body and soul' a proud exponent of his own *habitus*; in symbiosis with it he forms one body, one system of knowledge.

9.2 *Murai* – The Human Expert System

The gradual transformation of an ordinary 'unmarked' student into a 'marked' expert who can serve as a 'vessel' (Skt. *patra*)[3] that contains a highly specific and 'powerful' content, is achieved in careful interaction with the *habitus*. Bodies naturally imbibe the qualities of the soil of their family roots, of their own birth and of their actual domicile. Daniel mentions that Tamilians who spend long stretches of time outside their 'native place', or even outside Tamilnadu, are advised to return to their country from time to time and stay there in order to reaffirm and recharge their natural *rapport* with its nature and the qualities of its soil.[4] The same holds true for expert knowledge: its functionality assures its roots in the land and the locus of application. 'Cultural capital' is exclusive on grounds of birth, and all the natural rights that go with this fact. To be born in a family of temple-courtesans (Skt. *devadasis*), right behind the temple in upper Tiruttani, *eo ipso* meant to have certain rights established by custom. These included the right to one of the nine houses assigned to initiated *devadasis* and their families, some land, some rice and clothes from the temple during their lifetime, and funeral rites arranged by the temple in the event of her death.

This right by birth was not automatically met with, nor was birth always a restrictive factor. Girls could be adopted from 'outside' and, sometimes, a girl form inside could be refused admission to the initiation ceremonies. The first is attested by texts, inscriptions, travelogues and oral accounts, and, by the fact that *devadasis* belonged to several castes.[5] The second case, of a girl 'from inside' who was not accepted, happened in Tiruttani, during Ranganayaki's lifetime:

> There was a girl who was refused admission to the initiation ceremony, in spite of the fact that she was well trained in song and dance, beautiful to look at and, personally, of a good reputation. The authorities justified their decision on the grounds that her mother lost her virginity as a girl, before obtaining her status as *devadasi*. Her family was therefore no longer considered respectable and was hence unfit to offer a daughter to the temple. The unfortunate girl finally obtained permission to be dedicated to a shrine in Kanchipuram where the rules of ritual purity were less strictly observed.[6]

This anecdote underlines once more that the principle at work here was not a structural fixity of caste by birth but the flexible eligibility to apply for a function. I fully agree with Daniel that the study of caste has been overrepresented in the sociocultural studies of two generations of South Asian anthropologists. Whether analysed as a 'uniquely' Indian institution or as an extreme manifestation of its 'rudimentary or vestigial' counterparts, the studies of caste became autonomous, closed systems of inquiry that prevented scholarly inquiry from escaping its own confines and from taking into account other symbolic constructs that are more pervasive, regnant and natural than 'caste'.[7]

In the case of the tradition of royal and temple courtesans in particular the focus on caste has not done their cause much good. In line with the 'spiritual, morally puritan' fashions of colonial Victorianism that held sway over India, in some parts until today, the phenomenon of the temple courtesan who was dedicated to god, on the one hand, and bore children to a patron, earning her livelihood with song and dance on the other hand, could not bode much good. To answer the pressing question of their moral rectitude: the dichotomy either nun, or public woman, became the burning issue of an anti-*devadasi*, anti-*nautch* campaign that lasted for over a century and that was resolved in abolishing the *devadasi* marriage and dedication ceremony.[8]

The stigma that had become attached to the issue *'devadasi'* was hard to generalise on the level of function; therefore it was located in 'caste' – a presumed caste, though. The *devadasis* themselves refer to their own tradition as *devadasi murai* or *devadasi vrtti*. The Tamil *murai* refers to 'order, arrangement, system, regularity, turn by which work is done, time, birth, manners, custom, approved code of conduct, relationship by blood or marriage, justice, antiquity, fate, nature',[9] while the Sanskrit *vrtti* means 'a mode of life, common practice, rule, profession, activity, function'. Both definitions indicate that 'to be a *devadasi*' means to perform a given task, execute a function, lead a particular type of professional life, but does not refer to a social structure termed 'caste'.

The self-enclosure of the studies of caste is revealed in the fact that the term itself has hardly ever been reflected upon critically. Terminology may reveal or confuse much, depending on the use that is made of it. Caste, for instance, is not an Indian word; it was introduced in the sixteenth century by the Portuguese, who broadly defined the many divisions of Indian society as *castas*.[10] Let us suppose that the term *casta* corresponded to *varna*, which literally means 'colour', and indicates the four main strata of Indian society (that is, *brahmana, ksatriya, vaisya* and *sudra*); then the coinage of a *'devadasi varna'* would find no Indian advocate. Whereas if *casta* should correspond to *jati*, which means 'birth, production, genus',[11] then the term *devadas jati* should be known in society. But it is not; *devadasis* did not 'sprout' like flowers, trees, birds or *jatis*; rather, they were born in several *jatis* and made to fit the life and tasks of a *devadasi*. This transformation of an ordinary girl to a *devadasi* applicant was achieved through a pedagogic process (*marga*, Skt. 'road') and various rites of passage (*samskaras*, Skt., lit. 'making together', 'making beautiful') to which we will return further on, that assured the reproduction of certain qualities and substances as part of daily life.

Devadasi murai did not equate to '*devadasi* caste', but to the natural aptitude to become a *devadasi*. To apply for such a post in a temple from 'outside', from a totally unrelated background in terms of language, region or family culture, would seem a theoretical construct without any support from 'common sense', especially at beginning of this century. Any application in those times would be firmly rooted in 'natural rights by custom'. The customs dictated by ritual tradition prescribed that a girl should be dedicated before puberty;[12] but again, owing to English legislation on 'child-marriage', the age for initiation was set as seventeen. In Tiruttani, when a girl aspiring to become a *devadasi* reached the age of sixteen, an application to be allowed to have the dedication ceremony performed for her would have to be sent to the king of Karvetinagar. Such a petition, called *arji pettukovala* (Te. 'application to be supported', i.e. by the temple or the state), had to be countersigned by ten priests and ten *devadasis* employed in the same temple. Generally, six months passed before such a petition was granted. During that time the girl was guarded very strictly: she should not leave the house, so that no man could set his eye on her. Once the permission was granted an auspicious day would be fixed, in accord with her horoscope, the stars and the ritual calendar, for her solemn marriage and dedication. For one month before that day, the house should remain in a ritually spotless clean state; any menstruation or other form of ritual pollution was warded off, to the extent that all women of the family and even the aspirant *devadasi* had to stay in the house of another relative during that period. Strictly watched and thoroughly cleansed, she was prepared by other *devadasis* and elderly ladies in the family for the grand, auspicious event.[13]

9.2a *Marga*, 'way'

The training that prepared for the status of *devadasi* was a graded curriculum in the arts of language, music and dance. The *Kamasutra* mentions sixty-four arts that were to be mastered by aspirant courtesans, including the preparation of drinks, of unguents, and of perfumes, decorative arts and several games played for entertainment.[14] Some of these subsidiary arts have survived in the skills of drawing *kolams*, the large rice-powder figures on the doorstep of traditional South Indian homes and in temples;[15] the decoration of the wedding pavilion and of the bride; and the preparation of soothing pastes and substances against the evil eye, as well as the innumerable, funny, entertaining songs that were sung at weddings, sometimes accompanied by a simple game. Ranganayaki's grandmother composed many such songs, among which the 'Song of the Chicken' (Ta. *Kolippattu*) is a beautiful example:

> They say that the chicken said:
> – when people say: the basket has been placed upside down, I say: I have set the tent;
> – when people say: all feathers have been spread, I say: I have purified all members;
> – when people say: we have placed [the chicken] in the fire, I say: I have seen *Agni Bhagavan* [god of fire];
> – when people say: we have cut [the chicken], thrusting it on the knife, I say: a disagreement has arisen between us and the knife;
> – when people say: we have tied [the chicken], after rubbing it with *masala*, I say: I have applied *mancal* ['auspicious, turmeric paste or powder': SK];
> – when people say: we chew [the chicken], after having put it in the mouth, I say: I have seen the sixteen teeth;
> – when people say: we swallow [the chicken] from the tongue down, I say I have reached *Sivaloka*;
> – when people say: we have eased ourselves, placing [it] on the rock, I say: I have seen *Surya Bhagavan*.[16]

Smt. P. Ranganayaki (*b*. 1914) was trained by her grandmother Smt. Subburatnamma (1871–1950) as the only granddaughter out of six. She recalls how, at the first lesson in dance, chaff (Ta. *umi*) was spread on the floor. For that occasion a small image of the elephant-headed god Shri Vinayaka was formed out of saffron powder.[17] *Puja* was performed for this image, to bless the event, the student and the teacher and to invoke the successful growth of Ranganayaki's knowledge. The dance-master told her to stand on the chaff, and, while holding her ankles, he made her perform the first step of the 'way of dance' (*marga*) *teyya tey*,[18] beating vigorously the soil and its products.[19] A training in music and languages (Telugu, Tamil and some Sanskrit) was added to this beginning in dance.

The curriculum of word, sound and image shows a remarkable systematicity in its build up: from *drills* of 'minimal units' that are mastered easily by young children and stored in their somatic memory, the teaching transforms into the *skills* that have been discussed earlier in Part II. *Competence* is acquired by mastering one standard suite in dance and vocal and instrumental music. This suite completes the *marga*, and is publicly displayed in a formal 'debut'. In dance it is called *gajjai puja* 'worship of the ankle-bells', and serves several purposes: artistically it is the first time that the student performs with full orchestra and before the public; ritually, it marks the end of the teaching assignment, celebrating this success by handing over the second half of the tuition fee, the gift of betel leaves and new clothes to the dance teacher. On the other hand the ceremony *gajjai puja* also formed the transition through the rite of passage that generated the student's new ritual status.

9.2b *Samskaras* – transformations

Three important rites mark the transformation from a student into a *devadasi*:

(1) Initiation, celebrated by the above mentioned *gajjai puja*, held five days before the marriage ceremony;
(2) Marriage, '*kalyanam*' (Skt. 'auspicious event'); and
(3) Dedication, '*muttirai*', literally 'branding'.

Marriage
On the day of the *kalyanam* and *muttirai* functions the bride should observe a fast. While she waits at home in a room that has

been kept ritually clean (Te. *mati*), elderly *devadasis* (that means those who are beyond the menopause) prepare the present for the 'bridegroom': a small loincloth, a flower garland and other 'auspicious items'. Accompanied by the auspicious instruments (Skt. *mangalavadya*) such as the *nagasvaram*[20] they set out for the temple, to offer their presents in worship to the image of the god Murugan as Velayudhan 'the one with the spear'. After the priest has clad the image in the loincloth, garlanded him with the flowers and spoken the appropriate formulae, he returns to the ladies the cloth and the flowers as well as the spear (Ta. *vel*) that is held by the statue in his right hand[21] to take it home to the girl, waiting in her 'pure' room. With full musical support they arrive and instal the spear in that realm of ritual purity. The girl re-enters, dressed like a traditional bride, and seats herself under the wedding canopy, taking the spear from the temple in her lap. The home-priest (Skt. *purohita*) performs all the traditional rites (*kalyanam*) for the girl and the spear, and finally, one of the elderly *devadasis* should tie the marriage-necklace (Ta. *tali*) with its pendant (Te. *bottu*) around the girl's neck. Grandmother's sister Smt. Jayaratnamma tied the *bottu* for Smt. Ranganayaki.

After this ceremony with the spear for 'groom', the *vel* would be returned to a specially pure pedestal in the room. While the 'marriage' ceremony, the auspicious *kalyanam*, was going on the dance-master (Ta. *nattuvanar*) arranged a *puja* ('worship') for the nine planets (Skt. *navagraha*) in the hall of the house. After the tying of the *bottu*, the newly wedded bride enters into the hall, clad in a new *sari* ('dress for women') fully ablase with her bright *kasi pottu*, the large mark on the forehead worn by married women. The nine planets receive their worship; and, after this important event, the aspirant *devadasi* dances regular concert items. Even after this performance she receives only milk and fruits, while the guests are offered a sumptuous meal and take some rest till the early evening.

Dedication
At 7 p.m. the group sets out in procession to the temple.[22] There, the girl dances for the first time in the presence of god as part of the lustration by burning lamps (Skt. *diparadhana*): first *puspanjali* – 'salutation by flowers' followed by a full concert. Hereafter, the crucial rite is performed: the temple priest (Ta. *kurukkal*) imprints the mark of the trident on her upper arm, as an 'imprint',

muttirai, of her status as *devadasi*, servant in the temple and participating in ritual worship. He hands over to her the 'pot-lamp' (Skt. *kumbhadipa*) to remove the evil influences from the image by rotating the pot with its burning flame three times around the god and once from head to foot. The performance of the 'removal of the evil eye' (Skt. *drstiparihara*) substantiates her new, transformed life. As a sign of her 'auspicious status' the young *devadasi* receives a silk headcloth, a coconut and other offerings touched by the god.

The big band (Ta. *periyamelam*) of the temple accompanies the procession back home. There, the spear is guarded on its pure pedestal, waiting for the bride. As the girl reclines on the bed, the spear is placed next to her to celebrate the ritual *garbhadana* (Skt. 'giving of an embryo' accompanied by a *santihoma* (Skt. 'peace oblation') by brahmin priests. Other *devadasis* sing lullabies and wedding songs[23] and offer freshly ground sandal paste.[24]

Early next morning, one of the elderly *devadasis* takes her bath, prepares herself ritually, and replaces the spear on its own pedestal in the house. The new *devadasi* takes her bath, and only then she is allowed to break her fast. In the early afternoon a swing ceremony is celebrated: the girl, now in a full, nine-yards sari called a *matisar*[25] and pyjamas, and with the marital mark on her forehead, is seated on the swing with the spear, swinging to the tunes of swing-songs, lullabies and boat-songs.[26] The pain from the branding was not bad, although it would take some time to heal; but 'if a girl had lied about her physical state', Ranganayaki remarks, 'she would suffer badly and the wound would not heal'. After the swing-ceremony, the group moves again back to the temple to return the spear to the priest. In the pavilion of 'flower salutation', the *puspanjali mandapa*, right opposite the image of the god, the new *devadasi* dances *puspanjali* for him, fully aware of her new life.

9.2c *Prayojanam* – 'application'

After one month, usually, a public concert is arranged for which a cultural, sophisticated, aristocratic and well-to-do public is invited. This audience should be composed of *rasikas* in the true sense of 'persons of refined taste'. Traditional Hindu logic does not favour asceticism in the young, and certainly not in women, who are in the midst of the creative, fertile force of their lives.[27] Moreover, a young girl dedicated to the temple has a husband, and cannot become a 'loose', wanton woman. On the contrary, her sexuality is in 'essence' enjoyed by the god, not unlike the offerings of food. In the same vein, he returns the gross *materia*, sanctified by his touch, to his devotees. Such returned flowers, food and people are considered *prasada* (Skt. 'auspicious equanimity'); therefore to maintain a *devadasi* is considered a great privilege, to be enjoyed only by deserving patrons.[28] Thus *prayojanam* meant 'putting to use' and 'recycling' the auspicious power of her intimate symbiosis with the god to the world of ordinary men and women. Smt. P. Ranganayaki explains this custom as follows: 'We were godfearing. After we received our status as *devadasi* we could decide for ourselves. If some were deserted by men, they still had their profession, which afforded them a living. We had our own discipline.'[29]

9.2d *Sampradaya* – 'tradition'

The transmission, or – in other words – the 'assembled' (Skt. *sam-*) 'over' (Skt. *pra-*) 'giving' (Skt. *daya*) of an expert system that is rooted far and wide in space and time and that is concretised in human bodies and human interaction can hardly be imagined as occurring in another form than that of live, somatic transmission embedded in an entire 'way of life'. In this sense, the *devadasi murai* as a 'human expert system' can be traced from the earliest strata of Tamil culture known to us right through to contemporary informants' accounts. In spatial terms Tamil textual sources, Sanskrit temple manuals and recent practice in village cults, 'royal' courts and temples reveal a shared *structure*, *identity* and *application* of the '*devadasi* tradition'. Tradition functions as it were as a complex expertise that contains propositional, practical and intimate knowledge; its working conditions presuppose familiarity and sympathy.

Structure
The structure of initiation, marriage, dedication and application in the world streamlines the propositional knowledge of the *devadasi murai*. *Gajjai puja* marks the prerequisites for a

professional life as *devadasi* that cannot be imagined without the dance-bells worn round the ankles.³⁰ This life commences with the rites of ritual marriage and dedication. The object figuring as the groom ranges over the period of 1500 years from a pole, a pot, a lamp, or a sword to a trident and a tree; the marriage ritual consists mainly of bathing and garlanding the 'groom'. The auspicious event, *kalyanam*, is proclaimed to the entire universe: by means of a circumambulation through the town on the king's chariot, with the state-elephant and the drum of victory (*c.* 450 AD); a circumambulation through the village or around the temple; or a circumambulation around the 'nine planets', the elders and other *devadasis*. The dedication comes to its ultimate articulation after the concert in the king's presence, or in front of the god during the worship at dusk. It is as if the act of 'branding' the mark of the *trisula*, the trident, contains all the force and energy that were bundled in the past preparations concentrated into a burning focus in that moment, serving to imprint the imagination of any onlooker with the assurance of the force and energy of her dedication to her status in the future.

This mark, the *muttirai*, epitomises in a poignant way the entire reality of *devadasi murai*. The anguish of that particular moment of imprinting the human flesh with the burning meaning of the trident reminds one of the 'anguish of the Hebraic *ruah*' that unites wind, breath, soul or spirit. 'Only in God are breath, spirit, speech and thought, absolutely identical; man can always be duplicitous, his speech can be other than his thought.'³¹ The engraving of the trident in her arm should be One with any of her 'speech' past, present or future; this writing in the human flesh is the writing of the 'only one book on earth', that is, according to Leibniz, the law of the earth.³² The proposition expressed in the burning mark is the proposition of 'truth' as absolute identity of 'spirit', 'thought', 'speech', 'soul', 'action' and 'being'. By preparing herself for the ceremony and by feeling the burning iron, the young girl makes a statement of 'truth' in Indian terms of *mey* (Ta. 'body') or *satyam* (Skt. 'beingness'). The anguish of the moment, the expectations that brought her there, the presence of the elders, the priest, all these in front of God do not allow any duplicity or ambiguity: the mark on her arm is real, as is her body and her status. The world has witnessed the event and is awaiting her committed action. The logic of her commitment is written down in the same way: in the body of reality, the earth. It is according to this logic, the 'law of the earth' that her new status is applied to the world through the ceremony of *prayojanam*.

Identity
The knowledge of familiarity is contained in the realisation of 'identity'. This identity is at the same time one's self-image and self-respect. The Tamil term *tanmanam* ('mind over self') covers both, as an individual being part of a 'circle'. Daniel's work outlines the concentric circles of 'relatedness' that the concept may absorb in its practical use. One of the most intimate circles of identification is one's sexual partner. As we saw above, the aspirant *devadasi* is married to a ritual object, ranging from a tree to a pot, a lamp, a sword or a trident. On a closer look, it turns out that all these ritual objects are synonyms of the great goddess, especially of her aspect of 'power', *Sakti*, the vitality of the sun that makes nature sprout, grow and blossom. The weapons of a god are usually considered to be his *sakti*, his power and potency; the spear (Ta. *vel*) of the god Subrahmanya-Murugan in Tiruttani is no exception to this logic. This brings us to the observation that *devadasis* like Smt. Ranganayaki were in fact 'married' to, or rather, merged with the goddess. Only after this merger of her own female powers with those of the goddess she was fit to be dedicated to the god Murugan as his *dasi*. As a result, the identity of the *devadasi*, the respect which society owed her, is derived from the fact that she is in fact a *cala-devi*, a 'moving goddess' a *pars pro toto* of the divine, the auspiciousness of the great *Sakti*, to be applied on a human level in the processes of the world. This explains her 'ever-auspicious status' (Skt. *nityasumangali*), her dignified, noble bearing, and the right of wearing the powerful red mark of auspiciousness, the *kumkuma-pottu*, on her forehead, while adorned with beautiful jewellery and rich, traditional saris.

Formerly Ranganayaki used to wear even the ritually, 'very pure' dress of the nine-yards *matisar*, a size and way of tying the female dress that is the privilege of women born in the caste of Brahmins.[33] The natural identity of *devadasis* with the goddess and close relationship to the god in the temple were expressed in the funeral honours bestowed on them until recently:

When a *devadasi* dies, the god has to observe pollution, called *munnumukkalu gatti* (Ka. 'hardness for three times three-quarters of an hour'). No *puja* would be conducted during this period. When the funeral litter arrives at the temple tower, a garland is taken from the god and given to the corpse of the *devadasi*, and an umbrella is held over the stretcher. After the cremation of the deceased *devadasi* the temple must be purified; on that day the god is served a curry of bitter vegetables.[34]

When a *devadasi* has died, her funeral pyre must be lit with fire from the temple-kitchen. Usually a funeral procession should not stop anywhere, but in the case of the funeral of a *devadasi*, the bearers stop for a moment at the *gopura* of the temple and place the bier for a moment on the floor. A garland is removed from the statue of the god and is given to the corpse, as well as a new *sari*, sandalwood, flowers and *prasadam*. A *devadasi* always gets a funeral of a *sumangali*, i.e. a woman who still wears her *tali* because her husband is still alive.[35]

Application
The quality of 'eternal auspiciousness' that characterises the *devadasi* is the key to her tradition and all that it implies: ritual objects, implements, jewellery, costumes, make-up, ritual actions, and the ritual repertoire of songs and dances. As was indicated earlier, the large, marked canvas of the world, the *ilakkiyam*, was believed to contain markers (*ilakkanam*) that could be applied and operate accordingly for the benefit of mankind. The traditional expertise of *devadasis* covered all spheres of divine influence: the personal private world, especially during the crucial moments of the rites of passage; the political, through attendance on the king; and the purely ritual, in the performance of temple worship. The element of manipulating and influencing the divine energies that they all share is strongly reminiscent of the activities of the medieval alchemist. Song and dance are primarily instruments to this end; their aesthetic quality and effect comes second. The most salient application of the *devadasi* status and identity is found in the task that all *devadasi*-informants remembered to have performed: the waving of the pot-lamp in order to remove the destructive influences of the 'evil eye'. The method is a triple clockwise rotation, concluded by a sweeping gesture from the head of the image to its foot.

These movements are performed with implements that are considered to be powerful 'antidotes' to the vicious energy of the evil eye (Skt. *drsti* 'glance'). First and foremost among them are lamps (*dipa*), of which the pot-lamp, the *kumbhadipa* (Skt.), is held to be the most effective.[36] The pot, being a synonym of the goddess, and the *devadasi*, being a *pars pro toto* of the goddess, instil the cleansing fire on top of the pot with a triple energy. In addition, the same movements may be performed with plates (ta. *tattu*) containing substances to absorb or counteract evil influences; substances such as solutions of charcoal powder, red *kumkum* powder, yellow turmeric powder and lemons serve this purpose well.[37]

To know these objects, substances and actions, coupled with the performing arts of song and dance and the knowledge when to dance or sing what and where, constituted the practical knowledge of the *devadasis*. The application of their propositional statement, their vast familiarity with the gods and the alchemy of the world, and their practical skills in how to go about human welfare and render the atmosphere 'auspicious' earned them great prestige and made them indispensable until the beginning of this century.[38] Even today, the belief in the efficacy has far from died out, and modern Indians continue to find gaps in the mesh of the law to answer the need for this expertise.[39]

Tradition embodied by human experts is stronger than jurisdiction. Its complexity, flexibility and pragmatic interaction with the domain obey deeper necessities in space and time than the temporary dictates of social power.[40]

Notes

1. In terms of the Indian student–teacher relationship one may speak of *bhayabhakti*, 'devotion filled with fear'.
2. The line of transmission through Smt. Nandini Ramani and Smt. T. Balasarasvati goes back to the Tanjore court of the eighteenth century; see also CD-i Content-Time-on Performers.
3. Cf. CD-i: Content-Time-Image-Performer.
4. Cf. E.Valentine Daniel, 1984, paperback 1987, *Fluid Signs, Being a Person the Tamil Way*, Part I, *Toward Compatibility*, pp. 59–225.
5. Cf. S. C. Kersenboom-Story, 1987 and S. C. Kersenboom, 1991b.
6. S. C. Kersenboom, 1991b, p. 134.

7. E. Valentine Daniel, 1987, pp. 1–2.
8. Cf. *Devadasi Act*, 1947, quoted in full in Kersenboom-Story, 1987, p. xxi.
9. *DED* 4115.
10. Cf. Basham, 1967, *The Wonder that was India*, London, Sidgwick & Jackson, 3rd revised ed., p. 149.
11. Cf. Skt. *jan-*, 'to be born'.
12. Cf. Kersenboom-Story, 1987, Ch. III, pp. 185 ff.
13. Cf. Kersenboom-Story, 1987, pp. 187–9.
14. The *Kama Sutra*, ascribed to Vatsyayana, dates back to the second/third century AD. Chapter 3 of this manual on erotic sophistication deals with the sixty-four arts to be mastered by courtesans.
15. See CD-i: Form-Time-Sound-Skill for an example of a *kolam*.
16. Kersenboom-Story, 1987, p. 67.
17. See CD-i: Content-Time-Word-Text for an image of the god Shri Vinayaka.
18. In the famous Sanskrit play *Malavika Agnimitra* by Kalidasa, the young girl is requested to kick a tree so that its flowers may blossom.
19. See CD-i: Form-Time-Image-Drill.
20. See CD-i: Content-Time-Sound-Performer, showing the group of musicians that constitute the 'big band' (Ta. *periyamelam*).
21. See CD-i: Content-Time-Word-World for the idol of Murugan–Velayudhan.
22. CD-i: Title introductory music sounding the *nagasvaram*.
23. See Kersenboom-Story, 1987, p. 159 *Lali*, p. 160 *Uncal*, p. 162 *Otam*.
24. See CD-i: Content-Form-Image-Text for grinding and offering sandal[paste].
25. This way of tying the *sari* is typical for Brahmin women; Ranganayaki remembered with great nostalgia the days that she was expected to wear her *saris* thus. Nowadays, she can no longer do so; for the sake of feeling and completeness she taught me too how to tie the *matisar*.
26. These compositions are still performed, even today, during the long wedding ceremonies; nowadays, they are sung by *su-mangalis*.
27. Cf. Kersenboom, 1990, in *Sangeet Natak Akademi Journal*, pp. 44–54, 'Devadasi Murai'.

28. Cf. Kersenboom, 1986, in: *Journal of the Institute of Asian Studies*, pp. 45–57, 'Samskaras of the Devadasis'.
29. Cf. Kersenboom, 1991b, p. 147.
30. An anecdote told by Smt.T. Balasarasvati underlines the importance of the *gajjai*, the dance-bells worn around the ankles: 'It was a time when I did not have many invitations to perform. One day, Konnakole Pakkira Pillai told me to go to dance at the Tiruttani temple in Murugan's *sannidhi* or presence, implying that this offering would help me to overcome the difficulties I was facing then. As a result of his suggestion, I got it firmly fixed in my mind that I should offer my art as a tribute to Lord Murugan at Tiruttani. However, because dancing in temples was now unlawful, I was feeling very unhappy that I couldn't fulfil my vow. It was then that Dr. A. Srinivasan, that wonderful man, told me when I described my unhappiness to him just to go ahead and perform at the temple. When I told him I doubted I would be permitted to do so, he smiled and replied that no one would know if I performed the hastas when the priest was conducting service. [...] We went to Tiruttani. We bought a large garland of roses and other materials for performing *abhishekam*, the ritual anointing of the idol. When we offered these to the officials concerned, we were told that the garland couldn't be used because it had *zari* or tinsel on it. So we requested them to place it at the Lord's feet. When the priest was offering worship, I quietly executed dance gestures with my hand, softly singing the song *Neelamayil vahano*. Yet I was dissatisfied. The high noon service was over and everyone left, that is, everyone but me and three other members of my party, all family members. We didn't feel like leaving the place. The watchman came along and said it was time to lock up the premises and suggested that we come again in the evening. We gave him ten rupees to fetch a packet of camphor for *deepa aradhana*. We had somehow to get him out of there, since I had to perform the dance without being found out by the police! Before the watchman could return, I quickly put on my *gajjai* – this is very important, you know; I danced the Tiruppugazh number called *Koorvale pazhittha vizhiale*. I don't quite remember what else I performed, but I danced spiritedly, possessed by a silent prayer to Murugan: *Swami, unakke naanum arpanam, en kalaiyum arpanam*: Lord I

offer to you humbly both myself and my art! It is a great privilege to have been able thus to perform a dance as an offering to God, under the holy flagpole, on full moon day. He, Murugan, accepted my offering!'
31. Jacques Derrida, 1978, *Writing and Difference*, p. 9 fn. 24.
32. Jacques Derrida, 1978, p. 8.
33. See CD-i Content-Time-Image-World for a photograph of Smt.P Ranganayaki; however, not in the nine-yards sari that I gave her for the sake of dear memories.
34. Kersenboom-Story, 1987, p. 192.
35. Kersenboom-Story, 1987, p. 192.
36. The pot-lamp (Skt. *kumbhadipa*) is considered to be the most powerful lamp in the effort of removing 'evil eye'; therefore it should be shown as the last lamp in the series of *diparadhana*, 'lustration by lamp fire'.
37. Kersenboom, 1990, 'Devadāsi Muṟai' in *Sangeet Natak Akademi*, p. 50.
38. The repertoire that was noted down by Smt. Subburatnamma, the maternal grandmother of Smt. P. Ranganayaki, includes a temple repertoire (*Koyil Sambandham*), a social repertoire (*Samskara Sambandham*) and an artistic repertoire (*Kacceri Sambandham*).
39. See Kersenboom-Story, 1987, pp. 192 ff. for variants that continue the central concepts of the phenomenon.
40. Tradition poses epistemes that are persistent and at the same time hard to abstract for the purpose of external representation and reflection.

Chapter 10

Objectification

10.1 Exteriorisation

Lyotard poses the question whether it is possible to think without a human body. This is, of course, the central question that stirs the imagination and acumen of Artificial Intelligence (hereafter: AI) to the absolute summits of cognitive theory and experiment.[1] Lyotard depicts the human expert as *hardware* in body and as *software* in language.[2] The demands for an expert system imply the quality of durability and the capacity for exact repetition to make the system 'workable'. The human body can not fulfil these demands. The human expert is subject to the workings of time and space; in consequence he will be affected in adequacy and efficiency. Moreover he may choose to veil his knowledge or to reveal it only partially; he may even cheat or lie deliberately, as he may be unwilling to share specific expertise. Also, he may suddenly die and take all his treasures with him for ever. The fear of irretrievable loss or whimsical delivery has prompted mankind to try to arrest and fix human expertise in lasting materials. Lyotard suggests that the frantic search for non-organic hardware carrying human software is aimed at preserving human knowledge even after the collapse of life on earth.[3] This image evokes the ultimate caricature of Modernity in its search for 'universal-validities-upon-which-all-certainty-in-history-rest'. Its hidden agenda aiming at 'control' is bound to succumb to the 'first law of culture' which says that 'the more man controls anything, the more uncontrollable both become' (Clifford and Marcus, 1986, p. 123). The challenge that results from that ambition has not died out yet, and is deeply rooted in academic attitudes.

In order to be able to program any organic, human expertise that occurs in real-time/ real-space, the first task seems to be to demarcate the 'object of study', to find the functional structures that make its processes coherent. In short, the demand for exteriorisation entails the effort of representation. According to Peirce, reality is made accessible to thought, reflection and discussion only through this effort, and is thereby capable of affecting us. The choice of materials and forms of representation may turn out to be a dominant factor in the analytic quest and its resulting database. As Clifford remarks, 'Cultures do not hold still for their portraits', however much we would like them to. Their essential quality is one of process; even though this can be grasped on an analytic level, it cannot be inscribed on paper. The concept of 'structure' as an essential, lasting trait seems to allow such static representation to a much higher degree. The codification that demarcated the static from the changing as separating 'essentials' from 'non-essentials' turned scientific representations into self-referential communications. Their agreement and affect relate therefore to the intellectual community, but do not necessarily relate that community to the world – its 'object at large'. The original, intellectual challenge that inheres in the ambition to externalise human knowledge dries up in the process of its static representation.

10.2 Materialisation

Knowledge become an object can lead many different lives. There is no natural relationship between any such object and its use. Books may be read, but they may also be carried around in procession, garlanded, sprinkled with water or displayed in a museum. Watches live manifold lives, as precise instruments coordinating the hectic schedule of a businessman or measuring the exact time achieved by a marathon-runner; or they may serve as a status object among the tribals in the Nilgiri mountains of South India. The ambition of recording knowledge in writing in order to provide a lasting base and instrument of control, is just one of the many possible applications of knowledge become object. Episteme and its 'expert objects' are organically interwoven: medium, codification, praxis, form and use are rooted in one and the same *habitus*.

The original question *enta prayogam* 'which use, which

application?' is born from unfamiliarity with the *habitus* of the object and its obviously totally uninspiring form. For instance, a watch may inspire many applications; but a publication representing a ritual seems a poor performance, devoid of alternative uses but for its occasional photographs. On the other hand, objects of traditional Indian knowledge are not always being questioned critically by Western scholars as to their natural use; many of these are immediately treated as if they were 'documents' and therefore to be 'read'. A closer look may reveal a totally different aim and use in their *habitus*. The critical factor is hidden in the relationship between the Sign of Knowledge and its World. Does it live a life in symbiosis with the world, as the Ancient Sign did in Foucault's terms, or, has it severed this organic relationship and does it pursue a life of its own? The latter is a disembodied sign that strives to represent lasting perfection; the former an embodied sign that makes use of a number of instruments to attain perfection during a human lifetime.

One such instrument is the *yantra* (Skt. 'instrument to complete one's integration' [free translation mine]), a mystical diagram, that appears to the Western eye as a synoptic representation of the cosmos. The so-called *Shri Cakra* consists of four triangles pointing upwards and five triangles pointing downwards, enclosing a central dot, all situated in two lotuses in full bloom on a kind of pedestal; it forms an instrument in the religious practice of integrating oneself with *Sakti*'s creation. This great goddess gradually unfolds and multiplies herself from the still centre, the *bindu*, 'dot', and contracts back into the same. Even the concrete, material diagram is not what it seems: when drawn on the ground, on stone, metal, or paper the *Shri Cakra* seems to be two-dimensional; but, in its more accurate forms it is a three-dimensional object, with the still centre at its top and the triangles and lotuses unfolding towards its base. In reality it is four-dimensional, that is, composed out of meditational practices, reciting *mantras* (Skt. 'instrument of thought', 'speech', 'formula') that generate the underlying essence and understanding, and, finally singing devotional hymns to enter into interaction with the beloved goddess.[4] It makes no sense at all to 'decipher' or 'read' this document; the *yantra* truly is an inscription considered as meaningful action.

This episteme holds that understanding is born only from

carrying out the processes that are contracted in the document: its unfolding generates a becoming that equals a temporary knowing. Therefore all representations are considered partial, either by their static nature or by the fleeting experience they generate. Knowledge cannot be materialised or stored in any conclusive way; all objects of knowledge are instruments in fully-fledged praxes of knowledge that involve the senses and the organs of cognition and action. The expectations around the objects of knowledge divulge the deep differences between epistemes and their 'expert systems'. This critical factor throws a new light on the representations of human knowledge in word, sound and image.

10.2a *Word*

The origin and status of the 'modern text' have been dealt with at length in the Introduction. The reductionist movements that finally yield an inscription of 'ideal sense meaning' stand in dramatic contrast to the Muttamil text that unfolds in space, time and multimediality. Tamil hermeneutics expand a three-line document into a complex event. The works of de Bruin and Hiltebeitel show how epic texts receive multiple treatment in South Indian villages: the *Mahabharata* is offered to the goddess Draupadi in rituals that address the entire population and that dominate their lives for several weeks.[5] First the manuscript is carried to the temple, where the text and its experts are worshipped; then it is recited, explained and embellished by song. After these two stages, that are quite lengthy in themselves, the epic is brought to life in dramatic performance – first on an improvised stage, and later on several locations right in the village.[6] Thus, the ancient text achieves a concrete and effective hermeneutic arc back into its own world.[7]

Several objects involved in this long process are considered 'knowledge representations': the manuscript, although of minor importance, the meaningful *kattai* ornaments[8] worn by the actors, the stone on which the make-up paste is prepared, the musical instruments, the idols and the temple with its roots in time. It is hard to say which is the most important; all play a part in the unfolding, witnessing and experiencing of the epic. Other representations of verbal art do not resemble texts at all: for instance, the CD-i demonstrates how a mango-leaf design is in fact a mnemonic instrument in rendering the text *varavina*.⁹ The time it takes to mark and draw the mango leafs equals the time and syllables it takes to complete the text. This device, called *kolam*, is a drastic example of a text that should be appreciated through meaningful action, instead of 'meaningful action considered as text'.

10.2b *Sound*

The tuning-fork and its derivative, the pitch-pipe, are a great success in Karnatic music. The metronome much less, because South Indian musicians as well as many members of the audience loudly beat their thighs or clap their hands to maintain a steady rhythmic pulse and precision.¹⁰ Absolute hearing, though, is a rare gift; and therefore the absolute fixity of the pitch-pipe is a blessing in a tradition of relative tones. The only reference to a fixed representation of musical knowledge is the so-called *melam*, the frets on the classical lute.¹¹ Unfortunately, the manufacture of *melams* is not standardised, but fashioned by individual workmanship out of highly unsteady materials: the wooden neck of the lute is covered with firmly pressed wax into which metal frets are sunk. This is procedure is quite risky, since the wax must be partially melted to receive the frets and then be allowed to harden. In this way, it is very difficult to find the right position for the frets by trial and error. As a result some *vina*s never give the right interval; others might have once done so, but gradually became affected by high temperatures during the hot season that soften the wax and thereby change the fixity of the frets.

The most prominent of Western representations of musical knowledge, the music score, is not followed at all. The sophistication of a Western music score enables the 'musically literate' to perform a composition initially correctly in notes, scale, rhythmical structure and timing, although the result is perhaps still lacking in feeling. An Indian score (*sargam*) shows only an enumeration of the initial letters of the names of the notes, set to a rhythmic framework.¹² It is virtually impossible to recreate music from this type of inscription without having studied it previously with someone who already knew the piece.

Objectification

Indian music scores serve only as memory aids, and it is considered bad taste and weak competence to read them while performing.[13]

In contrast to this Indian attitude rooted in praxis and familiarity, Western musicologists picked up the challenge of recording and notating this type of music. Immense difficulties emerged when analysing the production of tones and the ways of connecting them; several new musical graphemes had to be invented and inserted in a score of Indian music.[14] However, the freedom in interpreting and rendering tonal schemes and compositional frameworks turned Western notation of Indian music into Sisyphus' torment: not a single composition, leave alone *raga*, is rendered in an identical fashion on two occasions, not even by the same artist. The Western intellectual challenge never appealed to Indian musicians; what did appeal to them was the challenge of classification and neat representation of tonal schemes (*ragas*) and rhythmical schemes (*talas*) in graphics.[15] The *raga*-chart shown in the CD-i is hardly of any practical use; it just looks beautiful, orderly and erudite, but to operate it involves complex mathematical and alphabetical operations.[16] Certainly it does not fulfil the demands of 'expressive adequacy' and 'reasoning efficiency' that mark a 'workable expert system'; but it does function as a challenge to musical competence or as a kind of 'cult-object'.[17]

10.2c *Image*

Until the advent of film and video not a single system of the notation of dance could claim to be satisfactory. The foundation of the French Royal Academy of Dance in 1672 was accompanied by a rigorous classification of the steps into groups of exercises, plus the demand for a notational system. Even today the demand for a workable dance notation is felt in order to preserve choreographies.[18] In this century the systems of Benesh and Laban have been widely used, but always in combination with a choreologist and a dance-master who knows the ballets or parts from personal experience. Not unlike the Western musicologist who tries to notate classical Indian music, Western dancers and dance-experts have tried to use Western notational systems in order to record Indian dance. Annemette Karpen, a performer of and expert on Indian dance, who is by training a Western dancer, used to notate her own dance works. She feels that the written score gives a 'first-hand impression' while a video 'will be an interpretation of that particular director and her dancers, this will give us a second-hand impression'.[19]

When she set out to study Indian dance it seemed necessary to her to record the compositions she learned faithfully. Almost immediately several problems surfaced: (a) the absence of a rigorous, binding, written (i.e. lasting) codification of the steps and their physical analysis; (b) the absence of a widely accepted system of dance notation;[20] (c) complexities involving the minor limbs, such as hand and finger positions;[21] (d) mimetic manipulation of the eyes, eyebrows, and lips, in short of facial expression; (e) a greater variety of foot-positions[22] than those recorded in various Western dance traditions; and (f) the intricate rhythmical structure of dance-music, and hence an extreme density in coordination.

About her first efforts using Sutton dance writing she remarks: '... what soon began to worry me was that the scores I had written would not be understandable to other persons'. Although she exchanged this system for the notation devised by Laban (*Kinetographie*, 1928) her earlier impression still seems to hold true.[23] My own teachers of dance used to make fun of their Western students drawing figures and noting down descriptions. In fact, they did not like the attempt. To produce a 'first-hand score' seemed an anomaly to them; the only first-hand score is one's own memory, trained and soaked by the example of one's teacher. This interiorised score guarantees a certain amount of intimacy and professional privacy that belong to one particular line of transmission (Ta. *pani*). Notations are seen as 'second-hand scores', and can be read only by experts.

I have come across two indigenous types of notation: handwritten, two-dimensional notations, and paintings or stone sculptures in temples as three-dimensional notations of dance. The handwritten recording of dance makes use of mnemonic syllables that are used by drummers and by dance-masters, but not by dancers or students of dance. The words 'ta ka di ku ta diṅ gi na tōm' are recited by the dance-master in concert and sounded by the *mrdangam* drummer. These can be noted down on paper, and imply the third step in the 'dit dit tey' family known to dancers.[24] Thus the roles and expertise are divided to ensure mutual dependence. Democratic accessibility is certainly not favoured, nor the preservation of personal expertise beyond personally transmitted and approved application.[25]

The three-dimensional sculptures on the walls of South Indian temples have always spread an 'auspicious atmosphere' for those entering through the huge gates.[26] They also marked explicitly the purpose of pavilions meant for dance. In this century these sculptures have been interpreted as 'dance notations' and even as 'prescriptive'. Some dancers specialised in such *karanas*, and inserted them as 'dance-poses' in every possible choreography.[27] Whatever may be their original or derived purpose, no three-dimensional record can express a four-dimensional creation adequately or efficiently. Dance seems to oppose reductionism in the most powerful and convincing way: there simply is no method that can improve on the live, human, embodied expert.

10.3 Flexibility

The 'burning question of today' in 1926 was 'the overcoming of statics, the expulsion of the absolute' as 'the essential turn for the new era' for Roman Jakobson. To make this essential turn, however, has proved far more difficult than his vision assumed. Basically, the move from statics, away from the aspiration for 'absolutes', is a move away from the episteme of modernity and its expert systems of inscription. And although postmodernism has proved its intention of setting out to make this move, at least conceptually, it has proved too that it is hard, if not impossible, to move away from a 'critical' representation of knowledge implying a static and linear form. Jakobson's 'burning question' imposes a few burning demands, namely: flexibility, that means, flexible expert systems, flexible users, and interactivity.

A flexible expert system or knowledge representation is sensitive to the context of time and place. The classical model for such systems is set by various surviving traditions. Their vitality taps the regenerative quality of their manifold, flexible logic apparatus and requires the recognition of various types of knowledge as valid, and, in consequence of the various forms of knowledge representations, expressions and receptions of knowledge as valid. The modern model for such systems is the ongoing challenge of Artificial Intelligence. The critical epistemological questions 'how knowledge is acquired, represented and used' precede implementation in flexible systems that can be extended, or that can explain their actions.[28]

Jackson identifies Classical, Romantic and Modern Periods in AI.[29] The first was concerned mostly with game-playing and theorem-solving; the second with research into the computer's 'own' understanding; and the third, which covers the period from the latter half of the 1970s to the present day, with expert systems that perform well on non-trivial tasks. The power of its problem-solvers lies in the explicit representation of the knowledge that the program can access, rather than in a sophisticated mechanism for drawing inferences from the knowledge. In other words, the composite representation of its world should be compatible with that world, rather than a limited representation with a powerful theory of interpretation.

Modern expert systems generally have two components: a *knowledge base*, which contains the representation of domain-specific knowledge, and an *inference engine*, which performs the reasoning. Jackson observes that these systems tend to work best in areas where there is a substantial body of knowledge connecting situations to actions.[30] Tradition as embodied expert system spends enormous time and effort to imbue the body with domain-specific knowledge and make it compatible with its world; the inference engine gradually ripens for the tradition in terms of *aucitya* 'propriety' and *manodharma* 'realm, frame or grasp of the mind'. In Bourdieu's terms 'body *hexis*' sets the inference engine in motion.[31]

Jackson admits that Modern expert systems still avoid the 'deeper representations of the domain in terms of spatial, causal or temporal models', but suggests that 'these are problems that a general knowledge representation system cannot side-step quite so easily'.[32] Tradition does not side-step these problems. As we will see further on, the ancient Indian expert on *mimesis* Bharata reminds experts in the dramatic mode of dissemination of knowledge that transmission should follow two types of precepts: *marga*, Skt. 'road', indicating the normative, 'codified' norms, and *desi*, Skt. 'regional, relating to locally and thereby coevally prevalent norms'. This advice is followed even today by the *Kattaikkuttu* performers of Tamilnadu. Hanne de Bruin quotes their success formula as *kiramattin istam* 'the wish of the village', and works out its practical implications in great detail.[33] The great systematicity within traditional flexibility deserves detailed study and reflection.

An attempt has been made in designing the CD-i demo following a 'formative logic' and a 'referential logic' determined by the dimensions 'space' and 'time'. This program was evolved on the basis of almost twenty years of apprenticeship in Tamil dance, to which were added training in vocal and instrumental music, and a similar period of involvement in the Tamil language and its textual tradition. Its poetry and poetics reveal an amazing systematicity in exactly these three problems of spatial, temporal and causal coordinates,[34] coupled to a vigorous flexibility that has found its way as far as into Tamil films.[35] Knowledge of the Tamil world is flexible *per se* and defies reduction to any static medium. Its aim is not to control this world but to understand it, in order to optimalise living in it. In terms of AI the power of the problem-solver, i.e. Tamil intelligence, lies in the explicit representation of the knowledge (here: embodiment), that the program, (here: the individual), can access. In this way, the CD-i demo is still a static representation; however, tomorrow's dream might be to achieve flexible knowledge bases with sensitive inference engines, not to equal Tradition but to understand its beauty and workings.

Flexible expert systems require flexible users, willing to connect 'knowledge situations' to 'knowledge actions'. Wittgenstein's perception of 'a concept as a *set of activities that follow a rule*', in contrast to regarding the concept as a rule to be applied,[36] opens the way for practice as the method to understanding. 'How-to' books are clumsy both as literature and as guide for action. Synoptic models and graphs may help, but require a special intelligence to infer the four-dimensional from the two-dimensional. Practical examples seem by far the most ideal device. However, these place us back in space and time immediately. A new, radical Hermeneutics that situates learning in the world of training, how-to apprenticeship, and trial and error, determined by objective and subjective factors of time and place, seems to be so radical that it may force Jakobson to wait till the turn of this millennium. However, Humanities fashioned in this curriculum would allow both Self and the Other to share in Time, Place and Representation.[37]

The aim of such flexible representation by flexible users would be to 'practise', to 'practise gradual familiarity with life', to acquire 'competence in the human condition restored to its original difficulty'.[38] This expert system and its underlying episteme do not aim for 'disembodied thinkers', as does the challenge put by Lyotard. Life is infinitely more complex than any reified representation of it. Lyotard diagnoses as one of the causes of disenchantment with 'representation machines' that their cognitive dynamics can not grasp the non-binary logic that forms the greater part of human thinking. Intuitive and hypothetical configurations are hard to program, whereas reflexive thinking mediated by perception seems inaccessible to a machine. Perception implies 'sensory perception' and reunites body and thought; these two are analogues to each other and stand in an analogous relation to their existential milieu.[39]

'The power of a problem-solver lies in the explicit representation of the knowledge that the program can access' means in this context that the expert system has to be an analogue to the human body and human thought in their analogous relation to Being. It has to position itself amidst its data; data that are alive, dynamic and in complex syntheses. Lyotard wonders whether such a representation will ever be achieved.[40] Probably not, and only 'hard AI-ers' will defend such optimism. The aim of the challenge is not in the achievement of such a final, conclusive representation. The aim is to catch Life in its complexity at the point where it attempts to grasp itself, right before it formulates metaphysical propositions or interpretations on its own Being.[41] Interactive multimedia afford us a playground of maximal description of the fullness of an existential moment as well as the possibility to interact and 'practise' with it. Not unlike the performing artist, it creates a secondary Presence of Being and allows us to capture part of its flux. During this moment we can enter Being again; its accessible Presence allows us to gradually become acquainted with it.[42]

No secondary representation can be complete or eternally valid; the organic nature of its *physis*, as well as its changing form through *kinesis*, do not allow such conclusive statements.[43] Therefore flexible representations of knowledge *eo ipso* serve temporary purposes that are set by their relation to the world in the form of application by flexible users. Thus they keep us on the alert as long as the question of Being – in the terms of Heidegger – is open.[44] To grasp Being as Presence and to apply its manifold possibilities to the world through various representations is to stand in a dialogical relation to it. The construction of a secondary 'presence', such as CD-i, can be understood as the Phenomenological perspective made concretely explicit; its deconstruction through interactive practice forms a powerful instrument to enter into such a dialogical challenge. The vitality of a dialogue is in its interactive nature: Being as World as Representation, Mankind as the Other, talk back – if we care to listen. Interactive multimedia do respond to interactive users as they prepare for understanding the real, doubly interactive dialogue, out there in the world, by means of repeated trial and error.

Clifford diagnoses Ethnography as 'still very much a one way street'. In quoting Michael Fischer he sees 'Post-modernism' as 'more than a literary, philosophical, or artistic trend. It is a general condition of multicultural life demanding new forms of inventiveness and subtlety from a fully reflexive ethnography.'[45] That demand can be met by dynamic multimediality, cognitive dimensionality, interactivity and, in future, flexibility. Such representations encourage the assessment of complexity, diversity, idiosyncrasy and constant transformation of the human condition. By repeated dialogue and flexible re-creation of its forms, practice does not mean repetition of the same, but 'a creative production which pushes ahead, which produces *as* it repeats, which produces *what* it repeats, which makes a life for itself', and for the apprentice, in the midst of Life – in its original, fluctuating difficulty.[46]

Notes

1. The computer engineers in the Center for Knowledge Technology in Utrecht pointed out to me that among those who pursue Artificial Intelligence a basic distinction should be made between 'Hard AI', that is the research that believes that the human brain can be simulated artificially, and 'Soft AI', that is the research that does not subscribe to this belief, but that is convinced that a great deal of discovery and insight can be gained in the course of this pursuit.
2. Lyotard, 1988, *L'inhumain: causeries sur le temps*; Dutch translation, 1992, *Het Onmenselijke*, pp. 23 ff.

3. Lyotard, 1988, Dutch trans. 1992, pp. 19–20.
4. Gupta, Sanjukta, 'The Religious and Literary Background of the Navāvaraṇa–kīrtana of Muttusvāmi Dīkṣitar', p. 23, in *Sacred Songs of India*, Diksitar's Cycle of Hymns to the Goddess Kamala, Part I, 1987, ed. E. te Nijenhuis and S. Gupta.
5. Cf. de Bruin, H., 1994 Ph.D. dissertation Leiden University, Kattaikuttu: The Flexibility of a South Indian Theatre Tradition, and Hiltebeitel, A., 1988, 1991 *The Cult of Draupadi*, Vols. I and II.
6. The video-material that is available with both authors shows these stages very clearly.
7. This type of 'hermeneutic arc' is expressed by the ritual gifts that are returned to the devotees, sudden fits of possession and, finally, the recitation of an auspicious verse *mangalam* at the end of the entire ritual; ritual fees are given to the actors and the musicians as well as token of ritual status and honour.
8. According to Hanne de Bruin (Leiden, 1994) it is especially the arm-ornaments called *kattai* that mark the auspicious, ritual nature of the play.
9. Cf. CD-i Form-Time-Sound-Skill.
10. Cf. CD-i Form-Time-Sound-Drill.
11. Cf. CD-i Content-Time-Sound-Text.
12. Cf. CD-i Form-Space-Sound-Drill/Skill/Competence.
13. This experience is bound to occur while studying Karnatic vocal music; as a commentary on the decay of classical standards one may find innumerable jokes on 'modern practices' of 'singing music from paper' in the prestigious music and dance magazine *Sruti*, The Sruti Foundation, Madras.
14. Cf. E. te Nijenhuis, 1987, *Sacred Songs of India*, Vol.II.
15. Cf. CD-i Content-Time-Sound-Text and Form-Time-Sound-Drills.
16. Cf. CD-i Content-Time-Sound-Text for the Melakarta and Janya Raga Chart, compiled and designed by A. Krishnasvamy; the so-called *katapayadi* formula given by him combines a computation of the first two syllables that make up the name of a *raga* in terms of numbers that are attributed to the syllables in the alphabet – the resulting value has to be reversed to find the serial number of the *raga*. For example,

the *raga mayamalavagaula* reads: *ma* = 5 and *ya* =1; their value 51 has to be reversed, resulting in the serial number 15.
17. Cf. the vocal feat *Mela-raga-malika-chakra*, formulated by Venkatamakhi (seventeenth century), a composition performed by among others Smt. M. S. Subbulakshmi, vocally supported by Radha Viswanathan, EMI/CD/PMLP 5031.
18. In 1979 I tried to apply the dance-notation systems designed by Benesh on the one hand, and Laban on the other hand, to an Indian dance choreography called *Ganapati kautvam*. The MA thesis that shows the results of both argues that both systems are either too reductionist or too elaborate and reductionist at the same time to be used efficiently by dancers aspiring to master this composition. As a compromise I offered a Benesh-based notation, registered from the back 'en dos', covered by a transparent page showing a photograph of the same sequence 'en face' (front).
19. Annemette Karpen, 'Laban notation for Indian dance, in particular Bharata Natyam', paper read and demonstrated at the 11th European Conference on Modern South Asian Studies, Amsterdam, 1990.
20. Cf. CD-i Content-Time-Image-Text.
21. Cf. CD-i Form-Space-Image-Drills.
22. Cf. CD-i Form-Time-Image-Drills.
23. Cf. Karpen, 1990, conclusion.
24. Cf. CD-i Form-Time-Image-Skills/Competence.
25. Following a logic similar to 'divide and rule'.
26. Cf. CD-i Content-Space-Image-World/Word-performer and Content-Time-Image-Text.
27. This trend was very popular in the mid-1980s but seems to loose ground now.
28. Ringland and Duce, 1988, p. 2.
29. Ringland and Duce, 1988, pp. 2–3, quoting Jackson, 1986, *Introduction to Expert Systems*, London, Addison-Wesley.
30. Ringland and Duce, 1988, p. 3.
31. Bourdieu, 1990a, p. 87.
32. Ringland and Duce, 1988, p. 3.
33. Hanne de Bruin, 1994, discusses at length this mechanism of flexibility on pp. 257ff.
34. Cf. Takahashi, Takanobu,1989, Poetry and Poetics, Literary Conventions of Tamil Love Poetry, Ph.D. dissertation, Utrecht

University.
35. Cf. Thiruchandran, Selvy, 1993, The Ideological Factor in the Subordination of Women, Ph.D. dissertation, Vrije Universiteit Amsterdam, who analyses Tamil poetic conventions and modern Tamil film alike to elicit Tamil female role models.
36. Göranzon and Josefson (eds), 1988, p. 11.
37. Cf. Fabian, J., 1983, *Time and the Other, How Anthropology makes its Object*, New York, Columbia University Press.
38. Cf. the Introduction of Caputo, J., 1987, *Radical Hermeneutics, Repetition, Deconstruction and the Hermeneutic Project*, Bloomington, Indiana University Press.
39. Cf. Lyotard, 1988, Dutch trans. 1992 (trans.), Ch.2 'Hij'.
40. Cf. Lyotard, 1988, Dutch trans. 1992 (trans.), Ch.2 'Zij'.
41. Caputo, 1987, pp. 1 ff. as a central task in 'restoring life to its original difficulty'.
42. By grasping the *varnam* in its moment of performative presence CD-i allows the user to become acquainted with that presence by means of practical knowledge and knowledge of familiarity.
43. Cf. Caputo, 1987, pp. 2–3 and Part I 'Repetition and the Genesis of Hermeneutics'.
44. Cf. Caputo, 1987, Introduction, his elaboration of the theme Being as inspired by Heidegger's *Being and Time*.
45. Cf. Clifford, J. and Marcus, G., 1986, *Writing Culture, The Poetics and Politics of Ethnography*, p. 22–3.
46. Cf. the CD-i, the Conclusion of this work and the Introduction of *Radical Hermeneutics*.

Chapter 11

Translation

In Latin *translator* means 'one who carries to the other side'. It is understood that he delivers his cargo 'without embezzling funds'. Linguistic messages never arrive intact because of translation. All the linguistic *translator* can hope for is to deliver the structure of a specific discourse, emerging from a specific ground of practices functioning within a specific form of life, reproduced in his own language. How that structure is reproduced will depend on the *genre* of the message, on the *resources* of the translator's language as well as on his own *interests* and those on 'the other side'. Talal Asad sees the reproduction of structure as the reproduction of coherence; this, he feels is difficult enough a task. To stretch one's ambitions into 'letting the language of translation go, so that it gives voice to the *intentio* of the original not as reproduction but as harmony, as a supplement to the language in which it expresses itself, as its own kind of *intentio*',[1] seems a hazardous enterprise to him. First of all, a good translation should precede a critique; interpretation is a concern of the receiver, not of the messenger. The type of critique and interpretation a translator has to go through is one of internal critique, based on some shared understanding, a joint life, that generates a way of thinking that comes as close to the original, natural coherence as an 'outsider' can get. Even then the task of evoking that alien harmonious *intentio* demands critical reflection before rushing into its production. It is true that the rewriting of the deeper intentions of the 'other' constitutes the 'hidden agenda' of the audience: it is waiting to read *about* another mode of life and to manipulate the text it reads according to established rules, not to learn *to live* a new mode of life.[2]

This interest is not only specific for this type of audience, but requires a very specific belief in the representational power of language – to which we will return later. Moreover, it is not a concern that is always shared by both sides of the event. Many authors, texts, auctors or cultural expressions do not aspire to be 'carried to the other side', certainly not in terms of categories and attributions that they cannot subscribe to. They cannot, technically, because they do not conceptualise their own heritage in terms of *intentio* or 'hidden meanings', nor can they, emotionally, because they feel 'exposed, cheated or reduced' as if something got lost on the way. The exposure resembles the helplessness of a client at a psychoanalyst's reading of 'hidden meanings', whereas the construction of 'original intention' may differ greatly from the common-sense experience of the native speaker. He may feel manipulated by an alien cosmology, while the reduction of 'live texts' to publication seems poor and ephemeral to his life-experience.[3]

This apparent impoverishment of the cargo carried from one side of *auctores* to the other of *lectores* is very much linked up with the genre of texts under translation and the resources of the language of the translator.[4] Asad argues that the 'texts' that are being translated by anthropologists are not literary texts but entire cultures and societies. Unfortunately, society is not a text that communicates to the skilled reader. It is people who speak. And the ultimate meaning of what they say does not reside in speech events. In this sense translation may indeed require mechanical reproduction, but *how*: in what modes of representation and with what kind of resources? Asad suggests that 'under certain conditions a dramatic performance, the execution of a dance, or the playing of a piece of music might be more apt' than the representational discourse of ethnography. 'These would all be *productions* of the original, not authoritative textual representations of it.'[5]

According to Tyler, the scientific (ethnographic) text failed 'because it could not reconcile the competing demands of representation and communication'.[6] A new type of 'polyphonic writing, evolved in a cooperative collage of various fragments of discourse', should 'evoke in the minds of both reader and writer an emergent fantasy of a possible world of commonsense reality, and thus provoke an aesthetic integration that will have a therapeutic effect'.[7] According to him, the whole point of 'evoking' rather than 'representing' is that it frees ethnography form *mimesis*.[8] But which is the critical form that should trigger off such evocation, how should it enter and work on the consciousness of its receivers, leading them to therapeutic aesthesis? Only very great literature has that power. For the less talented writers, the banal fact remains true: in the attempt to 'evoke worlds', writing lacks two dimensions to which performance can have recourse. Time and space generate form, sight, touch, sound, taste and smell, which can easily reconcile the demands of representation and communication.

Even then, allowing the polyphonic text to speak for itself: in what language or languages does it speak? Asad raises an extremely important issue, namely, the inequality of languages, which upsets the entire paradigm of translation.[8]

> Our translations, even the best ones, proceed from a wrong premise. They want to turn Hindi, Greek, English into German instead of turning German into Hindi, Greek, English. Our translators have a far greater reverence for the usage of their own language than for the foreign works ... The basic error of the translator is that he preserves the state in which his own language happens to be instead of allowing his language to be powerfully affected by the foreign tongue. Particularly when translating from a language very remote from his own he must go back to the primal elements of language itself and penetrate to the point where work, image and tone converge. He must expand and deepen his language by means of the foreign language.[9]

This long quotation from Rudolf Pannwitz serves to state a simple point: which language, that is, which speakers are willing to push beyond the limits of their habitual usages, to break down and reshape their own language through the process of translation? These tasks are extremely difficult, for the individual, too, but especially for society or culture at large, since matters of power, prestige and asymmetric gain are involved. Lienhardt outlines what it implies: 'In the field the process of translation takes place the very moment the ethnographer engages with a specific mode of life – just as a child does in learning to grow up within a specific culture. (...) When the child/anthropologist becomes adept at adult ways, what he has learnt becomes *implicit* – as assumptions informing a shared mode of life, with all its resonances and areas of unclarity.'[10] Imagine the practical difficulty of producing a polyphonic text with these *curricula* of all participants in mind as well as the communicative vitality to a 'general reader'.

Polyphony on the conceptual level underlies any such polyphonic production. In this context, the Tamil concept of translation reveals both the uneasiness with the medium 'writing' as a communicative moment and the asymmetrical capacity to transform in order to deploy foreign cultural concepts. The term 'translation' is caught in a neologism, *molipeyarppu*, literally, 'utterance-displacement': the subversion of spoken words into other (written) words is as far as the Tamil concept can allow. To impart to *molipeyarppu* the prestige of 'meaning', 'intention' is awkward: this power is reserved for *karuttu* 'design, plan, intention, meaning'. The *karuttu* of *iyal* ('word') can be expounded in 'commentary'; true polyphony is heard in investigating the Tamil term for 'commentary': it is *urai*, meaning 'utterance, speech', but also 'rubbing', 'touch of gold or silver on the stone', 'fame', 'roar', 'sacred writing'. In short, to comment on meaning is an activity, rubbing a stone in order to bring out its excellent qualities, and it is a sound 'roaring' loudly a hero's fame, the recitation of sacred writings. Indeed, the live communicative setting of the commentary is proved by its many 'enpa's', i.e. 'they say'.

Both the text, the original, and its translation into more accessible 'meaning' and *intentio* are live, doubly interactive events between senders and receivers. Evocation is known only as *vac* 'utterance', like Tiruvacakam. These 'holy utterances' are texts performed as *prabandhams*, that is, composed out of word, sound and image. In Part I we discussed their repeated translations into events of face-to-face communication between senders and receivers. The Western concepts of 'knowledge, meaning, intention and evocation' cannot be grasped by this traditional Tamil milieu away from communicative application. Therefore these activities are glossed by a strange neologism that attempts to frame these seemingly weird activities and products.

Molipeyarppu, 'utterance-displacement' for 'translation' functions as a mirror to the Western enterprise of expressing and disseminating knowledge. Such mirrors prove that the forms of dissemination of human knowledge cannot be taken for granted. They become most critical in the choice of their vehicle and their expressive milieu – in consequence, so does translation.

11.1 Vehicle

The primary vehicle of expression has traditionally been the spoken word As Foucault remarks, Antiquity considered language its prime treasure as the sign of things. From the depth of its being, and by means of the light that never ceases to shine through it since its origin, it adjusted to things themselves, it formed a mirror for them and emulated them; language was to eternal truth what signs were to the secrets of nature, it possessed an ageless affinity with the things that it unveiled.[11] The 'prose of the world' expressed itself in lively metaphors, endowing a verbal passage with the sensuous materiality of song, dance and mimetic presentation. This synthetic rendition allowed a parallel processing and simultaneity that is natural to life and to associative thought. The 'prose of imagination' that was to follow was moulded by the demands of the practices of writing. Script cannot but represent thought in a successive, linear order, and thereby suits analytic propositions of arbitrary equation. Lyotard argues that the flexibility in modulating relationships between elements of attribution depends largely on the mediating capacity of a 'middle term'.[12] An examination of pertinent middle terms reveals the aim, form and character of both primary proposition and secondary translation.

11.1a *verbum existentiae*

Identities, differences and interpretative relations between entities can be understood by tradition, belief, or revelation, or by attribution. The middle term in these propositions is the *verbum existentiae* 'to be', its referential base the noun. Foucault distinguishes four theories of meaning in bestowing 'names': proposition, articulation, designation and derivation. The first two form the dynamic tension between particular and the general, the second two a similar tension ranging between substance and quality.[13] The point of gravity in these expressions lies in the verb 'to be'. As a middle term the *verbum existentiae* is highly flexible: it connects all truths and falsehoods in the same manner. As a result the authoritative load of its referential power had to be defined: the grammarians of Port-Royal assigned the power of the verb 'to be' to its capacity of affirmation, i.e. the affirmation of an idea on identity, difference or meaning. 'But is the affirmation of an idea also the expression of its existence?'.[14] Yes and no, the *verbum existentiae* points both at the 'essence' of things and at its actual manifestation, in which essential quality and occurrence are in symbiosis. The 'essence' of things does not change, even if no concrete manifestation can prove its existence; the example, on the other hand, has to be presented again and again to prove this vital symbiosis.

The Tamil linguistic situation forms a dramatic contrast. To begin with: there is no *verbum existentiae*. Whereas the Western 'to be' can mediate between elements of attribution that are present or absent, that are concretely material or abstract essences, Tamil expresses such relations in terms of qualifiers of agents, space and time added to nouns, linking the two in one and the same body. Absence of such a relation is indicated by modifiers that express absence, i.e. *il* 'not', or difference, i.e. *al* 'different'. The particle *ul* 'inside' hints at an existential immanence of being, but does not function independently as a *verbum existentiae*. Therefore, to 'name' is to establish the thing, to bring it into existence in whatever spatial or temporal form. To attribute meaning is to incite *osmosis*, the gradual transformation of the two becoming one. The poem from *Kantaranuputi*, lit. the 'becoming towards Skanda', by the saint Arunakirinatar (fourteenth century AD) forms a telling example:

> uruvāy aruvāy uḷatāy ilatāy
> lit.: *uruvu* 'form' + *ay* 'verbal marker 2nd p.S. "you"',
> *aruvu* 'different form' (*a-uruvu*) + *-ay* 'verbal marker 2nd. p.S. "you"',
> *ulatu* 'inside it' (*ul* + *atu*) + *ay* 'you', *ilatu* 'absent it' (*il* + *atu*) + *ay* 'you'.

In this way the god Skanda is not only 'form and beyond form, immanent and absent, he also is fragrance and blossom, the jewel and its lustre, body and breath, the road and its destiny, the teacher, always potentially bestowing grace.[15]

The Western *verbum existentiae* mediates between the concrete, material world and its presumed abstract essence *sub specie aeternitatis*. Writing provides both middle term and elements of attribution a lasting, objectified base as continued evidence.

Tamil *osmosis* of attribution provides a processual transformation, a phenomenon that has to be repeated again and again in order to prove its point. Translation in these two examples is transported by totally different vehicles. While the first, the *verbum existentiae*, stands at the genesis of a long line of externalised vehicles such as the book, the camera, the computer, the second has remained incorporated in human embodiment.

11.1b *mimesis existentiae*

The Tamil 'prose of the world' lacks the *verbum existentiae* because it does not need it. Its logic postulates equation of words with things as resemblance. Their natural immanence in each other manifests itself in the process of 'becoming'. The quadrilateral that constitutes the 'name', in the terms of Foucault,[16] is here the gradual unfolding of the 'name' through mime. A noun like *moha* ('intoxication, infatuation') is developed in a creative field where the 'general' encapsules the 'particular' and where its substance fosters its potential 'quality'. The performance brings all in focus in a non-linear, associative order, orchestrating its effect with great care, sensitivity and skill. The *varnam* becomes the truly sensuous metaphor of the full quadrilateral of that particular noun; it engages the senses of sight and sound, suggesting smell, taste and touch to a maximum of sympathy and identification. This type of utterance is a language of action, spoken by the body; it has as its base and as its target human experience, and therefore it is capable of evoking identification in those who witness it. Just like the Ancient Sign, it does not point only at day-to-day experience but at its cosmic embeddedness as well: the realisation of the beauty and order into which microcosm and macrocosm are enfolded. Translation of its complexity, diversity and essence coincides with its expressive articulation. Its vehicle is not the spoken word alone; it is the expression of the entire body gradually realising this organic sameness. This direct, primary vehicle of translation carries the eternal potentiality into an activity that is known as *natya* (Skt. *'nat-'*, 'to dance', 'to shine'). The legendary sage Bharatamuni recommends *natya* to gods and men alike as a felicitous activity. The great god Brahma himself designed it to apportion good and bad luck,[17] he instructed Bharata in the science of *Natya* and requested him to practise it with the help of his one hundred sons. In the first chapter of his *Natyasastra* Bharata reveals the origin and purpose of this applied science

> From the onset of the silver age people became characterised by the codes of village life; passions like lust, greed, power, joy, anger, etc., created the experience of well-being (*sukha*) and unhappiness (*dukha*). The gods kind of 'lost contact' because the people following the sensuous *gramya dharma* ('village life') were not allowed either to recite or to hear the four original (ritual) *Vedas*. So, the gods too, wanted to sway with emotion and sensuous experience. They asked Brahma to create some form of play (*kridaniya*) that would engage both the eye and the ear. Only in this way could communication be restored. Brahma went into deep concentration (*yoga*), distilled the sensory essence from the four existing *Vedas*, and 'processed' this knowledge into a fifth *Veda*: the *Veda* of *natya*, or – in other words – knowledge concretely represented and experienced through the senses. *Natya* relates the state-of-being of the three worlds (*trailoka*), their interrelatedness (*sutra*), by presenting them in performance. Thus, it serves as a method of instruction, it supports this world and it maintains the 'codes of eternity' (*dharma*).[18]

Natya is far from a by-product of culture in village life. It contains the total sum of knowledge on micro- and macrocosmic levels, and determines the very fate of gods, men and anti-gods. The effect of this type of knowledge is immense: it touches the entire continuum of the three worlds and all that live in it. The heavens, earth and nether regions do not exist in isolation, nor do the gods and other divine forces restrict their influence to their home-region: their power is *in flux* and can be felt at any moment and place of human existence.[19] Therefore it is of the utmost importance to identify all possible forces, their character, their power and their effect, in order to keep them in check and harmonise them with happiness and prosperity. The other sages, colleagues of Bharata, ask the very same questions that information technology would pose: from where is information derived, to what purpose, how is it stored, which are the guiding principles, and how is it to be applied?[20]

The crucial nexus in the method of *natya* is the knowledge of Signs: (a) correct diagnosis of the forces at work (Skt. *laksana*), and (b) correct application in the formation of a marker (Skt. *laksya*). The physical nature of 'translation into concrete equation' is the feeding ground of success as well as of disaster.

> Brahma advises all gods to engage themselves in *natya*; they will enjoy worship that brings them good luck (*subham*) when they descend through *natya* in the world of mortals (*martyalokagatah*). However, great care has to be taken in preparing the pavilion (*mandapa*) and stage (*ranga*) of the *natya*-performance. Once everything has been ritually consecrated, the performance attains the same validity as the [Vedic] *yajna* ritual. Not only the gods who descend in *natya* enjoy *subham*; the organiser and the performer of the ritual will enjoy good luck, happiness and wealth (*artha*) as well; finally, they will even reach heaven.[21]

In the final analysis, *natya* can be understood as a meticulous method of embodiment of the macrocosm into the microcosm. Performance is a *trans-latio*: the establishment of the cosmic order through incarnation. The logic of embodiment is followed from beginning to end. The *Natyasastra* enables us to set up a basic structure of *natya*. Within this structure, variables are determined by the divine 'filler' and the 'occasion' of performance:

(1) Preparing the locus and platform for performance;
(2) Preliminary rites:
    (a) propitiatory rites;
    (b) identificatory rites;
(3) Performance proper: transformatory process; and
(4) Withdrawal rites and purificatory rites.

This procedure gradually draws the divine into the mundane, human world, and fixes it there for some time in order to invigorate it, celebrate it and allow the auspicious, osmotic process to take place; thereafter it is ultimately again released. All the ingredients in the performance are constructed out of physical, human norms and materials. From the size of the stage, which is measured out in analogy to the limbs of the sacrificer, to the actors, who incarnate the divine character, all vehicles are human bodies.

This aspect comes out best in the identificatory rites that form part of the preliminary rites. The process of identification with the characters to be staged is crucial in the production of a *natya* performance. Anyone who wishes to obtain *subham* ('well-being') should scrupulously follow the rules of *aharyabhinaya* ('representation through costume and make-up', NS XXIII 1–3). Identification is achieved by three important proficiencies: (1) ritual skills in preparing and applying suitable costumes and make-up; (2) effective mental preparation; and (3) knowledge of characters that are suitable for impersonation and of those that are not. The ritual skills of make-up are exercised in the greenroom (Skt. *nepathya*), which can be compared to the wombhouse of a temple (Skt. *garbhagrha*). The entire production emerges from it (*tasmin pratisthitah*, NS XXIII 1); here the characters are shaped (*prakrtayah*) and given their direction (*sucitah*). Only then, they can enter without effort into their concrete manifestation by means of their physical features, limbs, etc. (*angadibhir abhivyaktim upagacchanti ayatnatah*, NS XXIII 3).

After stating the three materials by which a character is given its shape (i.e. make-up paste, ornaments and painting of the limbs), Bharata lists a fourth element: the process of bringing the character to life. This process is described in *Natyasastra* XXIII 82–6: by applying the *dharma* (code) of *natya*, the shaping of a character takes place. The involvement of the actor is supposed to be total: 'after one has shed one's own colour and *atman* (Skt.'soul, life-principle'), the form of the character whose shape must be taken up is to be made by means of colours and costumes'. Just as a living being may transform himself into another body [and] another state of existence by having recourse to the body of a ghost (Skt. *bhuta*) after he has shed his natural state of existence and himself, so a man should transform himself into that other state of existence, once he is covered by paints and costume, of the character whose dress he wears.

Natya proves to be much more than mere 'play' or 'interpretation', it means impersonation, human incarnation almost to the extent of human sacrifice.[22] Which character can be impersonated and which cannot? NS XXIII 86 gives a simple rule of thumb: those who possess *prana* (Skt. 'vital breath'), that is, the *jivabandha* (Skt. 'group of the living') can be impersonated: gods, demigods, nymph-like beings, nature-gods, demons, but not hills, palaces, instruments, shields, armours, banners and weapons. However, under certain circumstances the *natyadharma* ('code of impersonation') may bestow *jiva* ('life') on them as well; in that case they can be portrayed as characters endowed with *prana* ('vital breath'). This instance shows once more the belief in the actual transformatory power of the theatrical codes and their application.[23] The actor knows how effectively to 'empty' himself from his own existence, in order to become a vessel (Skt. *patra*) ready to receive the identity of the character he has to impersonate.[24] His translation is literally *trans-latio*, a 'bringing to the other side', leaving his cargo intact, offering his own body as its vehicle.

11.2 Reception

These two different vehicles travel along very different hermeneutic trajectories. The written translation of another text or cultural event attempts to lay down in the form of verbal representation true equations, coining legitimate names for objects and phenomena. Whether false or true, all the structures of its language converge to 'naming'; from there language can enter into a relation with the truth according to which it will be judged. But once that name has been spoken, all language that has led up to it, or that has been crossed in order to reach it, is absorbed into it and disappears. Once that name has been written its reader gropes towards this boundary of absorption; but, in surviving it privately *tête à texte* he pushes its boundary further away. His naming, his writing will travel a similar track, continuing the suspension of the sovereign act of nomination, towards the place where things and words are conjoined in their common essence. This journey is basically a solitary one, contemplating through interior dialogue 'universal validities upon which all certainty rests'. Its reception and hermeneutics are characterised by the one-way activity *tête à texte* that tries to evoke an experience of the essence of Being through 'right' interpretation and understanding. Its joy is the solitary flight of imagination.

The vehicle of performance prospers in a milieu of multiple interactivity: the entire cosmos is present and alert in its process. The gods, the anti-gods, the actors impersonating the gods, the king, the sacrificer and the public, all are involved in complex interlocked behaviours.[25] These behaviours are mutually contingent and produce multiple interactions that flow back and forth through the three worlds; they affect the gods, the anti-gods, the king, the country and all sentient beings in it. This interactive flux is not entirely accidental; earlier we saw that the performance of *natya* is highly structured. The four major cycles through which the *natya* evolves deal with different interactive conglomerates.

Bharata learnt this lesson from empirical evidence: the first celebration of *natya* was spoiled by the anti-gods, who identified their status in the play as inferior; therefore, out of spite and envy with the gods who received better treatment, they paralysed the speech, movement and memory of the actors through their magical powers (*NS* I 66). Bharata then introduced the preliminary rites that pacify these evil spirits, propitiate them by the sound of their own fame and by the gifts they like to receive; he also decided to fence off the accessibility of the playground by effective rites of protection. Moreover, he assured them that the *Natyaveda* was composed in such a way that it would apportion good and bad luck to all parties involved in the three worlds (*śubhāśubha vikalpakah*, *NS* I 105). Thus, the four stages of the *natya* evolve developmental sequences that tend to structure the socio-cultural life of the group by the very fact of their repetition.

The convergence of interactions yields structure from within, especially then the aims are formulated so naturally and loosely: *subham* 'well-being' for the king, the country, the sentient beings in it, the gods and the three worlds at large. The performance of *natya* is believed to invigorate life as such. How is its impact felt? Bharata describes the success of *natya* as *siddhivyanjaka*, that is, 'the making manifest of power' (*NS* XXVII). It is this experience of power emanating from the socio-cultural event of *natya* that legitimizes the performance proper.

The beneficial effect of such celebrations is described eloquently and in great detail by Bruce Kapferer in *A Celebration of Demons* (1983). The performance amounts to a large transformatory process in which the demon is exorcised out of a patient by means of the healing aesthetics of impersonation and gradual identification with the Buddhist forces of life. In this case, the *natya* checks and breaks the power of the demons, it reinforces the working of Buddhist gods and the Buddha himself; it reintegrates the suffering, isolated patient back into society and culminates in the assertion of auspiciousness and sociability. In terms of the 'social psychology of organising' the *natya* is brilliant, especially when we realise that it has already persisted for some two thousand years.

In contrast to the individual experience which emerges from the single interaction between reader and text, the multiple interaction generated by performance is experienced both by the individual and by all the participants in the process. The success of performance as the 'making manifest of power' is identified as being twofold: one manifestation is 'human power', and is expressed by smiles, praising words and other encouragement; the other is *daiviki siddhi*, 'divine power', and is recognisable by an excess of *sattva*, or 'beingness' (*NS* XXIV 1–3 and 16). *Sattva* is the experiencing of 'the essential' that inscribes itself into the human sensory body: it becomes manifest in spontaneous gooseflesh, shivering, tears and other spontaneous affects. Whereas the reader struggles to 'name' the essential 'truth', the participant of a *natya* concentrates to experience 'beingness'.

This type of experience is probably what Peirce hinted at in his category 'firstness': a quality of total feeling, of freshness, life, freedom. The power of *sattva* rests coiled up in the communicative setting: through mimesis, reaching out (Skt. *abhinaya*) towards a sympathetic public (Skt. *sa-hrdaya*, i.e. 'with-hearted') it engenders an identification with the characters, with the group, with the world, with life-at-large, up to the degree of 'tasting' (Skt. *rasa* 'juice', 'taste'). This experience, the final double interaction emerging from the multiple interactions, is the magic of *communio*, that 'extra' which Huizinga would term *beatitudo*; which *natya*, in turn, would term *mangalam* or *subham*; and which theorists on organisational psychology see as the stable component in organisational growth and decay.[25]

Ultimately, it is the experience which is binding, not the norm, consensus or ideology. The aim of 'universal-validities-upon-which-all-certainties-in-history-rest' is very restrictive and prescriptive at the same time; coupled to a disturbed social dynamics of solitary, introspective, single interactions the flexibility of its cosmology is impaired. In contrast to this 'essentialist' aim, the 'eternal consensus', the *Sanatana Dharma* presents a more experiential and existential phenomenon. The predominance of 'experience' over correct normative behaviour is voiced in the withdrawal rites, where the gods are invited 'to take leave, and go back to their regions' to the accompaniment of purificatory rites. A prayer of flexibility accompanies these last rituals:

sādhuvāsadhuvā karma yad yad ācaritam mayā/
tatsarvam devadeveśa gṛhāṇa ārādhanam param//

whatever deed wise or unwise performed by me/
that in total, Oh god of gods, please accept as supreme lustration//

Notes

1. Clifford and Marcus, 1986, p. 156.
2. Clifford and Marcus, 1986, p. 159; cf. also the earlier quote from George Steiner's 'To civilize our gentlemen'.
3. The general uneasiness that one detects among informants about the final representations that their data receive may also, to some extent, be caused by the different types of scholarship: in terms of Bourdieu, that of *auctores* versus the scholarship of *lectores* (Bourdieu, 1990b, pp. 94–5).
4. Clifford and Marcus, 1986, p. 161.
5. Clifford and Marcus, 1986, p. 159.
6. Clifford and Marcus, 1986, p. 123.
7. Clifford and Marcus, 1986, p. 157.
8. Clifford and Marcus, 1986, pp. 156 ff., 'The Inequality of Languages'.
9. Clifford and Marcus, 1986, p. 157 quoting Walter Benjamin, 1969, *Illuminations*, New York, Schoken, pp. 80–1.
10. Clifford and Marcus, 1986, p. 159; this advice reminds me of my own mental resolve that I took when I first started to live in Nandini's house. Sushama, Nandini's daughter was about five years old by that time; I made a point of it that my own efforts should be those of a similar mental age. We started vocal music in almost the same season, while Sushama's dance classes commenced shortly after mine. Unfortunately, I was not able to keep pace with her tempo and development owing to my absence over long periods. However, Sushama's debut in dance took place in October 1987, while mine followed in March 1989.
11. Foucault, 1970, trans., p. 33.
12. Lyotard, 1988, Dutch trans. 1992, (trans.), p. 15.
13. Foucault, 1970, trans., p. 94.

14. Foucault, 1970, trans., p. 95.
15. Cf. CD-i Content-Time-Word-World for a recitation of this hymn.
16. Foucault, 1970, trans., pp. 115 ff.
17. NS I.105, where the *natyaveda* is defined as *subhasubhavikalpakah*.
18. NS I 7 ff. and NS I 108–15.
19. Cf. CD-i: Content-Space-Image-World.
20. NS I 4–5: *katham, kasya, katyangah, kimpramanas, prayoga*.
21. NS I 124–6.
22. Kersenboom, S. C., 1989–90, 'Natya – the Desi Yajna' in *Indologica Taurinensia*, Vol. XV–XVI, pp. 187–205.
23. By way of this logic the spear of the god Murugan could be understood as the marriage partner to Smt. P. Ranganayaki, or the pot (*kumbha*) as a synonym of the goddess.
24. Cf. Weick, 1979, *The Social Psychology of Organizing*, Ch.4, p. 110.
25. Cf. Weick, 1979, pp. 89ff.

Conclusion

The wise say: 'Do not read: "start at my sanctuary", but "start at those who sanctify me".'
— Talmud *Sabbath*, 55a[1]

The *devas* ('gods') ate together while the *asuras* ('anti-gods') ate alone, for themselves.

This work has been dealing continuously with both aspects: practice and interaction as conditions for human knowledge. In a kind of 'radical hermeneutics' the humanities are played out in the open, among fellow human beings, taking as their vehicle the four dimensions of shared presence that unite time and place. Human time and human space, man-made presence, are the only rift into 'general, physical time' and 'general, physical space' that opens up to us. All that we can achieve or know, we perform or learn in that 'clearing'; it constitutes our stage, our opportunity. Our performance is our effort to feel intuitively the hall and the audience, to express and open ourselves to an answer. It is limited, in space, in time and in means; nevertheless, we try to make the best of this opportunity: it is ever unique, acute and fresh to our individual experience. On that stage of our lifetime, lit by the lights of real-life circumstances, we chisel our presence with the limited means we can dispose of. Our bodies are quite capable of such expression: words, sounds and images are all we have, but how rich they are! They form the media of expression as well as the model for a successful reception of our urge. The hall around the stage, however, remains dark; it can be felt but not assessed. Still, we act, reaching out with our lives for life. Human culture is a performing art. It dwells in the four dimensions of space and time. Only under these conditions can it unfold in full. Any reduction is a loss of complexity and hence of information, know-how, feel and intimacy. Therefore the

Conclusion

representations of culture will always fall short; this does not mean that they serve no purpose. The inscription of guidelines, of structures and of formulae such as the three lines of the *varnam*, or even the larger manuscripts of the Hindu epics, serve excellently as 'memory aids' to groups of professional performers. It is their expertise to *render the text into meaningful action*. On the other hand, to *reduce meaningful action into text* and to sever its umbilical cord to presence, runs the danger of a permanent loss of dimensional complexity which can never be retrieved away from its original milieu. Taking culture as a performing art we must come to the conclusion that there is *no meaning without practice*.

It is the practice of culture that allots an opportunity to every member of society. Practice, first and foremost, guarantees activity, application and exchange – if only on the artisanal level. The practice of culture is the concerted effort of 'chiselling the presence of culture'. Not unlike the processes that made up the ancient science of Alchemy, the practice of culture can be seen as an Alchemy of Presence in which the human body forms the central instrument, norm and medium. Human bodies, cast in the process of life, mix and mingle, constituting together their Fantasy that Works. For this to work, Fantasy has to hold beyond the single, isolated individual; Fantasy must 'reach out', it must be able to accommodate a 'grand sweep' of imagination: right and left, up and down, high and deep; it must have the power to enthuse others, its graceful attraction must point beyond, beyond even the grasp of words and imagination. This 'Grand Sweep' starts off with 'Exteriority', that reaching out for the Other, for Life and ultimately even Beyond.[2] Such reaching out is the intuitive reaching out into the dark hall, the innumerable dimensions that are at work there, perhaps, but that cannot be determined in human terms on a human stage lit by the four dimensions of matter and time. In essence, it is an attitude of openness, receptive to the unknown, entering into a relation with it, without determining the conditions of that relation. In Indian terms this is understood as the fundamental attitude of devotion, of *bhakti*, the 'melting to become part of'.[3]

Ultimately, the belonging is not known; the Face of God, is in the Face of the Other: the Divine is encountered as tree, as worm, as stone, as man, as woman, as guest, as icon in temples. In the end, the Divine is beyond representation, hidden in the act of worship.⁴ Images serve only to stimulate the relation, the direction outwards, reaching beyond the Ego; they appear to the individual perception in accordance with its natural grasp to comprehend, to be enthused and to shift its own limitations. The final expectation of the 'beyond' is 'Bliss': *sat-cit-ananda* 'being-consciousness-bliss'.

Older thoughts maintained *neti neti* 'not according to said, not according to said', generally translated as 'not so, not so', avowing that human speech cannot coin any term to express the Beyond.⁵ Language can, at most, suggest and incite an attitude that is directed towards experiencing the Beyond, but can never describe it in full. The concentration on a unifying concept and absorption of the experience of life in terms of essences that can be transformed into a meta-reality called 'truth', is basically an introspective activity.

Such Interiority is not without danger. First of all, the inward direction of the quest precludes further open-ended testing in the world. As we saw earlier, the entire procedure of 'eliciting meaning from an event' consists, according to Ricoeur, in a gradual distanciation from any referential reality. Once the 'data' have been gathered, the corpus for reflection is closed off at the danger of arbitrary limitation and loss of compatibility with the 'real-life' performance. This danger increases all the more with the growing distance between the locus of reflection and the world, and with diminishing the need for applying the results of that reflection back into the world. The chance of a 'hermeneutical arc' that never returns to the human soil is implicit in this procedure. The attitude of Interiority prospers in this suspension of the dimensions time and space. Nevertheless the question remains: to what does the interpreter lose himself in the process of absorbing his text by reading it over and over again? What is revealed to him in such a mysterious manner: 'meaning' as universal reality, the experience of 'understanding', or the lapse into complete solipsism by the workings of entropy?

At their extreme poles both attitudes seem to border on madness. Vital epistemes that propound 'Fantasies that work' and that last for several generations move within this polar continuum, either as a strategy for a fertile life or as an example of one successful lifetime; they never rotate around one pole only. Thus Indian tradition provides us with one such example: the Buddha, who concentrated on his self-enclosure in yogic, meditational exercises to the extent of exhaustion and starvation without success, only to attain enlightenment in a simple setting under a *bodhi* tree. It is telling that this moment did not fulfil him with total interior conviction and satisfaction: therefore he touched the soil as a witness to attest the exterior 'referentiality' of his experience. In modern terms one might say that, for the Buddha, *the test of the theory is the touch of the earth*.[6] At the end of his long journey of interiority lay a return to exteriority; even in his reaching *nirvana* (Skt. 'evaporation') he considered his wisdom to be complete only in the act of returning to the world of mankind. After all, he was born in a human shape and still continued to live that life. Wisdom and metaphysical experience can be translated on the level of human existence only into embodiment that poses a concrete example of understanding. In Buddhism this is *karuna*, empathy, an outgoing involvement in all life. The fundamental principle of 'not-harming' (Skt. *ahimsa*) is an example of 'applied Exteriority' in the confrontation with the 'Other'. The example that was set by the Buddha (6th century BC) has inspired entire continents for millennia.

However, for the individual man or woman it may take several rebirths to achieve this ripe, practical wisdom. In a single birth, one may hope to apply successfully the strategies for equilibrium that are handed down by tradition. The *sanatana dharma*, 'eternal coherence', grades and amalgamates attitudes of exteriority and interiority throughout the several phases of an individual lifetime. Hindu *mores* envisage the trajectory of human life as evolving in four stages. First as a child, where the main concern is to grow and gain physical strength in the nourishing warmth of the love of others – at such a stage the little girl and boy are considered gods; the image of God as a naughty child is therefore a very plausible one. Hereafter follows the period of study: in a setting of teacher–student interaction the pupil is taught whatever he needs to know in order to earn a living, either as priest, as dancer, as musician, as sculptor or as Tamil expert. Any expertise is transmitted in that period, before the awakening of sexuality. Once these forces have blossomed in their bodies, it is advisable to make them enter the stage of a householder. Thus commences the application of learning to the flourishing of life: growth, children, wealth and happiness are the natural share of that period.

Finally, when one's first grey hairs appear, the time seems ripe to withdraw from immediate action, and take contemplation seriously. This meditative movement, narrowing the circle of interaction with the world and focusing upon metaphysical understanding of life, cannot be entered into before one has experienced the fullness of the application of life. Its vitality is revealed in the fulfilment of human needs such as material wealth (*artha*) and sexual pleasure and intimacy (*kama*), both within an appropriate, natural slot in one's *habitus* (*dharma*). Abstraction, metaphysics and ultimate transcendence (*moksa*) require the solid basis of an actual 'having experienced' the complexity of human existence. Before that stage in life, any abstract mission that requires withdrawal from daily interaction is possible only for the very, very few, such as a saint or a child touched by the grace of god. Such very 'potent' persons might qualify for bearing the heavy load of the metaphysical quest.

Anyone who enters such a situation without due preparation and natural strength, or who lands in a situation of isolation that is similar to religious seclusion, runs the risk of what Bruce Kapferer diagnoses as *tanikkam noy* 'the illness of self-confinement', or 'the suffering of alone-ness'.[7] Physical isolation, living alone, or being alone among others, marked by a gradual withdrawal from sensory 'feedback' and interaction with the world, form situations that are potentially very dangerous. Usually such conditions develop as a result of mental–emotional isolation or shock; but they can be self-induced as well. They prepare a feeding ground for demons and spirits of the deceased that could not quench their thirst for life during their own lifetime. As a result they are in search of other, living bodies that they can invade and inhabit to live out their passions. Men and women afflicted by these dark, virulent forces tend to disappear into a deepening solipsism unless they are helped by their community to re-enter into real, double interactivity.[8]

The work of Bruce Kapferer shows that these practices are at the same time very powerful knowledge representations. In the course of a continuous ritual process they offer not only propositional knowledge on Existence and the human condition within it, but also practical knowledge that makes human life comfortable, and knowledge of familiarity that renders the human span of life worthwhile and precious. The ritual process is multi-medial and interactive *par excellence*; it is very flexible and adaptable to individual circumstances. It has to be so,

Conclusion

because its main aim is not to explain 'meaning' or to teach dogmas, but to transform, to interact with Existence in order to improve the conditions of human life. Therefore, the ritual has to know and understand Existence deeply. It does; being an 'ancient Sign' it enters the Grand Sign via the temporal sign (both *ilakkiyam*, Ta. 'the marked'), embodied in the ritual specialists and in the patient, and it sets things right.

Whether it does so 'objectively' and *eo ipso* metaphysically may be a matter of doubt to us. At the level of the participants it works and heals the community, restoring the individual human life in the only 'clearing' that we can know in one lifetime. In order to represent such critical knowledge, the ritual appropriates all dimensions: it demands a sensory presence, a sharing of space, time and sympathies. In the course of twelve hours crossing midnight, the demon is invited, celebrated, challenged, matched, drained of his powers and fragmented into ridiculous proportions, while the patient is gradually released from his interior confinement and step by step 'cleansed' from the forces that draw him back into his inner darkness. He is 'opened up' and carefully guided back into communication and social interaction. The procedure is not one of reading out of sermons, insights, good counsel or generalities; on the contrary, the procedure is the concrete practice of the dancing exorcists, their recitations, the appearance of the gruesome demon, his penetrating stench, the blaze of the *dummala* fire-torch, the telling of ageless stories, the burning of lamps, hacking and slicing of fruits, the coarse humour and obscene jokes and finally, the impressive destruction of the palace from where the patient emerges as a newly born member of society, ready to share the grand communal meal.[9] From its beginning to the end, the ritual is one gigantic flexible, adaptable, multimedial, doubly interactive representation of all-encompassing knowledge. To reduce its practice to mere structure or to a 'gist' of propositions would render the entire effort impotent and ineffective. Moreover, the ritual is meant not to be conclusive. In its need for repetition, a deepening sense of familiarity and sociality seem to be safeguarded.

In a similar vein the *varnaprabandham mohamana* moves from total Interiority to freeing Exteriority. The declaration of *moha*, of infatuation as a sensuous snare, remains unanswered by the god. His fame and renown in the world of *dharma* shake the devotee out of her self-enclosure and transform the experience of *moha* 'intoxication' into *bhoga* 'delight'. The arrows of the god of love (*Kama*) descend on her in the course of her reaching out and interaction with the exterior, experiential reality (*artha*). The sound of the birds, the touch of the evening breeze, the beauty of the moon rays force her not to lapse back into an interior self-delusion, but prepare her for the final reaching out and surrender to the embrace of the Absolute (*moksa*).[10] The struggle from debilitating interiority to all-encompassing exteriority is achieved in various ways: in the rituals of demon exorcism, the battle between the forces of isolation and those of sociality is embodied by various characters and played out in an 'epic performance'. In contrast to this trajectory, the *varnam* situates this raging combat right within a single individual – the devotee, the girl in love. Through her receptive vulnerability, her drunken infatuation transforms itself into a power of love that is capable of transcending any narrow confinement to self-defined realities. The essence of this lyrical poetry is not to reduce 'the unknown' to categories of the known but to 'let go' the known, opening a space for the 'unknown'.

Challenge

The demand of human knowledge to be represented in order to become accessible to thought as well as to life, confronts us with a number of facts, questions, problems and choices. In contrast to the 'four-dimensional intertextuality' of ritual practices, the practices of 'two-dimensional inscription' reveal a different dynamism. The mediating principle that brings such representations alive is *conceptualisation*. It lies at the root of all activities involved in writing, reading and interpreting, all facilities such as libraries, museums, universities, publishing houses, etc. The interactive moments in the life of this type of knowledge are the classroom, seminars, conferences and the like, where propositional knowledge is offered in the format of some twenty or sixty minutes' verbal text, spoken while seated or standing and listened to by an audience that is invariably seated so that it can note down details of interest, agreement or disagreement. The real celebration of the interactive event is in

Conclusion

the discussion, the exchange of ideas.

Without trying to depict a caricature of academic life, the vast gap between the two practices of knowledge representation must yawn at us in scaring, abysmal proportions. It is painfully evident that the task of representing human knowledge is not tackled in uniform ways. 'Modern' demands for 'measurement, order, universals and control' are being questioned today in many disciplines of Western scholarship.[11] In spite of these discussions we do not seem to be able to move beyond the stage of reflections, theories and propositions on the problems involved. Why? Perhaps, on the one hand, because of the media of expressing these concerns; these are still mainly static, two-dimensional representations that are capable of accommodating only linear, analytic description and theory. Simultaneity, process, organic complexity and synthesis do not remain intact in written publications, not to mention change and flexible interactivity. On the other hand, we may still not have fully given up our hope for the 'Elusive, Unifying Truth Principle' – the altar of modernity.[12]

Imagine, instead, a different *episteme* that goes with a different attitude: not pursuing a paradigm of abstract generalities or universals but one of concrete particulars; namely, an *episteme* of 'effective communication'. *Sarasvati*, the goddess of Speech, encompasses all levels of abstraction and concretion in her *'power of utterance'*.[13] Taking communication as a first given, the 'new' scientific pursuit revolves around a 'what' coupled to a 'how' in order to achieve successful interactivity between senders and receivers on all planes of 'Being'. Such an episteme is rooted in a practice of *exteriority*, dwelling and unfolding in the particularities of shared *presence*.[14]

The contemporary demand for flexible knowledge systems and representations has many facets: first, representations should be able to convey more than propositional knowledge alone; second, no representation is expected to be 'conclusive' but should, ideally speaking, remain open to 'updating'. This aspect is new and paves the way to two types of use: either within the old paradigm of the 'growth of human knowledge', or within a new paradigm of interactivity and practice. The Compact Disc Interactive used in the latter way implies a dynamic representation of human knowledge in its ancient capacity of 'memory aid' and 'device in a live practice'. In terms of cognitive psychology it affords the brain a chance to test and work out its imaginative artistry in the representational workshop of the interactive program.[15] The true challenge of interactive multimedia is in the *différant* ways of storing, representing and using human knowledge. To break away from the agenda of Modernity may imply the breaking away from its media of representation. The printed book seems to be the 'knowledge representation' *par excellence* of Modern Science. The challenge of today consists not only in opening up new horizons of thought but also in treading fresh methodological soil and finding better ways of representing human knowledge.

A 'Radical Hermeneutics' demands an immersion in the world of practice, a truly 'dialogical' confrontation with the Other, sharing Time and Space in a committed presence. The expertise, familiarity and ease with cultural processes that are concrete, dynamic, complex, organic and synthetic, coupled to a virtuosity of representing these in ways that are adequate for practising understanding, will free us from the accusation of an 'anthropological sleep'. Foucault diagnoses the 'critical analysis of what man is in his essence' as a condition of sleep – a sleep 'so deep that thought experiences it paradoxically as vigilance', drawing into its analytic dream everything that can, in general, be presented to man's experience.[16] He envisages a solution in the destruction of the 'anthropological quadrilateral'[17] in its very foundations, in the tearing ourselves free from all 'ismic' prejudices. The promised land that stretches behind these feats of growing up is 'nothing more, and nothing less, than the unfolding of a space in which it is once more possible to think'[18] – which shuttles us back right to the start of modernity.

'Questions about the limits of thought' as well as 'general critiques of reason' are formed out of the same propositional temperament and epistemic aims and committed to similar forms. Perhaps it is not possible to think radically different thoughts as long as the underlying activity and media of representation remain unaltered. In contrast to purely discursive thought, Anthropology is one of the disciplines that takes us to the field, to the real-time, real-place confrontation with the Other. The enigmatic presence of Foucault's void may turn out to be the vital presence of the Other. The unfolding of the space to think may be revealed in the practices of the Other, in interaction, labour and suffering. Practice and practising may turn out to be a *conditio sine qua non* to crack the self-confinement in concepts and to open up the experience of the 'Beyond'; that is, beyond formalisation, codification and even articulation.

This type of research does not aspire to unravel what 'man essentially is', but rather what man can be in concrete particulars. Instead of the fixation of 'universal' truths, it needs devices for practice, instruments and occasions for interactivity in order to experience an infinite variety of existing 'truths'. These devices should be representations that are dynamic and that open themselves up to an active acquisition of their content. To analyse and describe phenomena is no longer enough: to synthesise them again, in accordance with their inner logic, into working order and to allow the users repeated experiments with the program until they can imagine and reason along with the organic process of the phenomenon, is a contemporaneous demand. CD-i may therefore be considered a representation of human knowledge that is 'post-modern' in the contrastive sense of the term: organic, flexible and concretely practical, communicative and playing with the categories of time and space.[19]

The real challenge lies in the world, here and now. Good representations of knowledge should take us right there, well prepared, well practised, to experience for ourselves. In Indian terms all acts of worship, and therefore, all possible representations of knowledge, are necessarily limited; they do not aspire a conclusive power of measurement and control. On the contrary, the ultimate aim of the act of sacrifice is *tyaga* 'letting go', 'surrender', 'renunciation', renouncing even the meaningful purpose of the rite. Thus it substantiates the essential 'reaching out', Exteriority, the communicative, vulnerable groping for a relation with the unknown. To dance the *varnam 'mohamana'* implies offering all efforts of training, practice and memory to the 'King of Tyaga', Shri Tyagaraja. To publish the *varnam 'mohamana'* as a book and a CD-i implies offering all efforts to bold imagination.

May it live there.

Notes

1. This motto is taken from Lévinas, Emmanuel, 1974, *Autrement qu'être ou au-delà de l'essence*, Paris, Livre de Poche, repr. 1990: 'Les sages ont dit: "Ne lisez pas 'commencez par mon

sanctuaire' mais 'commencez par ceux qui me sanctifient' . . . comme l'enseigne le Traité talmudique *Sabbath*, 55a (Commentaire de Rachi in Ezechiel IX, 6)'.
2. Lévinas can be considered the most eloquent advocate of 'Exteriority' in his *Totalité et infini, essai sur l'exteriorité*, dating back to 1961, reprint, 1984, The Hague, Martinus Nijhoff Publishers.
3. *Bhakti*, understood as 'melting to become part of', forms one of the main streams of Hindu devotion. Lyrical texts such as *padams* and *varnams* belong to a particular type of devotion: *srngara bhakti* 'devotion urged by eros' – not as an individual thirst and gratification but as the encompassing embrace of the unconditioned, infinite experience of bliss. Again, Lévinas voices similar notions beautifully within a Western context. In his series of lectures delivered in 1946/7 at the Collège Philosophique, under the title 'Le temps et l'autre', the fourth lecture deals with desire for 'the other' as desire for 'otherness' in terms of mystery, of elusive but evocative two-sided communication that is carried by the erotic yearning developing its own wings to carry both lovers beyond all categorisation and articulation.
4. The non-representational character of the Divine is strongly felt in Hinduism. However, such insight does not come easily to anyone and certainly not to everyone. Therefore Hinduism sees images of the Divine that are concretised in idols as possibly indexical of the Divine; for those whose mental grasp cannot surge beyond the concrete, these images form a locus of getting into and maintaining a relationship with Divine presence. Images are carefully designed in accordance with the nature of the Divine that should enter them. Once the image (Skt. *murti*) has been completed, a priest will invite the Divine to take residence in the icon; it is by the very act and continuity of worship that the Divine is made to be present among mankind. Tradition holds that when the basic quantity and quality of worship (fire, water, flowers) is interrupted, the god or goddess leaves the idol: the indexical presence is thereby reduced again to a material icon. It is the practice of worship that transforms the three-dimensional icon into a four-dimensional presence, or vice versa. Hinduism envisages a very wide range of representations of the Divine: from natural phenomena (mountains, trees, rivers, etc.), to

meticulously detailed anthropomorhic images, to creations of a highly abstract level. For instance, the god Shiva is often represented by the *linga*, lit. the 'index' of his presence, usually identified by Western scholars as a phallus. Apart from this rather common representation, in Tamilnadu Shiva is also worshipped in the forms of a *linga* made out of the 'five elements' (*panca bhuta*): earth, water, fire, air and aether. This last is to be found in the temple of Chidambaram (*citampalam* 'hall of consciousness') where the aether-*linga* is present, although it cannot be seen by the eye. To mark its presence the priests traditionally suspend a *bilva* leaf in the 'empty' sanctum.

5. The aversion from conclusive representations of the Divine, in either mental or material articulations, points at the experiential nature of the Divine. Basically, it is held to inhere in a practice that generates an experience. Its quality is *ananda* 'unboundedness', accessible through *cit* 'consciousness, experiential centre', and its locus is *sat* 'being'. Life cast into conditioned Form and Time cannot perceive the Divine in its natural, unconditioned 'being'. However, a 'relational flux' between the two can generate the experience of the Divine that dwells in the 'first dimension', beyond Time (dimension four), Form (dimension three) and Postulate (dimension two).
6. *Buddha bhumi sparsa mudra* ('gesture of touching the earth').
7. Cf. Bruce Kapferer, 1983, *A Celebration of Demons, Exorcism and the Aesthetics of Healing in Sri Lanka*, Chapter 4 'Demonic Illness: Diagnosis and Social Context', pp. 49–92.
8. This is an ancient belief that is still to be found in South Indian villages; see for example *The Village Gods of South India*, by Whitehead, reprint 1983, New Delhi, Cosmo Publications, *Les dieux et les hommes*, by Reiniche, 1979, Paris, Mouton, and, for Sri Lanka, *Medusa's Hair*, by Obeyesekere, 1981, Chicago, Chicago University Press.
9. Cf. Bruce Kapferer, *Sorcery and Sacrifice*, forthcoming, 1995–6, Berg Publishers Oxford.
10. Through the transformation of the self-centred drive of desire that belongs to frenetic Interiority, into the groping surrender to the mysterious charisma of love, the practice of Exteriority attains its intimations of Divinity. The character of Erotic charm suggested by Lévinas was well understood by the

original royal and temple courtesans. *Srngara bhakti* was handled by them in most delicate and suggestive ways, to incite the mystery of the Other in terms of the attraction of Eros rather than to spell out the particulars of its sexual implications. However, the so-called 'puritans' who earnestly took it upon themselves to 'upgrade' the performing arts to 'respectability' so that South Indian housewives could 'save' it from total disintegration, carefully selected 'decent' compositions from the traditional repertoire, in addition often censored it according to Victorian norms, and added a number of new compositions that were considered 'spiritual' or 'purely devotional'. Obviously, *srngara bhakti*, 'erotic devotion', was no longer understood nor welcome. Dancers like Smt. T. Balasarasvati, who belonged to the old, mystical finesse of the temple and court tradition, defended their heritage against Theosophists and other new authorities. With gusto T. Sankaran retells a joke that was current in those days: 'Balasarasvati is famous for *srngara bhakti* ("erotic devotion"), modern dancers for *akar-bhakti* ("incense devotion")'.

11. Cf. the chapter 'Representing' in *The Order of Things* by Foucault, 1970, pp. 46–78.
12. A concise survey and critical history of Modernity and its 'hidden agenda' are to be found in Stephen Toulmin's 1990, *Cosmopolis*, The Free Press, New York.
13. Skt. *Vaksakti*, meaning *vac*- 'utterance', *sakti* 'power'. See CD-i Content sub sound-time-world for her iconography.
14. Note that one of the Sanskrit synonyms for temple is 'presence': *Sannidhi*.
15. Ideally speaking such a workshop should be part of a CD-i program; owing to lack of funds we had to decide to skip the sub-programs 'variants' and 'workshop'.
16. Cf. Foucault, *The Order of Things*, 1970, p. 341.
17. Cf. Foucault, *ibid.*, pp. 342–3.
18. Cf. Foucault, *ibid.*, p. 342. In the light of the 'sterility' of discursive thought as the saving grace, we may point out that the question of 'tacit knowledge', its varying nature (practical, familiar) and loci (body and world) arises again in the context of a dynamic concept of 'knowledge'; 'knowing' is understood here as residing in a flux between multiple dimensions flowing back and forth between the first

Conclusion

dimension of pure experience and the fourth dimension of time and beyond. Such flexibility sets new demands for data, analysis, vision and their implementation.
19. The design and programming of a CD-i title requires detailed practical knowledge, broad and deep familiarity with the life-world of the object of expression, analytic and synthetic thinking combined in a non-linear, multiple stream conglomerate of organic messages.

Select Bibliography

1. Primary sources

- *Sanskrit*
  - *Nāṭyaśāstra,* Vols I and II, ed. and trans. by M. Ghosh, 1967, Calcutta, Granthalaya
- *Tamil*
  - Cilappatikāram, with commentary by Atiyarkkunallar, ed. Dr U. V. Caminataiyar, 1892, Madras, reprint, 1985, Tamil University, Thanjavur
  - Poṉṉaiyā Maṇimālai, by Kittappa, K. P. and Civanantam, K. P, ed. Sarabhai, M., 1961, Ahmedabad, Darpana
  - Tirumantiram, ed. with commentary by G. Varatarajan, 1978, 1983, Madras, Palaniyappa Piratars
  - Tiruvācakam: *The Tiruvacagam or "Sacred Utterances" of the Tamil Saint and Sage Manikka Vacagar,* ed. and trans. by G. U. Pope, 1900, Oxford, Clarendon Press
  - Tolkāppiyam, 1967, with commentary by Naccinakkiniyar, ed. K. Cuntaramurtti, 1952, repr., 1974, Madras, The South Indian Saiva Sidhanta Works Publishing Society
  - Yāpparuṅkalakkārikai, with commentary by Kunacakarar, ed. M. V. Venugopala Pillai, 1968, Madras, Pari Nilayam
- *Telugu*
  - Pallaki Sēva Prabamdhamu, by Shahaji Maharaja, ed. in Tamil and Telugu by Sambamoorthy, P., 1955, Madras, Gnanodaya Press

2. Secondary sources

- *Interviews*
  - Interviews with T. Balasarasvati by N. Pattabhi Raman with Anandhi Ramachandran in *Sruti, South Indian classical music and dance monthly,* 1984, January–February, 1984, pp. 17–32, and, March, 1984, pp. 17–40, 46

241

These and other interviews and reminiscences were collected and published by T. Sankaran, in a special bumper issue of *Sangeet Natak*, Journal of the Sangeet Natak Akademi, 1984.
- *Public address*
  - Smt. T. Balasarasvati, 'Reflections', 1978 Committee on research in Dance (CORD), printed in *NCPA Quarterly*, 1982, Vol. XI, Nos. 3 & 4, pp. 5–15, Bombay, National Centre for the Performing Arts, translator unknown
  - Smt. T. Balasarasvati, 'Bharata Natyam', Tamil address read out by her daughter Smt. Lakshmi Knight, in Tamil Icai Sangam, December 1975, trans. by S. Guhan in *Marg*, Vol. XXIV No. 3, pp. 37–45, also in *Bala on Bharata Natyam*, compiled and translated by S. Guhan, 1991, p. 23, Madras, The Sruti Foundation
- *Authors*
  - Adams, P., 1972, ed., *Language in Thinking*, Harmondsworth, Middlesex, Penguin
  - Baker-Reynolds, H., 1980, 'The Auspicious Woman', in: *The Powers of Tamil Women*, Syracuse, Syracuse University Press
  - Bourdieu, P., 1990a, *Outline of a Theory of Practice*, 7th edn, Cambridge, Cambridge University Press
  - Bourdieu, P., 1990b, *In Other Words*, Oxford, Polity Press
  - Brand, S., 1988, *The Media Lab, Inventing the future at M.I.T.*, Harmondsworth, Middlesex, Penguin
  - Brodsky, J., 1987, *Less than One*, Harmondsworth, Middlesex, Penguin
  - Brooks, D. R., 1992, *Auspicious Wisdom, The Texts and Traditions of Srividya Sakta Tantrism in South India*, New York, State University of New York Press
  - Bruin, H. de, 1994, Kattaikkuttu: The Flexibility of a South Indian Theatre Tradition, Ph.D. Dissertation, State University, Leiden, Holland
  - Busch, T. W. and Gallagher, S., eds, *Merleau-Ponty, Hermeneutics and Post-Modernism*, New York, State University of New York Press
  - Caputo, J., 1987, *Radical Hermenutics, Repetition, Deconstruction and the Hermeneutic Project*, Bloomington, Indiana University Press
  - Clifford, J. and Marcus, G., 1986, *Writing Culture, The Poetics and Politics of Ethnography*, Berkeley, University of California Press
  - Daniel, V., 1984, *Fluid Signs, Being a Person the Tamil Way*, Berkeley, University of California Press
  - Derrida, J., 1978, *Writing and Difference*, Chicago, University of Chicago Press
  - Eco, U., 1976, *A Theory of Semiotics*, Bloomington, Indiana University Press

- Fabian, J., 1983, *Time and the Other, How Anthropology makes its Object*, New York, Columbia University Press
- Foucault, M., 1970, *The Order of Things, An Archaeology for the Human Sciences*, New York, Pantheon Books
- Göranzon, B. and Josefson, I., 1988, *Knowledge, Skill and Artifical Intelligence*, Heidelberg, Springer Verlag
- Gupta, S., 1987, see Nijenhuis, E. te and Gupta, S.
- Hiltebeitel, A., 1988, 1991, *The Cult of Draupadi, Mythologies: from Gingee to Kuruksetra*, Vols. I and II, Chicago, University of Chicago Press
- Hiriyanna, M., 1978, *Essentials of Indian Philosophy*, London, Unwin Paperbacks
- Holton, G., 1988, *The Origins of Scientific Thought*, Cambridge, Mass., Harvard University Press
- Huizinga, J., 1955, *Homo Ludens, A Study of the Play Elements in Culture*, Boston, repr. London, Routledge, Kegan and Paul
- Jakobson, R., 1990, *On Language*, ed. Waugh, L. R. and Monville-Burston, M., Cambridge, Mass., Harvard University Press
- Jakobson, R. and Pomorska, K., 1980, *Dialogues*, Paris, Flammarion
- Kapferer, B., 1983, *A Celebration of Demons, Exorcism and the Aesthetics of Healing in Sri Lanka*, Bloomington, Indiana University Press
- Kersenboom-Story, S. C., 1987, *Nityasumangali, Devadasi Tradition in South India*, Delhi, Motilal Banarsidass
- Kersenboom, S. C., 1990, 'Devadasi Murai', in: *Sangeet Natak*, Journal of the Sangeet Natak Akademi, Delhi, no. 96, pp. 44–55
- Kersenboom, S. C., 1991a, 'Natya – the Desi Yajna', in: *Indologica Taurinensia, Vol. XV–XVI (1989–90)*, pp. 187–205
- Kersenboom, S. C., 1991b, 'The Repertoire of Tiruttani Temple Dancers', in: *The Hindu Woman*, ed. Leslie, J., London, Pinter
- Kristeva, J., 1981, *Le Langage cet inconnu, Une initiation à la linguistique* Paris, Editions du Seuil
- Lévinas, E., 1974, *Autrement qu'être au delà de l'essence*, Paris, Livre de Poche, 1990 repr.
- Lévinas, E., 1979, *Le temps et l'autre*, Paris, Fata Morgana
- Levinson, S., 1987, *Pragmatics*, New York, Cambridge University Press
- Lyotard, J. F., 1988, *L'inhumain: causeries sur le temps*, Paris, Editions Galilée
- McLuhan, M., 1962, *The Gutenberg Galaxy*, Toronto, University of Toronto Press
- Mookerjee, A., 1982, *Kundalini, The Arousal of Inner Energy*, London, Thames and Hudson

- Muilwijk, M., 1992, The Divine Kura Tribe, Kuravanci and other Prabandhams, Ph.D. diss., State University of Utrecht
- Nijenhuis, E.te and Gupta, S., 1987, *Sacred Songs of India, Diksitar's Cycle of Hymns to the Goddess Kamala*, Part I and II, Winterthur, Amadeus Verlag
- Olsen, D. R., Torrance, N., Hildyard, A., 1985, *Literacy, Language and Learning, The Nature and Consequences of Reading and Writing*, Cambridge, Cambridge University Press
- Ong, W. J., 1982, *Orality and Literacy, The Technologizing of the Word*, London, New York, Methuen
- Ponnusvamy, S., 1972, *Sri Thyagaraja Temple, Tiruvarur*, Govt. of Tamilnadu State Dept. of Archaeology
- Ramanujan, A. K., 1970, *The Interior Landscape*, London, Peter Owen
- Reiniche, M.L., 1979, *Les dieux et les hommes, Etude des cultes d'un village du Tirunelveli*, Paris, Mouton
- Ricoeur, P., 1981, *Hermeneutics and the Human Sciences, Essays on Language, Action and Interpretation*, Cambridge, Cambridge University Press
- Ringland, G. A. and Duce, D. A., 1988, *Knowledge Representation, An Introduction*, Letchworth, Research Studies Press
- Said, E., 1978, *Orientalism, Western Conceptions of the Orient*, London, Penguin
- Seeger, Ch., 1977, *Studies in Musicology 1935–1975*, Berkeley, University of California Press
- Silverman, K., 1983, *The Subject of Semiotics*, New York, Oxford University Press
- Smith, F., 1985, 'Literacy: inventing worlds or shunting information', in Olsen, Torrance and Hildyard, 1985
- Steiner, G., 1969, *Language and Silence*, Harmondsworth, Middlesex, Penguin
- Stevens, J., 1986, *Words and Music in the Middle Ages, Song, Narrative, Dance and Drama*, Cambridge, Cambridge University Press
- Takahashi, T., 1989, Poetry and Poetics, Literary Conventions of Tamil Love Poetry, Ph.D. Dissertation, State University of Utrecht
- Tedlock, D., 1983, *The Spoken Word and the Work of Interpretation*, Philadelphia, University of Pennsylvania Press
- Vatsyayan, K., 1980, *Traditional Indian Theatre, Multiple Streams*, New Delhi, National Book Trust
- Weick, K.E., 1979, *The Social Psychology of Organizing*, New York, Random House
- Whorf, B. L., 1972, in: Adams, P., ed., *Language in Thinking*, Harmondsworth, Middlesex, Penguin

- Zimmer, H., 1974, *Myths and Symbols in Indian Art and Civilization*, Princeton, Princeton University Press
- Zvelebil, K. V., 1971, 'The Present Tense Morph in Tamil', in *Journal of the American Oriental Society*, Vol. 91, No. 3, pp. 442–7
- Zvelebil, K. V., 1973, *The Smile of Murugan, On Tamil Literature of South India*, Leiden, Brill
- Zvelebil, K. V., 1974, *Tamil Literature*, Wiesbaden, Otto Harrassowitz
- Zvelebil, K. V., 1992, *Companion Studies to the History of Tamil Literature*, Leiden, Brill

Glossary

abhinaya, Skt. abhinaya	– mime, expression; interactivity
acai, Ta. acai	– to move, shake; syllable
akam, Ta. akam	– inside; house; privacy
aksara, Skt. aksara	– unalterable, unit for counting length
alapana, Skt. ālāpana, Ta. ālāpaṇam, ālāpaṇai	– musical prelude, conversation
alarippu, Ta. alāri pū	– alari flower; opening dance, see kacceri
ananda, Skt. ānanda	– bliss; immanent reality
ananga, Skt. anaṅga	– one without limbs, Eros
anupallavi, Ta. anupallavi	– lines following on chorus, see pallavi
artha, Skt. artha	– matter, thing; meaning
arul, Ta. aruḷ	– grace
asura, Skt. asura	– anti- or counter-god, see deva
aucitya, Skt. aucitya	– fitness, suitableness, propriety; habituation
bhakti, Skt. bhakti	– devotion, belonging, worship
bharata natyam, Skt. bhārata nāṭya, Ta. pārata nāṭyam	– classical Indian dance originated in Tamilnadu
bhava, Skt. bhāva	– becoming, manner of being, emotion
bhoga, Skt. bhoga	– enjoyment
cakra, Skt. cakra	– centre, disc; nerve centre
cankam, Skt. sangha, Ta. caṅkam	– gathering, board of experts, academy

Glossary

cankattamil, Ta. caṅkattamiḷ	– refined, authorised Tamil
carana, Skt. caraṇa, Ta. caraṇam	– foot; lines inbetween chorus; peacock's tail
cem tamil, Ta. cem tamiḻ, centamiḻ	– auspicious Tamil
ceyyul, Ta. ceyyuḷ	– poeiesis; poetic making
cirappu, Ta. ciṟappu	– excellence, distinction
col, Ta. col	– utterance
cuvai, Ta. cuvai	– taste
darsana, Skt. darśana,	– showing, seeing, perception; visiting a temple in order to see and be seen by an idol
dasi attam, Skt. dāsi Ta. āṭṭam	– dance by devadasis or rajadasis
deva, Skt. deva	– god, *see* asura
devadasi, Skt. devadāsi	– slave of god; temple courtesan
dharma, Skt. dharma	– consensus, coherence, support; traditional applied law
dipa, Skt. dīpa	– lamp, *see* kumbhadipa
diparadhana, Skt. dīpārādhanā	– lustration by means of burning lamps
drsti, Skt. dṛsti	– evil eye
Skt. dṛstiparihāra	– removal of evil eye
etir, Ta. etir	– opposite, potentialis
gajjai, Te. gajje	– bells worn by dancers
garbhagrha, Skt. garbha gṛha	– inner sanctum, womb-house
gati, Skt. gati	– gait, *see* natai
gopuram, Skt. gopura	– town-gate, ornamented gateway of temple
guru, Skt. guru	– heavy; teacher; rhythmical mnemonic figure;
Ta. gurukkaḷ	– priest
Skt. gurukulavāsa	– living in the house of one's teacher
icai, Ta. icai	– sound, praise, meldoy, *see* muttamil
ilakkanam, Ta. ilakkaṇam Skt. lakṣaṇa	– marker, grammar
ilakkiyam, Ta. ilakkiyam Skt. laksya	– marker, marked; 'literature'

inpam, Ta. iṉpam	– delight, happiness; sexual love; marriage
iranta, Ta. iṟanta	– expired, past tense
iyal, Ta. iyal	– nature, order; natural word, see muttamil
jati, Skt. jāti	– birth, 'caste'
jatisvaram, Ta. jati Skt. svara	– choregraaphic phrases on solfège, see kacceri
javali, Te. jāvali	– song, see kacceri
kacceri, Arabic kaccēri	– public office, assembly; concert: dance suite comprising: alarippu, jatisvaram, sabdam, varnam, padam, javali, tillana, sloka; see also marga
kalam, Skt. kāla, Ta. kālam	– time; basic rhythmical pulse
kalyanam, Skt. kalyāṇa, Ta. kalyāṇam	– auspicious; wedding
kama, Skt. kāma, Ta. kāma(ṉ)	– eros, god of love
karana, Skt. karaṇa, Ta. karaṇam	– doing, making; writer, scribe; part of speech; dance-pose in sculpture
karu, Ta. karu	– embryo, born, creation
karuttu, Ta. karuttu	– object, design; intention; meaning, essence
kolam, Ta. kōḷam	– sphere, orb; circle, map
kotumtamil, Ta. kōṭu tamiḻ	– bent, crooked Tamil, biased Tamil
kumbhadipa, Skt. kumbha dīpa	– pot-lamp; synonym of goddess; see dipa
kurippu, Ta. kuṟippu	– mark, sign, allusion, hint
kuttu, Ta. kūttu	– drama, dance, see muttamil
mancal, Ta. mañcal	– Indian saffron, turmeric, curcuma longa
mandapa, Skt. maṇdapa	– pavilion; public resting place
mangalam, Skt. maṅgala	– auspicious
Skt. maṅgalavādya	– auspicious musical instruments, see for instance nagasvaram and parai

Glossary 249

manodharma, Skt. manas dharma	– realm of the mind, improvisatory scope
mantra, Skt. mantra, Ta. manttiram	– instrument of thought, speech, recitation of sacred text
maran, Skt. m ra, Ta. māraṉ	– death, god of death, Eros, *see* kama
marapu, Ta. marapu	– tradition, memory, worship
marga, Skt. mārga, Ta. mārkkam	– way, road; graded training; traditional suite of classical dance, *see* kacceri
marutam, Ta. marutam	– topos in Tamil love poetry; agricultural track, riverbanks, ricefields; flower in this type of countryside
mati, Te. maṭi	– ritual purity
melakkaran, Ta. mēḷakkāraṉ	– traditional name for performing artists *see* melam
melakkarta, Ta. mēḷakkartta	– graph representing melodic scales facilitated by the frets of the vina, *see* vina
melam, Ta. mēḷam	– fret on large lute called vina – drum, musical band
mey, Ta. mey	– body, 'truth'
meyppatu, Ta. mey pāṭu	– affecting the body, affect, experiencing
moha, Skt. moha, Ta. mōka	– infatuation, intoxication by love; loss of consciousness
moksa, Skt. moksa	– emancipation, liberation, release from worldly existence
mrdangam, Ta. mirutaṅkam	– doublesided drum
mukkalam, Ta. mu Skt. kāla	– three times: past, present, potentialis, *see* nikal, iranta and etir
murai, Ta. muṟai	– manner; order; turn, duty; right
murti, Skt. mūrti	– embodiment; idol, statue
mutal, Ta. mutal	– first, basic category in the taxonomy of the world comprising kalam and nilam

muttamil, Ta. mu tamiḻ	– threefold Tamil: word, sound and image, see iyal, icai and natakam or kuttu
muttirai, Skt. mudrā, Ta. muttirai	– seal, instrument for stamping; impression made by seal; positions of intertwining fingers
nagasvaram, Skt. nāga svara	– sound of the snake; type of oboe
natai, Ta. naṭai	– walk, pace; see gati
natakam, Skt. nāṭaka, Ta. nāṭṭakam	– drama, mimetic mode of Tamil, see muttamil
nattuvanar, Ta. naṭṭuvaṉār	– dance master
natu, Ta. nāṭu	– country, country-side
natya, Skt. nāṭya	– mimesis
nikal, Ta. nikaḻ	– happening, present tense
nilam, Ta.nilam	– space as part of mutal
nityasumangali, Skt. nitya-su-maṅgalī	– lasting-well-auspicious-female see also mangalam and sumangali
nrtta, Skt. nṛtta	– abstract dance
nul, Ta. nūl	– thread, book
olai, Ta. ōlai	– leaf, palmleaf manuscript
otuvar, Ta. otuvār	– singer of sacred Tamil poetry
pa, Ta. pā	– song, verse, weave
padam, Skt. pada, Ta. patam	– song, see kacceri
Ta. patavarṇam	– varnam to be sung for dance, type of prabandham
pallavi, Ta. pallavi	– sprout, shoot, chorus, refrain
pancabana, Skt. pañcabāṇa	– one with five arrows, Eros attacking the senses, see kama and maran
pani, Ta. pāṇi	– sign, mark; camp; style characteristic for one specific artistic group
parai, Ta. paṛai	– drum, see mangalavadya
parampara, Skt. paramparā	– line of succession
pati, Skt. pati	– husband, Lord; master
pasa, Skt. pāśa	– tie, bond, chain

Glossary

pasu, Skt. paśu	– cattle, domestic or sacrificial animal
patra, Skt. pātra	– vessel; actor, embodiment; incarnation
pattiyal, Ta. pāṭṭiyal	– normative treatise on the composing of songs
polutu, Ta. poḻutu	– time marked by micro and macro calendars, *see* also kalam, talam and aksara
pottu, Ta. poṭṭu	– round spot on forehead; round (golden) matrimonial token worn by Telugu women
prabandham, Skt. prabandha, Ta. pirapantam, Te. prabandhamu	– composition, 'literary' genre
prasada, Skt. prasāda	– purity, food offered to idol and received by way of blessing
prayogam, Skt. prayoga, Ta. pirayōkam	– joining, undertaking, application; discharge as of weapons; use; practice of magic; medicine; authority, quotation; example, illustration; horse
Skt. prayojana, Ta. pirayōcaṇam	– usefulness; profit, advantage; result of actions, good/bad reward; rites in wedding ceremony
puja, Skt. pūjā,Ta. pūcai	– worship offering various materials
pulavar, Ta. pulavar	– poet, learned man, expert in muttamil
puram, Ta. puṟam	– outside, politics, public
purana, Skt. purāṇa	– legends, stories of old
puspanjali, Skt. puspāñjali	– salutation by offering flowers, dance composition
raga, Skt. rāga	– melodic scale
raja, Skt. rāja	– king
Skt. rājadāsīs	– courtesans belonging to the king's court
rasa, Skt. rasa	– juice, taste

rasika, Skt. rasika	– taster, afficionado
ratha, Skt. ratha	– car, chariot
sabdam, Skt. śabdam	– word, dance composition, see kacceri
sadir, Ta. catir	– traditional term for female solo dance suite, see kacceri
sakti, Skt. śakti	– power, strength; ability; energy; goddess
samskara, Skt. samskāra	– putting together, rite of passage
sari, Hindi sārī	– long piece of cloth worn by women
sastra, Skt. śāstra	– treatise, 'how to' manual
sat, Skt. sat	– being
Skt. satguṇa Ta.aṉ	– he whose quality is being
Skt. sattva	– beingness, essence
Skt. satyam	– being, 'truth'
siddhi, Skt. siddhi	– accomplishment; substantiation, proof; success
sloka, Skt. śloka	– verse, benediction, see kacceri
smara, Skt. smara	– memory; love; worship god of love, see kama, pancabana
srngara, Skt. śṛṇgāra	– of the horns; love mood, erotic mood
su-mangali, Skt. su-maṅgalī	– well-auspicious-female
tala, Skt. tāla, Ta. tāḷam	– palm of the hand beating rhythm; rhythm cycle
tali, Ta. tāli	– marriage cord, marriage badge
tanikkam noy, Ta. taṉikkam nōy	– disease, suffering because of isolation aloneness
tillana, Ta. tillāṉā	– syllables used in singing, finale, see kacceri
tinai, Ta.tiṇai	– tribe, caste, race; class; soil, land; site; division of poetic themes, see marutam
tirmanam, Ta. tīrmāṉam	– decision, resolution; conclusion of interlude; salvo of dance steps
ter, Ta. tēr	– car, chariot
trikala, Skt. trikāla	– three tenses: past, present, potentialis, see mukkalam

senses, 3, 19, 41, 52, 59, 63, 73, 74, 85, 109n9, 154, 158n47, 173, 178, 199, 217
　sensation, 19
　sensorily, 7
　sensory, 16, 18, 42, 55, 59, 62, 104, 124, 151, 159, 206, 217–8, 223, 231
　sensuous, 4, 15, 20–1, 51, 53, 217–8
sight, 55, 57, 59, 63, 85, 139, 151, 213, 217
skin, 55, 159, 165
smara, 19, 93, 94, 120
　Kaman, 19, 55, 62, 163, 232
　see also memory
smell, 55, 57, 63, 77n54, 85, 153, 213
sound, xvii, xix, xxn4, 13–5, 33–4, 43, 47, 55 *passim* 63, 68, 77n54, 88, 90–1, 117, 120 *passim* 129, 134–40, 146, 149, 150 *passim* 154, 161–5, 172, 175, 185, 199, 213, 217, 226, 232
srngara, 103–4, 112n62, 113, 63, 114n63, 134, 160, 238n10
taste, 15, 43, 59, 77n51, 154–5, 213, 217
tongue, 55
touch, 55, 66, 85, 155, 160, 163, 188, 213, 217, 229, 232
tree, 64, 68, 80n70, 104, 152, 189, 190, 193n18, 227, 229, 236n4
uri, 48, 54, 69, 72–3, 75, 83
　see also perspective
voice, 19, 86, 124–5
　see also vac
water, 47, 55, 58, 63–4, 68, 78n62, 79n69, 81n85, 85, 96, 106n9, 164, 236n4, 237n4

WORDS – COL

alchemy, 192, 227
ankle-bells, 185
　see also gajjai
appropriation, 11–2, 35, 71
branding, 185, 187, 189
concert, 186–7, 189, 202
dedication, 182–3, 185–6, 188–9
devadasi, 40n18, 78n59, 91–2, 97–101, 108n17, 198n20, 110n39, 134, 181, 183–4, 186–92
distanciation, 10, 11, 14
episteme, 16, 20, 22, 154, 171, 174–6, 195n40, 197–9, 203, 206, 228, 233
example, 72, 88–9, 95, 134, 147 *passim* 152, 159, 161, 178, 202, 205
expert, 180–1, 199, 202
　human, 178, 180, 188, 192, 196, 203
　system, 174–6, 179–80, 188, 199, 203–4, 206
exteriority, 217, 229, 231–3, 235, 237n10
flexibility, 203, 205, 207, 215, 223
food, 64, 66–7, 188
gajjai, 194n30
　gajjai puja, 185, 188
　see also ankle-bells
grammar, xvi, xvii, xix, 2, 4, 5, 7, 13, 33, 34, 37, 39n14, 44, 48, 53, 74, 121, 126–9, 139, 143–5, 154, 158n47
habitus, 45, 47–8, 52–5, 74, 82,

129, 144, 147, 150, 161, 175, 178, 180, 197–8, 230
hermeneutics, xviii, 3, 5, 9, 11–3, 17, 21, 199, 221
  hermeneutic arc, 11, 199, 208n7, 228
  radical hermeneutics, 205,226, 234
history, 5,8, 12, 15, 20, 119–20, 122, 153, 196
humanities, ix, xi, xvi, xviii, 1, 5, 9
icon, 49, 50, 53, 84, 89, 161–2, 227, 236n4
iconoclasm, 21
ilakkanam, 13, 34, 43, 48, 53, 120, 191
ilakkiyam, 13–4, 32–4, 43, 46–8, 52–3, 82–3, 120, 174, 191, 231
index, 49, 50, 53, 57, 76n40, 84, 161–2, 236n4, 237n4
initiation, 181, 183, 185, 188
interactivity, 203, 207, 221, 223, 230, 235, 235
interiority, 140, 228–9, 231–2, 237n10
iyal, 7, 36, 134, 136, 146–8, 214
  see also rule
knowledge-
  body of, 95, 204
  of familiarity, 145, 147, 150, 153, 188, 190, 239n19
  formative, 150
  human, 173, 196, 199, 214, 226, 232, 234
  imagined, 173
  practical, 145, 150, 188, 192
  propositional, 145, 161, 188
  rational 171
  referential, 150

tacit, 144, 153–4, 238n18
totalising, 147
langage, 32, 34, 44–6, 52, 129, 144
lamp, 89, 186, 189, 190, 231
  potlamp, 187, 192, 195n36
langue, 34, 44, 52, 129
marapu, 19, 146–7, 156n17
  see also rule
memory, xvi, 20, 38, 59, 61, 74, 93, 121, 161, 202, 233
  mnemonics, 200, 202
  remembering, 19, 20, 89, 97, 128, 171, 201
  see also smara
mimesis, 36, 152, 155, 204, 212, 217, 223
modernity, 234
murai, 180, 182–3, 188–9
parole, 34, 44, 129
  perspective, 69, 72, 80n77, 103, 147, 207
  see also uri
phenomenology, 207
philology, xv, xix, 3–5, 9, 21
post-modern, 235
praxis, xix, 4, 13, 27, 44–7, 105n2, 121, 126–7, 144, 153, 174, 178, 197, 201
prayoga(m), xv, xvii, xix, 1, 21, 45–6, 83, 93, 144, 154, 197
prayojanam, xx, 187, 188, 190
rule, 83, 143, 145–8, 153, 156n18, 182
  see also iyal
  see also marapu
sign, 2–4, 9, 13–7, 21–2, 32, 37, 43, 47, 49–50, 52–4, 82–4, 90, 104, 125–8, 152, 159, 161–2, 171–4, 187, 198, 215, 217, 218, 231

Index

speech, xviii, 10, 16, 33–4, 42, 44, 46–7, 51–2, 85, 91, 107n10, 120–4, 128–30, 144–7, 158n47, 161, 189, 212, 233
  see also vac
symbol, 49, 50, 53, 84, 161–2
system, 9 *passim* 15, 33–4, 33, 50–1, 119, 123, 129, 143, 180–2, 201–3
  flexible, 204, 233
  somatic, 176
  notation, 209n18
theory, 174, 196, 229
  on discourse, 13
  in the head, 42, 48, 54, 56
  of interpretation, 9
  of language, 9
  of the world, 82
vac, 238n13
  see also speech
  see also voice

VOICES – *VAY*

Ahinava Gupta, 131
Abhinaya Darpana, 115n65
Allen, M, 110n47
Appakannu, 98
Appar, 6, 57, 68
Arthasastra, 147
Arunakirinatar, 71, 216
Asad, T, 211–3
Auvaiyar, 6
Balasarasvati, T., Bala, xv, 4, 87, 95, 97–8, 103, 105, 107n12, 107n16, 108n16, 110n39, 111n47, 112n63, 114n63, 115n63, 115n64, 115n 65, 115n66, 115n68, 132, 140, 141n31, 152–3, 160, 167n9, 194n30, 238n10
Benesh, 201, 209n18
Beschi, 7
Bharata, 131, 139, 147, 204, 217–8, 220, 222
Bourdieu, P., 2, 3, 12, 22n4, 45–6, 48, 74n9, 82, 144–5, 150, 179, 204, 224n3
Brinda, T., 97
Brodsky, Y., 16, 19, 20, 171
Bruin, H. de, 199, 204, 206n33
Cilappatikaram, 102, 108n19
Clifford, J., 22n3, 196, 197
Cuntarar, Cuntaramurtti Nayanar, 57, 68, 99
Daniel, V., 66, 79n68, 180, 181
Devadasi Act, 111n52, 193n8
Devisch, R., x, 77n50
Dhanammal, V(ina), 86, 87, 98, 110n40
Dharmasastra, 147
Duce, G.A., 174
Eco, U., 125–6
Fabian, J., ix
Foucault, M., 2, 14, 47, 75n27, 171, 174, 176n4, 215, 217, 234, 238n18
Ganesan, K(andappa), v, ix, 39n1, 95–6, 110n42
Gita Govinda, 113n63
Gnanasundaram, 105
Gonda, J., xv, 22n7
Göranzon, B., 144–8, 156n18
Gowri Amma(l), 87, 97–8
Grubert, N., 24n23
Guhan, S., 112n62, 141n31
Gupta, Sanjukta, ix, 131, 141n26
Heidegger, M., 206
Herder, J.G., 121
Higgins, J., 111n47

Hiltebeitel, A., 199
Holton, G., 8, 9, 12–3
Huizinga, J., 82, 223
Jackson, P., 204
Jakobson, R., 49, 50, 119–22, 125, 127, 129, 134, 140n1, 149, 203, 205
Janik, A., 152–3
Jayadeva, 112n62
Jayammal, 87, 98, 105
Jayaratnamma, 186
Jeevaratnammal, 98
Johanessen, K.S., 148
Josefson, I., 144
Kalidasa, 102
Kamakoti Ammal, 87, 107n16, 108n16
Kamalam, 99, 100
Kamasutra, 113n63, 147, 184
Kanammal, 98
Kandappa Pillai, 39n1, 88
Kandinsky, V., 135, 138
Kannan, Pulavar R., ix, 75n13, 81n85, 156n15
Kantaranuputi, 216
Kapferer, B., ix, x, 222, 230, 237n7
Karpen, A., 201
Kierkegaard, S., 16
Krishnamoorthy, B., ix, 97, 106n2
Kristeva, J., 74n7
Ksetrajna, 112n62
Kuppusvami Mudaliar, 97
Laban, 201, 204, 209n18
Lakshmi Knight, 112n61
Lessing, E., 121
Levinas, E., 235n1, 236n3, 237n10
Levinson, S.C., 123
Lévi-Strauss, C., 125

Lienhardt, S., 213
Lyons, J., 123
Lyotard, J.F., 196, 206, 215
Madhavi, 102, 108n19
Mahabharata, 199
Malavika, 102
Manikkavacakar, 34, 71
Manimekalai, 103
Marcus, G.E., 22n3, 196
Mcluhan, M., xvii, xx
Merleau-Ponty, M., 80n77
Muttusvami Dikshitar, 68, 84–5, 99, 110n38
Nageswara Rao, M., ix, 97
Nanacamoantar, 68
Nandini, Nandini Ramani, ix, 39n1, 77n55, 78n63, 80n73, 81n85, 95–7, 103, 106n3, 106n6, 108n20, 110n41, 111n47, 113n63, 115n65, 167n9, 180, 224n10
Natarajasundara Pilla, T., 156n17
Nattiez, J.J., 125
Natyasastra, 115n65, 131, 141n26, 147, 152, 154–5, 158n47, 218–9
Nijenhuis, E.te, ix
Ong, W.J., 39n2, 138–9
Pannwitz, R., 213
Paravai, 99
Paravai Nankaiyar, 101
Peirce, C.S., 49, 50, 53, 171, 197, 223
Periyapuranam, 99
Ponniah, 27
Powers, H., 140, 142n52
Poursine, K., 111n47
Priyamvada Sankar, 95, 110n41
Purandara Dasa, 142n41

Raghavan, V., ix, 77n55, 95, 97, 109n37, 110n38, 113n63
Ramani, R., ix
Ramiah, K., 96, 110n42, 157n37
Ranganayaki, P., ix, 91, 98–9, 108n20, 109n32, 181, 184–8, 190, 193n25, 195n33, 195n38, 225n23
Rasamanjari, 113n63
Ricoeur, P., 5, 9, 13, 15, 17–8, 20, 23n13, 23n19, 23n20, 31, 88, 228
Ringland, G.A., 174
Rukmini Devi, 112n63, 113n63, 114n63
Said, E.W., 3, 22n6, 75n19
Sambamoorthy, P., 78n59, 157n33
Sankaran, T., ix, 97, 110n39, 238n10
Sarada Raghavan, 95
Satyajit Ray, 167n9
Saussure, F. de, 119
Schoenberg, A., 138
Scriabin, A.N., 138
Scripps, L., 11n47, 115n65
Secenov, I.M., 120
Seeger, Ch., 127–8, 150, 172
Shahaji Maharaja, 78n59, 78n60
Shyama Sastri, 68
Smith, F., 42–3, 48, 74n3, 140, 143–4

Steiner, G., 1, 3, 22n1
Subburatnamma, 98, 109n32, 184, 195n38
Subrahmanya Bharati, 90
Sushama, V., 224n10
Sutton, 202
Svati Tirunal, 96, 111
Takahashi, T., 209n34
Talmud, 226
Tanjore Brothers/ Quartet, 27, 39n.1
Tedlock, D., 124–8, 130
Tevaram, 6, 76n41, 78n63
Tirumantiram, 7
Tirumular, 7, 81n84
Tiruvacakam, 34, 214
Tolkappiyam, xx, 53, 66, 145, 146, 154
Tolkappiyanar, 47, 553–6, 64, 69, 146–7
Trubetzkoy, N.S., 119
Tyagaraja, Saint, 68, 77n47
Tyagaraja Mudaliar, V.S., ix
Tyler, S., 212
Veda(s), 6, 106n7
Vinita Venkataraman, ix, 97, 142n47
Visvanathan, T., 95, 110n40
Weick, K.E., 24n.27
Whorf, B.L., 50, 51
Wittgenstein, L., 143, 145, 148, 205
Zvelebil, K.V., ix, xv, 22n8, 23n10, 28, 39n14, 75n19